DECISIONS UNDER UNCERTAINTY

with
Research Applications

Albert N. Halter, Ph.D.
Professor of Agricultural Economics
Oregon State University

Gerald W. Dean, Ph.D.
Professor of Agricultural Economics
University of California, Davis

Published by

SOUTH-WESTERN PUBLISHING CO.

Cincinnati   Chicago   Dallas   New Rochelle, N.Y.   Burlingame, Calif.   Brighton, Englan

H85

Standard Book Number: 0–538–08850–8

Library of Congress Catalog Card Number: 75–130034

2 3 4 5 Ki 5 4 3 2

Printed in the United States of America

Preface

The authors' motivation for writing this book stemmed initially from the experience of attempting to teach a course, or a portion of a course, on decision theory and finding the available texts to be unsatisfactory in one way or another. The courses taught by the authors have been either at the senior or graduate level in the field of agricultural economics. Since agricultural economics is an applied field of economics, one of the prime purposes of these courses has been to carry students beyond a purely theoretical discussion of decision theory and into the applications that have been made or which might be made. Most texts currently available either stop with the theory alone or, at best, present a few trivial examples of the theory. Our view is that advanced students would gain a greater appreciation of both the theory and its applications by studying some applications of the theory to real world problems. Therefore, Chapters VII to XI examine in depth some applications that have been made in the fields of agricultural economics, geology, climatology, and forest management. We hope the book will lead to a wider range of applications by the readers.

We realize that the first step in developing competence with the tools of decision theory is a systematic treatment of the theory itself. Here again, the authors have felt that some improvement over existing texts could be made in the organization and presentation of the subject. After the brief introductory Chapter I, Chapters II to V present the fundamentals of decision theory in some detail. The method of presentation and the ordering of the material are based on the experience of the senior author in teaching a graduate course in the area (over a number of years) at Oregon State University. The reactions of several graduate classes at Oregon State have led the authors to the present form of presentation. We owe a special debt to the spring quarter class of 1967 for their critical comments on the preliminary manuscript and for insisting on the expansion or clarification of particularly troublesome points.

Our feeling is that the book might be used in one of several ways. First, the book is well adapted in its present form for a one-quarter senior or graduate course in decision theory. In line with the emphasis on application, the student might be asked to submit a term report summarizing an attempt to apply decision theory tools in the solution of some original problem with which he is concerned. We have found that this experience is uniformly salutory; only after such experience do the elements of decision theory become embedded in the analytical apparatus of the student. Second, for those schools that do not teach a separate and formal course in decision theory, the present book could serve as supplementary reading for a section of other courses dealing with decision making under uncertainty. For example, a typical senior or graduate course in production economics devotes several weeks to the questions of decision making under risk and uncertainty. The instructor could select relevant sections and chapters for assignment in such cases, depending on the maturity and background of the students, and depending on the thoroughness with which the subject is to be treated. Third, we feel that the book will serve as a useful reference to researchers in natural resources and other applied fields of economics. The research applications in the text are sufficiently complete to lead the interested researcher into new avenues of application, as well as into challenging methodological problems.

A final word is perhaps in order regarding the level of mathematical and statistical preparation assumed for this book. The essential background material required to understand most parts of the book would be covered in an intermediate level undergraduate course in statistics and by mathematical training up to and including a first course in calculus. We have not felt it necessary or desirable to attempt to present the prerequisite statistics and mathematics as part of the book. This would constitute a textbook in itself, and many excellent texts of this type are already available. A smattering of set theory is used in reviewing probability theory in Chapter II, but the essential set concepts are developed as part of the presentation. Unfortunately, the more complex empirical applications occasionally involve more advanced concepts such as quadratic programming, Lagrangian multipliers, etc. These applications are likely to be of interest primarily to more advanced students or others interested in research. For the undergraduate student, several of the applications are quite simple and straightforward and can be followed with no preparation beyond the minimum indicated above.

A. N. Halter
G. W. Dean

Contents

CHAPTER I

Introduction

Decision making is an activity to which man allocates a good deal of time and effort. Of course, many times a choice among alternative courses of action is made with little conscious effort; a multitude of personal daily decisions, such as whether to shave, how to dress, and which route to take to work, are of a sufficiently routine or unimportant nature that they are made on a split-second basis with little conscious regard of alternative actions or consequences. A number of business decisions fall in the same routine category. However, major personal or business decisions often involve an agonizing experience of carefully weighing alternatives and consequences. Men with the ability and courage to make major decisions and live with them are rare. In fact, to a large measure, the status of a man in the world of business and government is determined by the scope and importance of the decisions he is entrusted to make. Decision making is the central coordinating concept of any organization, whether it is a family farm business, a giant industrial complex, or a governmental agency.

To view decision making in an organized way is itself the result of a decision. We (the authors) decided that it would be a worthwhile endeavor to evaluate the applicability of modern decision-making theory to agricultural and natural resource problems. The purpose of modern decision theory is to provide a systematic approach to decision making under conditions of imperfect knowledge. Agriculture would seem to be an especially relevant and fruitful field for applications of decision theory because of the extreme uncertainty facing farm managers and other decision makers in this sector of the economy. For example, prices, production coefficients, new technology, and human relations are factors with which the farm manager must deal and these are continually changing over time due to weather, markets, and other forces outside of his immediate control.

In this introductory chapter, we provide the general framework for decision making that will be used throughout the book.[1] The framework and its component parts are illustrated by specific empirical examples.

---

[1] The conceptualization of the decision-making problem given here follows that of Herman Chernoff and Lincoln E. Moses, *Elementary Decision Theory* (New York: John Wiley and Sons, Inc., 1959).

ILLUSTRATION 1: THE FOREST FIRE PROBLEM

To establish the components of our decision-making framework in concrete terms, we illustrate with an example from the field of natural resource management.[2] A forest fire suppression agency is organized in such a way that it must periodically maintain stand-by crews of fire fighters. The crews must be paid, but contribute nothing to the agency other than being available should they be needed for putting out fires. The problem for the agency's administrator is to decide upon the optimum size of the stand-by crew. If the crew is too large, there will be excessive wage and overhead costs. If the crew is too small, there will be excessive fire losses. The decision is one of finding the optimum balance between the two kinds of costs. These costs are often expressed in dollars. As discussed in detail in Chapter III, however, the administrator's utility values may be used as a more general measure of gains and losses. Utility is a measure of the subjective feeling the decision maker has toward particular monetary gains and losses. The intensity of this feeling is not necessarily proportional to the amounts of money involved.

The administrator defines the problem as follows: He first specifies several possible alternatives or *actions* that he might take. Suppose he specifies the following three alternative actions:

a_1 = stand-by crew of 10 men per day,
a_2 = stand-by crew of 20 men per day, and
a_3 = stand-by crew of 30 men per day.

Next he specifies the possible *states of nature*, defined as the size of forest fire that could occur in any one day, and measured in terms of acreage of timber burned per day. Although in our example the acreage burned per day is really a continuous variable from zero to 200 acres, we assume that three discrete states are defined:

θ_1 = 0–25 acres burn per day,
θ_2 = 26–100 acres burn per day, and
θ_3 = 101–200 acres burn per day.

Next the administrator specifies the *consequences* or outcomes (in dollars or utility) of each possible combination of action and state of nature. Table 1.1 shows the utility assigned by the administrator to each possible state-act pair. For example, the administrator assigns the greatest utility to the (θ_3, a_3) pair — where a large crew is on hand (a_3) and a fire

---

[2] We express our debt to Dr. Emmett F. Thompson, a former student at Oregon State University, for this example.

breaks out that could destroy over 100 acres of timber (θ_3). In such a case, the large crew could control the fire and reduce the loss. Contrariwise, he assigns the lowest utility to the (θ_3, a_1) pair where a small crew is on hand and a large fire breaks out. He assigns utility values to the other cells of Table 1.1 in a similar manner.

TABLE 1.1

**GAINS OR UTILITY TABLE FOR THE FOREST
FIRE PROBLEM**

	Actions		
States of Nature	**10-Man Crew** a_1	**20-Man Crew** a_2	**30-Man Crew** a_3
	Utilities		
0–25 acres burn θ_1	$u(\theta_1, a_1) = 50$	$u(\theta_1, a_2) = 40$	$u(\theta_1, a_3) = 20$
26–100 acres burn θ_2	$u(\theta_2, a_1) = 30$	$u(\theta_2, a_2) = 50$	$u(\theta_2, a_3) = 30$
101–200 acres burn θ_3	$u(\theta_3, a_1) = 10$	$u(\theta_3, a_2) = 20$	$u(\theta_3, a_3) = 60$

The likelihood of a fire on any particular day is primarily influenced by weather conditions. Knowledge of weather conditions should therefore be of some use in assessing the likelihood of a fire and therefore in determining the type of action (crew size) to select. Thus, each time the administrator must make a decision on crew size, he attempts to get additional information (called an *experiment*) by calling the ranger station to ascertain the fire-weather condition. (Fire-weather conditions are generally reported by a fire danger meter that the reader may have seen along the highway in forested areas.) From the past experience of the administrator with the fire-danger meter readings and actual occurrences of fires, he has determined the relationship between the fire-danger meter readings and the states of nature shown in Table 1.2. Low, medium, and high meter readings are designated as z_1, z_2, and z_3, respectively. In the past, when the true state of nature turned out to be θ_1 (0–25 acres burn), the fire-danger meter reading had been low (z_1) 70 percent of the time, medium (z_2) 20 percent of the time, and high (z_3) 10 percent of the time. More formally, the conditional probability that the fire meter reads z_1 when the true state of nature is θ_1 is written as $P(z_1|\theta_1) = 0.7$; the probability of z_2 given θ_1 is $P(z_2|\theta_1) = 0.2$; the probability of z_3 given θ_1 is $P(z_3|\theta_1) = 0.1$. The other rows of Table 1.2 are interpreted similarly. The probabilities in each *row* of Table 1.2 sum to 1.0; given the true state of nature (θ_i, $i = 1, 2, 3$), one of the three readings z_1, z_2, or z_3 must be ob-

TABLE 1.2
CONDITIONAL PROBABILITIES, $P(z_k|\theta_i)$, FOR THE PROBA-
BILITY OF A SPECIFIC FIRE-DANGER METER READING (z_k),
GIVEN THE STATE OF NATURE (θ_i)

States of Nature	z_k Observations: Fire-Danger Meter Readings		
	Low z_1	Medium z_2	High z_3
0– 25 acres burn θ_1	$P(z_1|\theta_1) = 0.7$	$P(z_2|\theta_1) = 0.2$	$P(z_3|\theta_1) = 0.1$
26–100 acres burn θ_2	$P(z_1|\theta_2) = 0.5$	$P(z_2|\theta_2) = 0.3$	$P(z_3|\theta_2) = 0.2$
101–200 acres burn θ_3	$P(z_1|\theta_3) = 0.1$	$P(z_2|\theta_3) = 0.5$	$P(z_3|\theta_3) = 0.4$

served.   Probabilities and probability functions are discussed in more detail in Chapter II.

The administrator now formulates the concept of a strategy.   A *strategy* is a decision rule or recipe that specifies the action (a_j, $j = 1$, 2, 3) which the administrator takes in response to a particular observation (z_k, $k = 1, 2, 3$) from the fire-danger meter.   The left-hand side of Table 1.3 lists all possible 27 strategies available to the administrator faced with three alternative actions (a_j) and three alternative observations (z_k).[3]   For example, strategy s_6 can be read as follows: If z_1 (low reading) is observed, select action a_1 (small crew); if z_2 is observed, select a_2; if z_3 is observed, select a_3.   Of course, many of the 27 strategies are intuitively nonsensical such as s_{22} which specifies a small crew when fire danger is high and a large crew when fire danger is low.   However, the 27 strategies are listed simply to exhaust all logical possibilities open to the administrator.

For any given strategy (s_t, $t = 1, \ldots, 27$), the administrator calculates the average utility which that strategy would bring should a particular state of nature (θ_i) occur.   These average utilities for each state of nature for each strategy are shown in the right-hand portion of Table 1.3.

The computational procedure for obtaining these average utilities is outlined for two selected strategies s_1 and s_5 in Table 1.4.   Strategy s_1 is defined as $s_1 = (a_1, a_1, a_1)$ meaning that action a_1 is taken regardless of the fire-danger meter reading z_1, z_2, or z_3.   First, *action probabilities* for each action are computed; that is, the probability of selecting action a_j when the true state of nature is θ_i.   Using the conditional probabilities $P(z_k|\theta_i)$ of Table 1.2 and the definition of the particular strategy s_t, the computation is straightforward.   For example, if θ_1 is the true state of nature, we observe z_1 with probability 0.7, z_2 with probability 0.2, and z_3 with probability 0.1

[3] There are "number of actions" raised to the power of "number of observations" possible strategies, $3^3 = 27$.

TABLE 1.3
COMPLETE LIST OF STRATEGIES (s_1 to s_{27}) AND AVERAGE UTILITIES DERIVED FROM EACH STRATEGY FOR GIVEN STATES OF NATURE θ_i

Strategies	Actions Taken for Each Observation			Average Utility for Each State of Nature		
	z_1	z_2	z_3	θ_1	θ_2	θ_3
s_1	a_1	a_1	a_1	50	30	10
s_2	a_1	a_1	a_2	49	34	14
s_3	a_1	a_1	a_3	47	30	30
s_4	a_1	a_2	a_1	48	36	15
s_5	a_1	a_2	a_2	47	40	19
s_6	a_1	a_2	a_3	45	36	35
s_7	a_1	a_3	a_1	44	30	35
s_8	a_1	a_3	a_2	43	34	39
s_9	a_1	a_3	a_3	41	30	55
s_{10}	a_2	a_1	a_1	43	40	11
s_{11}	a_2	a_1	a_2	42	44	15
s_{12}	a_2	a_1	a_3	40	40	31
s_{13}	a_2	a_2	a_1	41	46	16
s_{14}	a_2	a_2	a_2	40	50	20
s_{15}	a_2	a_2	a_3	38	46	36
s_{16}	a_2	a_3	a_1	37	40	36
s_{17}	a_2	a_3	a_2	36	44	40
s_{18}	a_2	a_3	a_3	34	40	56
s_{19}	a_3	a_1	a_1	29	30	15
s_{20}	a_3	a_1	a_2	28	34	19
s_{21}	a_3	a_1	a_3	26	30	35
s_{22}	a_3	a_2	a_1	27	36	20
s_{23}	a_3	a_2	a_2	26	40	24
s_{24}	a_3	a_2	a_3	24	36	40
s_{25}	a_3	a_3	a_1	23	30	40
s_{26}	a_3	a_3	a_2	22	34	44
s_{27}	a_3	a_3	a_3	20	30	60

(see Table 1.2). However, strategy s_1 specifies that action a_1 is taken regardless of the z_k reading. Hence, the probability that action a_1 will be taken when θ_1 is the true state of nature (the action probability of a_1 given θ_1) is 1.0. The action probabilities of a_2 and a_3 given θ_1 are then necessarily zero. By similar reasoning, the action probabilities of a_1 given θ_2 and θ_3 are also 1.0.

The computation of action probabilities for strategy $s_5 = (a_1, a_2, a_2)$ in Table 1.4 illustrates the procedure further. Again, if θ_1 is the true state of nature, the probabilities of obtaining z_1, z_2, and z_3 readings are 0.7, 0.2, and 0.1, respectively. Strategy s_5 specifies that action a_1 is taken if z_1 is observed while a_2 is taken if either z_2 or z_3 is observed. Hence, the action

TABLE 1.4
COMPUTATION OF AVERAGE UTILITIES FOR STRATEGIES s_1 AND s_5 FOR EACH STATE OF NATURE θ_i

For Strategy $s_1 = a_1, a_1, a_1$

States of Nature	Actions (Utilities)			Action Probabilities (Probabilities)			Average Utilities $G(\theta_i, s_1)$
	a_1	a_2	a_3	a_1	a_2	a_3	
θ_1	50	40	20	$P(z_1\|\theta_1) + P(z_2\|\theta_1) + P(z_3\|\theta_1)$ = 0.7 + 0.2 + 0.1 = 1.0	0	0	$G(\theta_1,s_1) = [P(z_1\|\theta_1) + P(z_2\|\theta_1) + P(z_3\|\theta_1)] \cdot u(\theta_1,a_1) + 0 \cdot u(\theta_1,a_2) + 0 \cdot u(\theta_1,a_3) = 50(1.0) + 40(0) + 20(0) = 50$
θ_2	30	50	30	$P(z_1\|\theta_2) + P(z_2\|\theta_2) + P(z_3\|\theta_2)$ = 0.5 + 0.3 + 0.2 = 1.0	0	0	$G(\theta_2,s_1) = [P(z_1\|\theta_2) + P(z_2\|\theta_2) + P(z_3\|\theta_2)] \cdot u(\theta_2,a_1) + 0 \cdot u(\theta_2,a_2) + 0 \cdot u(\theta_2,a_3) = 30(1.0) + 50(0) + 30(0) = 30$
θ_3	10	20	60	$P(z_1\|\theta_3) + P(z_2\|\theta_3) + P(z_3\|\theta_3)$ = 0.1 + 0.5 + 0.4 = 1.0	0	0	$G(\theta_3,s_1) = [P(z_1\|\theta_3) + P(z_2\|\theta_3) + P(z_3\|\theta_3)] \cdot u(\theta_3,a_1) + 0 \cdot u(\theta_3,a_2) + 0 \cdot u(\theta_3,a_3) = 10(1.0) + 20(0) + 60(0) = 10$

For Strategy $s_5 = a_1, a_2, a_2$

States of Nature	Actions (Utilities)			Action Probabilities (Probabilities)			Average Utilities $G(\theta_i, s_5)$
	a_1	a_2	a_3	a_1	a_2	a_3	
θ_1	50	40	20	$P(z_1\|\theta_1)$ = 0.7	$P(z_2\|\theta_1) + P(z_3\|\theta_1)$ = 0.2 + 0.1 = 0.3	0	$G(\theta_1,s_5) = P(z_1\|\theta_1) \cdot u(\theta_1,a_1) + [P(z_2\|\theta_1) + P(z_3\|\theta_1)] \cdot u(\theta_1,a_2) + [0 \cdot u(\theta_1,a_3)] = 50(0.7) + 40(0.3) + 20(0) = 47$
θ_2	30	50	30	$P(z_1\|\theta_2)$ = 0.5	$P(z_2\|\theta_2) + P(z_3\|\theta_2)$ = 0.3 + 0.2 = 0.5	0	$G(\theta_2,s_5) = [P(z_1\|\theta_2)] \cdot u(\theta_2,a_1) + [P(z_2\|\theta_2) + P(z_3\|\theta_2)] \cdot u(\theta_2,a_2) + 0 \cdot u(\theta_2,a_3) = 30(0.5) + 50(0.5) + 30(0) = 40$
θ_3	10	20	60	$P(z_1\|\theta_3)$ = 0.1	$P(z_2\|\theta_3) + P(z_3\|\theta_3)$ = 0.5 + 0.4 = 0.9	0	$G(\theta_3,s_5) = P(z_1\|\theta_3) \cdot u(\theta_3,a_1) + [P(z_2\|\theta_3) + P(z_3\|\theta_3)] \cdot u(\theta_3,a_2) + 0 \cdot u(\theta_3,a_3) = 10(0.1) + 20(0.9) + 60(0) = 19$

probabilities of a_1, a_2, and a_3 when θ_1 is the true state of nature are 0.7, 0.3, and 0 as shown in the bottom portion of Table 1.4. Likewise, given the conditional probabilities $P(z_k|\theta_2)$ in Table 1.2 of 0.5, 0.3, and 0.2, the action probabilities of a_1, a_2, and a_3 for strategy s_5 when θ_2 is the true state of nature are 0.5, 0.5, and zero; given the conditional probabilities $P(z_k|\theta_3)$ in Table 1.2 of 0.1, 0.5, and 0.4, the action probabilities of a_1, a_2, and a_3 for strategy s_5 when θ_3 is the true state of nature are 0.1, 0.9, and zero.

Given the computation of the action probabilities, it is now a simple matter to calculate the average utility obtained from following a particular strategy when the state of nature is θ_i. The right-hand portion of Table 1.4 shows how such average utilities or gains $G(\theta_i, s_1)$ and $G(\theta_i, s_5)$ are calculated for strategies s_1 and s_5. For example, the average gain of following strategy s_1 when the true state of nature is θ_1, $G(\theta_1, s_1)$, is simply the utility of action a_1 times the action probability of a_1, plus the utility of a_2 times the action probability of a_2, plus the utility of a_3 times the action probability of a_3; i.e., $50(1.0) + 40(0) + 20(0) = 50$. The average gain of following strategy s_5 when the true state of nature is θ_3, $G(\theta_3, s_5)$, is the utility of a_1 times the action probability of a_1, plus the utility of a_2 times the action probability of a_2, plus the utility of a_3 times the action probability of a_3; i.e., $10(0.1) + 20(0.9) + 60(0) = 19$.

Average utilities of following each strategy s_t when the true state of nature is θ_1, θ_2, or θ_3, $G(\theta_i, s_t)$, can be computed in like manner. These average utilities are summarized in the third column of Table 1.3. If the state of nature were known, then it would be a simple matter for the administrator to select an action that would provide him with the maximum gain or utility. In fact, if θ were known, the optimum action could be determined directly from the original Table 1.1. For example, if θ_2 were known to be the true state of nature, action a_2 would always be selected, providing a utility of 50. In Table 1.3, this would correspond to strategy s_{14}, which specifies action a_2 regardless of the fire-danger meter reading (z_1, z_2, or z_3), and gives the same utility of 50 when θ_2 is in fact the true state of nature. The real decision problem, however, is in those cases where the true state of nature θ is unknown at the time the decision must be made. The problem then becomes one of selecting the "best" strategy from among the 27 outlined in Table 1.3.

It is worth noting that some of the 27 strategies listed in Table 1.3 can be eliminated as irrelevant strategies on direct inspection. For example, s_6 is clearly superior to s_7 in that the former gives equal or greater utility than the latter for any of the three states of nature which could occur. In this case, we say that strategy s_6 *dominates* s_7. By the same token, s_{15} dominates s_{16}, s_{19}, s_{20}, s_{21}, s_{22}, while s_{18} dominates s_{23}, s_{24}, s_{25}, and s_{26}.

Unfortunately, there is no clear-cut final choice that can be made among the strategies using the idea of dominance alone. The selection of a relevant choice criterion among strategies has been much discussed in the literature and is treated in some detail in Chapter IV. At this point, we will simply argue that a very relevant piece of information to be used in making the decision is some knowledge of the relative likelihood of occurrence of the three states of nature θ_1, θ_2, and θ_3. If the probability of θ_1 occurring is relatively high, the administrator would intuitively lean toward a strategy that gives a high average utility for θ_1. On the other hand, if the probability of θ_3 occurring is relatively high, he would incline toward a strategy with a relatively high average utility for θ_3. More specifically, he might select that strategy which maximizes the expected utility (gain) over all possible states of nature, based on objective or subjective estimates of the probability of θ_i. Suppose the administrator assessed the probability of three types of forest fires as follows: $P(\theta_1) = 0.5$, $P(\theta_2) = 0.3$, and $P(\theta_3) = 0.2$. The expected or weighted average utility (gain) of each strategy can then be determined. For example, the expected utility of strategy s_1 in Table 1.5 is $50(0.5) + 30(0.3) + 10(0.2) = 36$. Upon cal-

TABLE 1.5

LIST OF UNDOMINATED STRATEGIES AND EXPECTED GAINS FOR EACH, GIVEN THE RELATIVE LIKELIHOOD OF θ_i

Strategies	Actions Taken for Each Observation			Average Utility for Each State of Nature			Expected Gain from Strategy s_t Given $P(\theta_1) = 0.5$, $P(\theta_2) = 0.3$, and $P(\theta_3) = 0.2$
	z_1	z_2	z_3	θ_1	θ_2	θ_3	
s_1	a_1	a_1	a_1	50	30	10	36.0
s_2	a_1	a_1	a_2	49	34	14	37.5
s_3	a_1	a_1	a_3	47	30	30	38.5
s_4	a_1	a_2	a_1	48	36	15	37.8
s_5	a_1	a_2	a_2	47	40	19	39.3
s_6	a_1	a_2	a_3	45	36	35	40.3
s_8	a_1	a_3	a_2	41	34	39	38.5
s_9	a_1	a_3	a_3	41	30	55	40.5
s_{10}	a_2	a_1	a_1	43	40	11	35.7
s_{11}	a_2	a_1	a_2	42	44	15	37.2
s_{12}	a_2	a_1	a_3	40	40	31	38.2
s_{13}	a_2	a_2	a_1	41	46	16	37.5
s_{14}	a_2	a_2	a_2	40	50	20	39.0
s_{15}	a_2	a_2	a_3	38	46	36	40.0
s_{17}	a_2	a_3	a_2	36	44	40	39.2
s_{18}	a_2	a_3	a_3	34	40	56	40.2
s_{27}	a_3	a_3	a_3	20	36	60	32.8

culating the expected utility for each of the nondominated strategies as shown in Table 1.5, s_9 is seen to be the optimum strategy since it provides the maximum expected utility of 40.5. Of course, if the agency administrator assessed the probabilities of θ_i differently, a different strategy would likely be optimal. The rationale behind this criterion is explored in detail in Chapter V. More efficient computational procedures also are discussed in Chapter V and become increasingly relevant as the size and complexity of the problem increases.

SUMMARY OF THE COMPONENTS OF A DECISION PROBLEM

The above example has illustrated the essential components of a decision problem. To fix these in mind, we summarize them below in a general statement, followed by specific reference to the forest fire problem. They are as follows:

General

1. The available *actions* that can be taken.

2. The *states of nature* which could occur.

3. The *consequences* (gains, losses, utilities) of each combination of action and state of nature (state-act pair).

4. An *experiment* or other device for obtaining knowledge about the states of nature. An experiment consists of:
   a. Possible observations that are related to the state of nature and which are observable at the time a decision is made.
   b. Estimation of a relationship that shows the dependence of the observations upon the states of nature in probabilistic terms.

5. The available *strategies* or recipes telling the decision maker which action to take in the event of a particular z_k observation from the experiment.

6. The consequences of each strategy for each state of nature, as determined by the *action probabilities*.

7. A *choice criterion* by which the decision maker solves the final problem of choice.

Forest Fire Problem

1. a_1 = 10-man crew
   a_2 = 20-man crew
   a_3 = 30-man crew

2. θ_1 = 0– 25 acres burn
   θ_2 = 26–100 acres burn
   θ_3 = 101–200 acres burn

3. Table 1.1 giving utilities for each crew size and forest fire state.

4. The weather conditions as expressed in fire-danger meter readings.

   a. z_1 = low meter reading
      z_2 = medium meter reading
      z_3 = high meter reading

   b. The conditional probability Table 1.2 showing $P(z_k|\theta_i)$.

5. The 27 strategies shown in Table 1.3.

6. The average utilities, $G(\theta_i, s_i)$ shown in Tables 1.3 and 1.4.

7. The criterion of maximizing expected utility, using $P(\theta_i)$, as illustrated in the last column of Table 1.5.

ILLUSTRATION 2: WET OR DRY

Many decision problems are of a type for which no experiment is readily available as a way of gaining information (z_k observations) to help in predicting the true state of nature θ_i. In such cases, called the *no-data* type of problem, the seven components of a decision problem listed above reduce to only four, numbers 1, 2, 3, and 7. In other words, a utility (gain, loss) table such as Table 1.1 is set up, probabilities of the states $P(\theta_i)$ are assigned, and the optimum strategy reduces to a single action that maximizes expected utility (gain) over the states of nature.

An example of this no-data type of problem (that is, a problem with no z_k observations) is a decision faced annually by several thousand California grape growers.[4] This decision involves a choice among alternative ways in which Thompson Seedless grapes can be produced and marketed. Thompson Seedless is a multiple-use variety that can be utilized for canning, fresh table consumption, wine production, or for sun-drying into raisins. The acreage of canning grapes and table grapes must be established at the beginning of the season because of contractual arrangements and different types of cultural practices for these uses. However, the remainder of the crop can be shifted late in the season to either wine grapes or to raisins. (The industry parlance for this decision is "going wet or dry.") This decision is made at a single point in time each year.

Suppose a grower has a given acreage committed to either wine or raisin usage. He could divide this acreage between the two uses in many proportions. For simplicity we analyze only the following three actions:

a_1 = allocate all of the acreage for raisins
a_2 = allocate all of the acreage for wine crush
a_3 = allocate half of the acreage to each use.

The possible outcomes of each action will depend primarily on weather conditions and prices, neither of which is known at the time the decision must be made. Prices in the two outlets are highly variable from year to year, and no price forecasting model is available to the grower. Weather conditions also are critical and highly unpredictable. Raisins in the area under consideration (around Fresno, California) are sun-dried completely in the open. However, it does rain occasionally during the drying period, which can inflict heavy losses on the grape grower who is going dry. If the grower is considering going wet, the grapes remain on the vines several weeks longer than their dried counterpart. There is very little chance of going dry after waiting for that period because of the increased probability of rain for late drying (see Table 1.6).

4 We owe thanks to Ernest Perelli-Minetti, a former student at the University of California, Davis for material included in this example.

TABLE 1.6
FIRST RAINS OF THE SEASON IN FRESNO,
CALIFORNIA, LIKELY TO DAMAGE
RAISINS (0.1 INCH OR MORE),
66-YEAR PERIOD, 1897 TO 1962

Item	Date	Number of Years
Years with rain by	September 20	8
Years with rain by	October 1	30
Years with rain by	October 10	66

The states of nature in this problem involve both drying weather and relative prices. Again, to greatly simplify the problem for illustrative purposes, we define only two sets of prices ("prices favor raisins" or "prices favor wine crush"), and only three sets of weather conditions ("no rain," "slight rain," and "heavy rain"). All combinations of these two unknowns form the following six states of nature:

θ_1 = prices favor raisins; no rain
θ_2 = prices favor raisins; slight rain
θ_3 = prices favor raisins; heavy rain
θ_4 = prices favor wine crush; no rain
θ_5 = prices favor wine crush; slight rain
θ_6 = prices favor wine crush; heavy rain.

The gains table for this problem is shown as Table 1.7. In this particular case, gains are expressed in dollars of profit per acre rather than

TABLE 1.7
GAINS (PROFITS) TABLE FOR WET OR DRY PROBLEM

States of Nature	Actions			
	a_1	a_2	a_3	
	All Raisins	All Wine	Half Raisins, Half Wine	$P(\theta_i)$
	Dollars Profit Per Acre			
Prices favor raisins; no rain θ_1	60.20	18.50	39.35	0.42
Prices favor raisins; slight rain θ_2	44.00	18.50	31.25	0.14
Prices favor raisins; heavy rain θ_3	− 3.88	14.80	5.46	0.32
Prices favor wine; no rain θ_4	28.00	41.96	34.98	0.04
Prices favor wine; slight rain θ_5	16.20	41.96	29.08	0.07
Prices favor wine; heavy rain θ_6	−23.20	33.57	5.18	0.01
Expected profit per acre	32.22	20.05	26.14	—

utility as in the forest fire problem. Each cell entry is determined by a budgeting analysis utilizing the relevant prices, damage factors, and costs for the associated action and state of nature. Table 1.7 provides components 1, 2, and 3 of the general decision problem outlined previously. The desirable next step would be to develop some type of experiment to predict prices and/or weather conditions. In this particular case, no such "data" are available to the grower; he has no price forecasting model nor weather forecasting device available. Therefore, components 4, 5, and 6 are irrelevant. However, the grower does have a subjective idea from past experience of the relative likelihood of various prices and weather conditions. Assume that he specifies the following probabilities of the six states of nature occurring:

$$P(\theta_1) = 0.42 \qquad P(\theta_4) = 0.04$$
$$P(\theta_2) = 0.14 \qquad P(\theta_5) = 0.07$$
$$P(\theta_3) = 0.32 \qquad P(\theta_6) = 0.01$$

Given these probability assignments, the grape producer can calculate the weighted average or expected value of each action. His strategy in a "no data" problem such as this is simply a single action. In Table 1.7, action a_1 provides the highest expected value:

$$60.20(0.42) + 44.00(0.14) - 3.88(0.32) + 28.00(0.04) + 16.20(0.07)$$
$$- 23.20(0.01) = 32.22.$$

Of course, a different set of probabilities, $P(\theta_i)$, could lead to a different action as optimal.

SUMMARY

The two examples included in this introductory chapter have served to introduce the framework and components of decision problems viewed from the perspective adopted in this book. The forest fire example illustrates a "data" problem where an "experiment" (z_k observations on weather conditions) is made. The grape marketing problem illustrates a "no data" problem where no "experiment" is conducted. The rationale behind these two types of problems will be examined in more detail in Chapters II through V. Chapters VI through XI present results of research studies employing this decision framework. These later chapters indicate a more direct method of obtaining optimal decision strategies than the "brute force" method employed in this chapter wherein all possible strategies and their consequences must be explicitly specified. More efficient methods allow solution of complex problems with little computational burden.

EXERCISES

1. Define a simple decision-making problem and solve it using the framework of this chapter. Be prepared to discuss it in class.
2. You are a student preparing for your final exam in a course in your major field. You have two possible actions—a_1, study for general type questions or a_2, study for specific type questions. There are three possible states of nature:

   θ_1, exam contains general type questions,
   θ_2, exam contains specific type questions,
   θ_3, exam contains both general and specific type questions.

   Three observations are possible:

   z_1, old exams contain mainly general type questions,
   z_2, old exams contain mainly specific type questions,
   z_3, old exams contain both types.

   Past experience shows the following conditional probabilities, $P(z_k|\theta_i)$

	z_1	z_2	z_3
θ_1	0.8	0.0	0.2
θ_2	0.1	0.6	0.3
θ_3	0.2	0.2	0.6

   List the action probabilities for what you consider to be reasonable strategies.
   Which strategy would you take?
   How did you arrive at your choice?

CHAPTER II

Some Concepts of Probability Theory

The intent of this chapter is to develop a point of view about probability that, to the authors, is prerequisite to the development of the theory of decision making under uncertainty and essential to the application of the theory to real world problems. We start with some elementary concepts of sets and functions, then we talk about probability functions, and finally discuss how probability functions can be specified in a number of different ways. We prefer this order of presentation, not because it is novel, which it is not, but because we want to leave the impression that probability does not necessarily depend upon the reader's intuition of what goes on when he is playing a coin-tossing game.

This chapter is not intended to be a short course in probability theory, nor should it serve as an introduction to statistics. Instead, it is to serve as a prelude to the development of a philosophical point of view about probability and its place in decision making under uncertainty.

SETS AND FUNCTIONS

Any collection of objects or events is called a *set*. The items in the collection are the *elements of the set*. Sets are frequently represented by indicating their elements within a pair of braces.[1] Examples of sets are: $\{\theta_1, \theta_2, \theta_3\}$, the possible states of nature in a decision making problem; $\{(H, H), (H, T), (T, T)\}$ the outcomes of tossing a coin twice when the order of toss is not distinguished, $H =$ head, $T =$ tail; and the integers between 1 and 1,000,000. These examples are all *finite sets* and are the kind we will be using in formalizing decision-making theory.

When a set A is composed of some of the elements of a set B, then A is a *subset* of B. A set with n elements has 2^n subsets, if we include as subsets the original set B and the empty set. The *empty set* is defined as one

---

[1] A set is denoted as a capital letter, for example, Θ is the set of states of nature $\{\theta_1, \theta_2, \theta_3\}$, A is the set of elements $\{a_1, a_2, a_3\}$. Subsets are usually denoted as a capital letter with a subscript, e.g., A_1 and A_2 are subsets of set A.

that contains no elements. As an example, consider the set of available actions in a decision-making problem $\{a_1, a_2, a_3\}$. Now let us consider subsets of actions. For any one subset, an action can either be included or not included. If all actions are included, we have the original set; and if none are included, we have the empty set. Thus, for each action there are two possibilities; and since there are three actions, there are 2^3 possible subsets. A listing of them may make this clear:

$$\{a_1, a_2, a_3\} \ \{a_1, a_2\}, \ \{a_1, a_3\}, \ \{a_2, a_3\}, \ \{a_1\}, \ \{a_2\}, \ \{a_3\}, \ \{\quad\}.$$

Two sets are said to *intersect* if they have elements in common. If they have no elements in common, then they are *disjoint*. $A \cap B$ (read A intersection B) is the set that contains those, and only those, elements which belong to both A and B. $A \cup B$ (read A union B) is the set that contains those elements which belong either to A or to B or to both. On the Venn diagram below, A and B are two sets. The double crosshatched area is the intersection $A \cap B$, and the total crosshatched area is the union $A \cup B$.

A rule that associates the elements (a) of one set A with the elements (*b*) of a second set B is called a *function*. The first set is called the *domain*

A   B

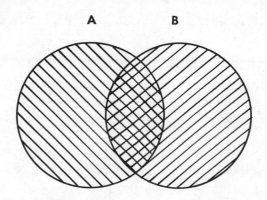

of the function and the second is the *range*. The elements of the set B can be written as $f(a)$. A function is a single-valued mapping of the elements of the set A upon the elements of set B as shown in the Venn diagram.

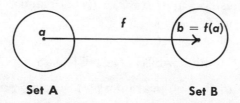

Set A   **Set B**

A graphical representation of the algebraic function $f(x) = x^3$ is shown below for a restricted domain. Here the domain is the set of all x between 0 and 2, and the range is the set of all $f(x)$ between 0 and 8.

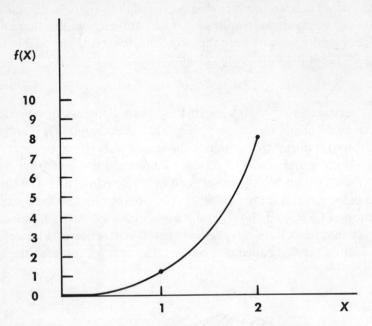

There is a function that assigns gains (or losses) to each action a_1, a_2, a_3 for the states of nature θ_i. Thus, for a_1, in the forest fire example presented in Chapter I, there is a function whose domain is the set $\{\theta_1, \theta_2, \theta_3\}$ and whose range is $\{50, 30, 10\}$. This particular function could be called a *utility function*.

Another special and interesting function is one that assigns a number to the possible events of nature, the possible outcomes of an experiment or possible outcomes of some other chance producing process. Thus, the set of outcomes of tossing a coin twice $\{(H, H), (H, T), (T, T)\}$ when the order of toss is not distinguished comprise the domain, and the numbers 1, 2, 3, are the range of the function f that assigns the 3 numbers respectively. The variable that represents the range of this function is called a *random variable*, X. It can be written $X = f(Y)$ where Y represents one of the outcomes. Thus, $1 = f(H, H)$, $2 = f(H, T)$, and $3 = f(T, T)$ are the values of the random variable X.

PROBABILITY FUNCTIONS

Still another function of great interest to decision making is the one that assigns numbers between 0 and 1 to certain subsets of the set of all possible states of nature in a particular decision making problem.[2] Let A be the set of all states of nature in a decision making problem, and A_1 and A_2 be two subsets. We denote $P(A_1)$ and $P(A_2)$ as the elements of the range of the function and notice that the subsets A_1 and A_2 are the domain. The function P, called the *probability function*, is a rule that assigns numbers between 0 and 1 to the subsets of the set A.

The function P has the following special properties where A is the set of outcomes or states and A_1 and A_2 are subsets:

1. $P(A_1), P(A_2) \geq 0$
2. $P(A) = 1$
3. For two subsets A_1 and A_2
   $P(A_1 \cup A_2) = P(A_1) + P(A_2)$ if and only if
   A_1 and A_2 are disjoint.

Now, it follows that if A_1 and $\tilde{A}_1$, ($\tilde{A}_1$ is defined as the subset of all the elements that are not in A_1) are disjoint, then $P(A_1) + P(\tilde{A}_1) = P(A)$ by property three, since $A_1 \cup \tilde{A}_1 = A$. Thus,

4. $P(A_1) + P(\tilde{A}_1) = 1$ by property two.

To obtain the property that $P(A_1) \leq 1$ consider that since $P(\tilde{A}_1) \geq 0$ by property one, then by property four, just derived, we have

5. $P(A_1) \leq 1$.

The probability of the empty set is 0. This follows since $\tilde{A}$ is the empty set and from property four, $P(\tilde{A}) = 1 - P(A)$ and thus from property two $P(\tilde{A}) = 1 - 1 = 0$. The empty set is frequently denoted as ϕ.

The probability of A_1, a subset of A, is always less than or equal to the probability of A. Let A_2 be another subset of elements in A which contains all elements not in A_1. Then $A = A_1 \cup A_2$ when $A_1 \cap A_2 = \phi$. Now by property three $P(A_1) + P(A_2) = P(A)$. But, by property one, $P(A_2) \geq 0$ and thus

6. $P(A_1) \leq P(A)$.

Another property of the probability of subsets is that

$$P(A_1 \cup A_2 \cup A_3) \leq P(A_1) + P(A_2) + P(A_3).$$

This differs from property three in that no restriction is made concerning the intersections of A_1, A_2, and A_3. Consider the following representation of the 3 subsets A_1, A_2, A_3.

---

[2] The set over which this function is defined could also be the possible outcomes of an experiment or the possible outcomes of some other chance producing process.

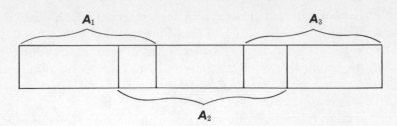

Let $B_1 = A_1$, $B_2 =$ the set of elements in A_2 but not in A_1, $B_3 =$ the set of elements in A_3 neither in A_1 nor A_2. The following represents the new and old subsets.

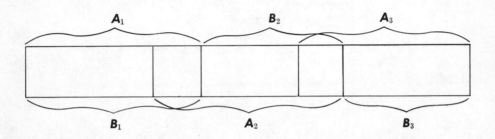

The subset A_1 equals the subset B_1 and A_1 is in a trivial way a subset of B_1. Further, B_2 is a subset of A_2 and B_3 is a subset of A_3. The subsets B_1, B_2, B_3 have no intersection, yet

$$A_1 \cup A_2 \cup A_3 = B_1 \cup B_2 \cup B_3.$$

Now, $P(A_1 \cup A_2 \cup A_3) = P(B_1 \cup B_2 \cup B_3)$
$$= P(B_1) + P(B_2) + P(B_3) \text{ by property three}$$

(extended). But, since

$$P(B_1) = P(A_1), P(B_2) \le P(A_2) \text{ and } P(B_3) \le P(A_3)$$

by property six, it follows that

$$P(A_1 \cup A_2 \cup A_3) \le P(A_1) + P(A_2) + P(A_3).$$

This inequality can be changed to equality if we subtract from the right-hand side the probability associated with the intersections that have been double accounted by the union, and adding the probability of intersection of all 3 subsets.
Thus:

$$P(A_1 \cup A_2 \cup A_3) = P(A_1) + P(A_2) + P(A_3) - P(A_1 \cap A_2)$$
$$-P(A_1 \cap A_3) - P(A_2 \cap A_3) + P(A_1 \cap A_2 \cap A_3).$$

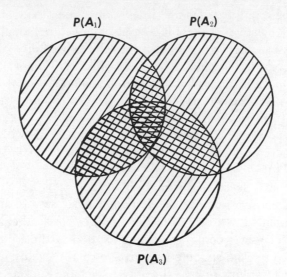

$P(A_1)$ $P(A_2)$

$P(A_3)$

The Venn diagram shows this situation, if each circle is thought of as containing the numbers that are the probabilities attached to the subsets A_1, A_2, A_3. The union $A_1 \cup A_2 \cup A_3$ includes the intersections and hence clearly

$$P(A_1 \cup A_2 \cup A_3) \leq P(A_1) + P(A_2) + P(A_3).$$

Now if each of the intersections

$$P(A_1 \cap A_2), \ P(A_1 \cap A_3) \text{ and } P(A_2 \cap A_3)$$

are subtracted, it is also clear that the intersection

$$P(A_1 \cap A_2 \cap A_3) \text{ (three hatched)}$$

has been subtracted three times when originally it was triple accounted in the union. Thus, it must be added in once again to obtain

$$P(A_1 \cup A_2 \cup A_3).$$

This demonstration is not a proof of the above assertion.

Development of Probability Functions

There are three ways of developing the values in the range of the probability function that will be discussed in this section. These are logical, empirical, and subjective. The logical is sometimes called the classical theory, and the empirical is sometimes called the frequentist theory of probability. Subjective probability is also called personal probability.

In the classical theory one determines the probability of an event or outcome by considering the logical possibilities. Thus, for example, suppose that we want the probability number, $P(H)$, for the event that an ideal coin when flipped will turn up heads. One could argue that since there are only two ways that the coin can fall, heads or tails, and since the coin is ideal, one would expect it to fall heads and tails with about equal frequency; hence, we would say that the value of $P(H) = \frac{1}{2}$. Likewise, the value of $P(T) = \frac{1}{2}$.

In the classical sense the probability function is developed by constructing the fraction: number of elements in subset A_1 divided by the number of elements in set A. Consider another classical case, tossing an ordinary die. The set A contains 6 elements, that is, the 6 numbered faces that may turn up. The six outcomes are mutually exclusive and equally likely to occur for a fair or true die. Now, let the subset A_1 be that the result of a toss is an even number. The subset A_1 contains 3 elements since 3 of the 6 possible outcomes are even numbered faces. Hence, $P(A_1 =$ even number$) = \frac{3}{6} = \frac{1}{2}$.

In the empirical approach to development of the probability function, the probability of an event or outcome is determined by considering the long-run regularity of a frequency ratio. For example, suppose we want the probability number, $P(R\text{-}4)$, for the possibility that it will rain on the Fourth of July. One could obtain historical weather records from which the number of rainy Fourth of Julys could be counted. Suppose one found that on 10 out of 30 of the Fourth of Julys of record it rained; then one would say that the value of $P(R\text{-}4) = \frac{1}{3}$ and $P(\text{not } R\text{-}4) = \frac{2}{3}$.

In the empirical approach the probability number, that is, the range of the probability function, is developed by constructing the fraction: number of observations in A_1 divided by the number of observations in A. In this case the A contains observations of events that can be repeated many times; the set A_1 contains those observations of events that satisfy certain similar conditions. While the event is repeated many times, there is an uncontrollable variation that is haphazard or random so that the observations are individually unpredictable. Hence, only after repeated observations can we speak of the relative frequency of the events in the set A_1 and the probability, $P(A_1)$. Since frequency probabilities can be calculated only after observation of events, it is sometimes called posterior probability.

Subjective Probability. In the subjective approach to assigning the values in the range of the probability function, the probability of an event or outcome is taken as a certain kind of numerical measure of the opinion of somebody about something.[3] This is why it is commonly called personal probability. In a talk in 1960 at Purdue University, Savage pointed to a plastic covered armchair on the platform and said ". . . consider what you think about the weight of that chair. . . . Suppose that I were to write a contract on a slip of paper promising the bearer $10 if this chair weighs more than 20 pounds, and to offer the contract up for auction. What would you bid? If you would bid as much as $5, I would say, roughly speaking, that you regard it as at 'least' an even money bet that the chair weighs more than 20 pounds. If you would pay just $9, I would take this as meaning by definition, that the probability of this event is exactly 9/10 for you. Thus, the personal probability of an event for you is the price you would pay in return for a unit payment to you in case the event actually obtains; in other words, a probability is the price you would pay for a particular contingency."

Savage points out that subjective probabilities are usually expressed in terms of odds, but the advantage of putting it in terms of a price is that it brings out the fact that personal probability is no more nonsensical, mysterious and unreal than the price that anyone would pay for a steak or a trip to San Francisco. One thing personal probabilities have in common with prices is that in neither case is there a right price or probability. Everyone is entitled to his own opinion. Another similarity with price is that it is difficult to say what one would give or take for a particular contingency. One has a sense of vagueness about it. Some people say that this is an objection to subjective probability; Savage sees it as a truth, something unpleasant but not to be escaped in the theory.

Two features of personal probability are (1) that it imposes the difficult responsibility to be honest with oneself and (2) that it requires a coherent person to formulate opinions. It is difficult to be honest with one's self about prices. It is hard to think about a price that would satisfy one in any buying or selling situation. But it must be done if subjective probabilities are to be generated.

A coherent person, according to Savage, is one who does not allow "book" to be made against him. He cannot be put into a position in which he is always paying no matter what happens; that is, if a person is offered a sequence of bets, he will not accept all of them, which would leave him with a negative net. Of course, real people make mistakes; but if a mistake is pointed out to a coherent person, he will generally correct it.

Savage has shown that if a person is consistent, his probability function

[3] Some of the material for this section comes from Leonard S. Savage, "Bayesian Statistics," *Recent Developments in Information and Decision Processes*, edited by Robert E. Machol and Paul Gray (New York: Macmillan Co., 1962), pp. 162–167.

has the first three properties listed on page 17; that is, the probability that he associates with each event is zero or positive, and the probability that one of two mutually independent events will occur is the sum of the two probabilities that each will occur.

Schlaifer's Standard Lottery.   In any decision-making situation there will be one and only one set of probabilities that comply with the three properties and express the decision maker's subjective feeling toward a set of exhaustive and mutually exclusive outcomes or events.   Schlaifer[4] has proposed that a standard lottery be used to find the set of probabilities which describes the decision maker's subjective feelings in any real decision problem.

The standard lottery is one in which the decision maker has a choice between the following two costless ways of attempting to win a prize of value V: (1) he wins the prize if he successfully draws a black ball randomly from a box of balls with different colors; (2) he wins the prize if some subsequent random event θ_1, occurs.   For example, suppose the decision maker is presented with a box containing 100 colored balls; 50 are black and 50 are orange.   He is asked if he would like to try to pick a black ball from the box or take his chances on event θ_1 occurring in order to get the free prize of value V.   If he chooses to pick from the box, he is implying that the probability of event θ_1 occurring is less than $\frac{1}{2}$.   The composition of the box is now changed to 40 black and 60 orange, and he is again given the opportunity to pick a ball from the box or take his chances on event θ_1 occurring to get the prize.   If he chooses to wait for θ_1 to occur, he is implying that the probability of θ_1 occurring is greater than 0.4.   The composition of the box could be changed again and the procedure continued until the decision maker says he is indifferent between picking a ball from the box or waiting for event θ_1 to occur.   In this case the decision maker is implying that for him the event θ_1 has a probability equal to the probability of drawing a black ball from the box. Knowing the proportion of black balls in the box allows us to calculate the probability of drawing a black ball and hence of calculating the decision maker's subjective probability of event θ_1 occurring.

In the wet-dry example of Chapter I there were six states of nature. The standard lottery procedure can be used to determine the subjective probability of each state.   These probabilities should add to one.[5]   If they

[4] Robert Schlaifer, *Introduction to Statistics for Business Decisions* (New York: McGraw-Hill Book Company, Inc., 1961), Chapter 2.
[5] It could also be that two decimal places in a probability do not adequately express his feelings.   In this case the number of balls could be increased to 1,000 to get greater accuracy in the estimate of the probability.

do not, then the decision maker was inconsistent and would correct these inconsistencies if they were pointed out to him.

Prices, Odds, and Probabilities. Another procedure for finding subjective probabilities is to ask the decision maker how much he would pay to have a prize of value V if the state of nature θ_1 would occur. For example, in the wet-dry problem the decision maker could be asked how much he would pay for a chance at $1.00 if θ_1 would occur; that is, if prices favor raisins and there was no damage due to early rains. Various prices that the decision maker could pay are shown in Table 2.1, along with the odds which are implied by the prices and the implied subjective probabilities of the event. Thus, if a decision maker says he would pay $.50 for a $1.00 return should θ_1 occur, he is telling us that the odds for θ_1 are 1 to 1, or that the subjective probability of θ_1 occurring is .50. The other odds and probabilities of Table 2.1 are associated with the prices in a similar fashion.

Given the probability of an event $P(\theta)$ we can say that the odds for θ are a to b if and only if

$$P(\theta) = \frac{a}{a+b}.$$

If the odds for θ are a to b, then the odds against θ are b to a. For example, if the probability of θ is .7, then

$$P(\theta) = \frac{7}{10} = \frac{7}{7+3}$$

and the odds for θ are 7 to 3, and against θ are 3 to 7.

Our discussion of odds and their relationship to subjective probability would apply equally as well to empirical or to logical probabilities, that is, the same interpretation in terms of odds can be given to any type of proba-

TABLE 2.1

RELATION BETWEEN PRICES, ODDS, AND SUBJECTIVE PROBABILITIES

Price for $1 Return if θ_1 Occurs	Subjective Probability	Odds for Event
.50	1/2	1 to 1
.667	2/3	2 to 1
.75	3/4	3 to 1
.375	3/8	3 to 5
.33	1/3	1 to 2
.706	12/17	12 to 5

bility. In fact, one could go one step further and say that if the probability of event θ_1 is $P(\theta_1)$, one should pay no more than $P(\theta_1) \times 1.00$ dollars for a chance at \$1.00 return in the event that θ_1 occurs. If you agree with the last statement, we see no reason why you should not agree when the statement is turned around to read, "The probability of an event θ_1 is the price you would be willing to pay for a \$1.00 return to you in the event that θ_1 occurs." The difference between empirical, logical, and subjective probabilities comes down to a mere difference of interpretation as to the source of the probability statement. We believe this distinction is an important philosophical point; but when it comes to solving decision makers' problems, we believe the recognition of the use of the calculus of probability is more important than the origin of the probability statement.

We believe the origin of the probability is unimportant because any prior probability can be revised in the face of new evidence and experience. The calculus of this revision is our next topic.

CONDITIONAL PROBABILITY

Suppose we have a set of outcomes A from an experiment or some random process and the set is divided into two intersecting subsets A_1 and A_2. Assume that we are given the additional information that all of the outcomes in A_1 have actually occurred. We are interested in knowing how this information affects the probability of A_2 (see Figure 2.A).

Because we know the outcomes in A_1 have occurred, the outcomes in $\tilde{A}_1$ have not occurred and can be eliminated from consideration. Hence, in the light of the added information, the subset A_1 replaces the whole set A as the set whose elements correspond to all possible outcomes of the experiment. The outcomes in A_2 are the ones for which we want the proba-

FIGURE 2.A

VENN DIAGRAM SHOWING SUBSETS A_1 **AND** A_2 **IN** A

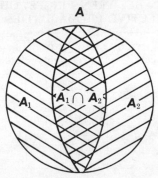

bility. Hence, outcomes not in A_2 but in A_1 are the ones of interest. This dependence between the subsets A_1 and A_2 is indicated by the set $A_1 \cap A_2$. The probability of A_2 given that A_1 has occurred is called the conditional probability and calculated by the formula:

$$P(A_2|A_1) = \frac{P(A_1 \cap A_2)}{P(A_1)} .$$

A simple example will motivate the plausibility of the definition of conditional probability, as well as illustrate the use of the formula. Two well-

TABLE 2.2
SUM OF FACES ON TWO DICE WHEN ROLLED, ONE CALLED, ONE UNCALLED

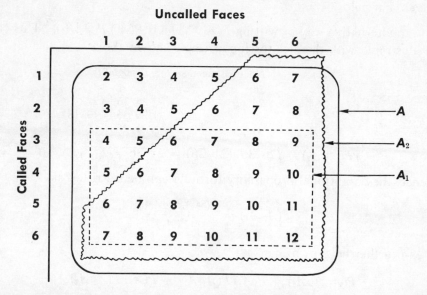

balanced dice are rolled by a friend. He tells you that one die shows a face three or greater. Given this information we are interested in the probability that the sum of the two dice is equal to or greater than six.

The logical possibilities are shown in Table 2.2. The outcomes of this experiment are the sums of the two dice, the set A. A_1 and A_2 are outlined by a dotted and wavy line respectively in Table 2.2. The subset A_1 contains those outcomes for which the called die shows a face equal to or greater than 3. The subset A_2 contains those outcomes for which the sum of the two dice are equal to or greater than six. By counting we can obtain the number of elements in each subset and the probability of each subset.

Subsets	No. of Elements	Probability
A	36	1
A_1	24	24/36
A_2	26	26/36
$A_1 \cap A_2$	21	21/36

Since A_1 replaces A as the set containing all possible outcomes of interest, the probability of a sum equal to or greater than six, given that the face of the called die is equal to or greater than 3, is $21/24 = 7/8$.

Alternatively, from the formula we obtain:

$$P(A_2|A_1) = \frac{P(A_1 \cap A_2)}{P(A_1)} = \frac{21/36}{24/36} = 21/24 = 7/8.$$

Bayes' Formula

An alternative way of writing $P(A_1 \cap A_2)$ is $P(A_2) P(A_1|A_2)$. This can be illustrated with the dice-tossing example shown above.

Subsets	No. of Elements	Probability
A	36	1
A_1	24	$24/36 = 2/3$
A_2	26	$26/36 = 13/18$
$A_1|A_2$	21	21/26

Now, $P(A_2) P(A_1|A_2) = (26/36) (21/26) = 21/36 = P(A_1 \cap A_2)$.

Hence, the conditional probability formula can be rewritten as:

$$P(A_2|A_1) = \frac{P(A_2)P(A_1|A_2)}{P(A_1)}.$$

It can further be shown that:

$$P(A_1 \cap A_2) = P(A_1) P(A_2|A_1) = P(A_2) P(A_1|A_2).$$

The conditional probability formula can be extended to any number of subsets; in fact, to the point where each subset contains just one element. In the latter case the set A with n elements is partitioned into n subsets,

$$\{a_1\} = A_1$$
$$\{a_2\} = A_2$$
$$\cdot$$
$$\cdot$$
$$\cdot$$
$$\{a_n\} = A_n.$$

The subsets $E \cap A_1, E \cap A_2, \ldots, E \cap A_n$, where E is any subset of A made up of one or more of the subsets A_i, are mutually exclusive and exhaustive of the subset E and hence partition the subset E.[5]

Now it follows that:

$$E = (E \cap A_1) \cup (E \cap A_2) \cup \cdots \cup (E \cap A_n)$$

and

$$P(E) = P(E \cap A_1) + P(E \cap A_2) + \cdots + P(E \cap A_n)$$

from property three extended (page 17).

From the definition of conditional probability we have that:

$P(E \cap A_i) = P(A_i) P(E|A_i)$ for $i = 1, \cdots, n$, and hence:

$$P(E) = P(A_1) P(E|A_1) + P(A_2) P(E|A_2) + \cdots + P(A_n) P(E|A_n)$$

Now we can write the conditional probability formula as:

$$P(A_i|E) = \frac{P(E \cap A_i)}{P(E)} = \frac{P(A_i)P(E|A_i)}{P(E)}$$

where E is any subset of A and A_i is a particular subset of A for $i = 1, \cdots, n$.

Substituting for $P(E)$, gives:

$$P(A_i|E) = \frac{P(A_i)P(E|A_i)}{P(A_1)P(E|A_1) + \cdots + P(A_n)P(E|A_n)}.$$

This is the celebrated Bayes' formula that will be used extensively throughout the remainder of this book. Its importance to the philosophy of decision theory will be referred to again in Chapter XII.

SUMMARY

This chapter has shown that a probability function over the states of nature of a decision-making problem can be defined in at least three ways. These were (1) by deducing all the logical possibilities for the states and their associated probabilities, (2) by empirically observing the frequency of the states from historical data, and (3) by subjective assignment. It was demonstrated that the rules of the probability calculus apply regardless of which way was used to define the probability function over the states. The final result was Bayes' formula, which will be used as the basis for further development of decision theory in subsequent chapters and the means for solving complex decision problems in research applications.

[5] Some of the subsets $E \cap A_i$ may be empty, otherwise $E = A$.

FURTHER READINGS

Goldberg, Samuel. *Probability*. Englewood Cliffs, N.J.: Prentice-Hall, Inc., 1960, Chapters 1, 2.

Good, Irving John. *The Estimation of Probabilities, An Essay on Modern Bayesian Methods*. Cambridge, Mass.: The M.I.T. Press, 1965, Chapter 2.

Kattsoff, Louis O., and Albert J. Simone. *Finite Mathematics*. New York: McGraw-Hill Book Co., 1965, Chapters 1,2,3,4.

Machol, Robert E., and Paul Gray (Editors), *Recent Developments in Information and Decision Processes*. New York: Macmillan Co., 1962.

EXERCISES

1. It is known that 0.4 of the 1,000 persons who own property favor a school bond issue, while 0.3 of those who own property are opposed to the new issue. Of the 200 persons who do not own property but can vote in the school bond issue, 0.2 favor and 0.1 oppose the new issue.
   a) What is the probability that a voter selected at random favors the bond issue?
   b) What is the probability that a voter selected at random owns property?
   c) What is the probability that a voter selected at random favors the issue or owns property?

2. A stockbroker in the past has successfully predicted the behavior of the market, using his own method, 80 percent of the time. What is the probability that he will make 10 bad predictions in a row? What assumptions must you make to obtain this probability? Would you change stock brokers if he made 10 bad predictions in a row?

3. Grocery stores usually stock special items to encourage sales. A given store advertises a special on milk and honey if purchased together. It is known that the probability of a customer buying both milk and honey is 0.07, while the probability of buying milk alone is 0.20. What is the probability that a customer who has purchased milk will buy honey also?

4. A saw-mill owner has four tracts of timber of equal size and density of trees. It has been found that 40 percent of the timber from tract 1 saws into low quality lumber, 30 percent of the lumber from tract 2 is low quality, and 15 percent from each of tract 3 and tract 4. If 70 percent of the trees on tract 1 are cut, 50 percent of tract 2, and 20 percent of tract 3 and tract 4, what is the probability of a low-quality log selected at random from the mill pond being from tract 2?

5. Three urns contain colored balls as specified below:

Urn	Red	White	Black
1	3	4	1
2	1	2	3
3	4	3	2

One urn is chosen at random and a ball is withdrawn. Suppose it is a red ball. What is the probability that it came from urn 2?

6. You know that urn *A* contains 2 green and 1 red ball and urn *B* contains 3 green and 2 red balls. One of these urns is selected at random, but you don't know which one is selected. You may perform one of the following experiments before guessing which urn was selected:
   a) Take one ball out of the selected urn and observe its color.

b) Take two balls out of the selected urn, replacing the first before drawing the second, and observe their colors.

c) Same as b) except that you do not replace the first ball before drawing the second.

Which of the three experiments would you prefer to use and why?

7. In a survey of producing firms over an extended period of time it was found that four maximum profit outputs were likely to occur. These are:

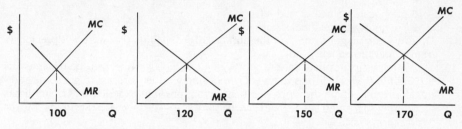

Let A_1 = the set of profit points where the output is between 0 and 100.
Let A_2 = the set of profit points where the output is between 0 and 150.
Let A_3 = the set of profit points where the output is between 0 and 170.
What can you conclude about the probabilities of A_1 or A_2 or A_3?

8. For the decision-making problem:

	Losses			Frequency Table			
	a_1	a_2	a_3	z_1	z_2	z_3	z_4
θ_1	1	2	3	$\frac{1}{2}$	$\frac{1}{2}$	0	0
θ_2	5	2	3	0	$\frac{1}{2}$	$\frac{1}{2}$	0
θ_3	7	6	3	0	0	$\frac{1}{3}$	$\frac{2}{3}$

and $s_1 = (a_1,a_1,a_2,a_2)$ indicate the point at which the assertion $P\{A_1 \cup A_2 \cup A_3\} \leq P\{A_1\} + P\{A_2\} + P\{A_3\}$ is used. Why does $P\{A_1 \cup A_2 \cup A_3\} = P\{A_1\} + P\{A_2\} + P\{A_3\}$ hold in this case?

9. Bowl I contains 3 red chips and 7 blue chips. Bowl II contains 6 red and 4 blue. A bowl is selected at random and then one chip is drawn from this bowl.
a) Compute P (chip is red)
b) Relative to hypothesis that the chip is red, find conditional probability that it is drawn from bowl II.

10. Consider tossing a pair of die. The set $A = \{(x,y)$ such that $(x,y) = (1,1), \ldots, (1,6), (2,1), \ldots, (2,6), \ldots, (6,6)\}$ contains 36 elements in its domain. Let the random variable $R = f(x,y)$ represent the range of this function, where (x,y) represents the outcome of one toss of the pair of die. If the numbers $1,2, \ldots, 36$ are assigned respectively to the various outcomes, then these numbers $1,2, \ldots, 36$ are the range of the function $f(x,y)$ which assigns the numbers: $1 = f(1,1)$, $2 = f(1,2), \ldots, 36 = f(6,6)$ as the values of random variable R.

Let the probability function be defined by $P(A) = \dfrac{\text{Number of elements in } A}{36}$

If A_1 is a subset containing $x = 1$ and A_2 is a subset containing $y = 6$ find $P(A_1)$, $P(A_2)$, $P(A_1 \cap A_2)$ and $P(A_1 \cup A_2)$.

11. Subjective probability may be developed for the weight of a mystery box. I offer for sale a contract promising to pay $10 to the holder of the contract if the box weighs more than 20 pounds. How much will you bid for the contract? If some-

one offers $8, how would you interpret this in terms of the probability of the box weighing over 20 pounds?

12. An experiment with 50 rats running through a maze showed the following results:
    25 were males
    25 were previously trained
    20 turned left
    10 were previously trained males
    4 males turned left
    15 previously trained turned left
    3 previously trained males turned left
    Draw a Venn diagram and find the number of female rats that were not previously trained and turned left.

13. Mr. Smith estimates that the probability that today's weather will be inclement is 0.2 and fair 0.8. He listens to an early morning weather forecast to get some additional information on the day's weather. From previous experience Mr. Smith has found the following conditional probabilities to describe the accuracy of the weather forecasts.

		Forecast	
Today's Weather	Fair	Inclement	Uncertain
A_1 Fair	0.7	0.2	0.1
A_2 Inclement	0.3	0.6	0.1

You are asked to determine the probability of fair weather given that Mr. Smith hears the forecaster predict fair weather. (Use Bayes' formula.)

14. Using the conditional probabilities of Table 1.2 and the prior probabilities $P(\theta_1) = 0.5$, $P(\theta_2) = 0.3$, and $P(\theta_3) = 0.2$, calculate using Bayes' formula the $P(\theta_i|z_k)$ probabilities.

15. Illustrate the property that $P(A_1 \cup A_2 \cup A_3) \leq P(A_1) + P(A_2) + P(A_3)$ for the following sets and probabilities. The probability function for the random variable X is:

X	0	1	2	3	4
$f(X)$	$\frac{1}{12}$	$\frac{1}{4}$	$\frac{1}{4}$	$\frac{1}{3}$	$\frac{1}{12}$

The sets are defined to be

$$A_1 = \{0,1,2\}$$
$$A_2 = \{1,2,3\}$$
$$A_3 = \{2,3,4\}.$$

16. Of the people in a town 25% read paper A, 30% read paper B, and 5% read both A and B. A person is randomly selected from the townspeople.
    a) What is the probability he does not read A?
    b) What is the probability that he reads A or B?
    c) Given that he reads B, what is the probability that he reads A also?

17. Prove the following using the results of problem 16 and Property #3.
    Let A be the set of outcomes with probability function P.
    If A_1 and A_2 are any two subsets of A, then

$$P(A_1 \cup A_2) = P(A_1) + P(A_2) - P(A_1 \cap A_2)$$

[Hint: A_1 and $\tilde{A}_1 \cap A_2$ are disjoint, so are $A_1 \cap A_2$ and $\tilde{A}_1 \cap A_2$]
Note that $A_1 \cup A_2 = A_1 \cup (\tilde{A}_1 \cap A_2)$ from Problem 16.

18. Assume that a graduate class consists of 16 male students and 4 female students. Among the male students 5 are Ph.D. students and 11 are Master students. Among the 4 female students 1 is a Ph.D. student and 3 are Master students. We write each student's name on a slip of paper and mix the slips in a hat.

   a) What is the probability of drawing a Ph.D. student, given that it is a male student?

   b) What is the probability of drawing a Master student, given that it is a female?

19. An urn contains 10 balls of which X are white and the rest 10-X are black. My friend is going to draw one ball at random from the urn and I guess the color of the ball that is drawn. I win if my guess is correct and lose otherwise.

Suppose I have the following strategies that can be used for making my guess.

   Strategy 1. I guess a white ball is drawn.
   Strategy 2. I guess a black ball is drawn.
   Strategy 3. I first draw a ball from the urn and replace it.
                If it is white, I guess a black will be drawn.
                If it is black, I guess a white will be drawn.

The probability of whether my guess is correct or wrong depends upon both the value of X and the strategy I decide to use.

Calculate the probability of my winning with each strategy and for values of X from 0 to 10.

CHAPTER III

Decisions Involving Expected Values (Utility Measurement)

The concepts of probability developed in Chapter II are vital in every decision problem under uncertainty. For example, in the "wet or dry" and "forest fire" problems of Chapter I, probabilities were used in computing the expected value (weighted average), monetary gain, or utility of each action or strategy. It was argued without much justification that choosing the action or the strategy with the maximum expected value appeared to be a reasonable criterion of choice. In this chapter, we provide the theory and rationale for using the maximum expected value of utility as a general criterion of choice in decision making under uncertainty. While maximizing expected utility is shown to be the general choice criterion, we also identify the class of cases in which maximizing expected monetary value is identical with maximizing expected utility and can therefore be substituted without error as a choice indicator. In the process, we will develop a precise definition of utility and demonstrate how it is derived in a practical setting.

To bring out the importance of the discussion of utility in this chapter, consider the following example:

States	a_1	a_2	$P(\theta_i)$
		Dollars	
θ_1	0	10,000	$\frac{1}{2}$
θ_2	0	$-10,000$	$\frac{1}{2}$
Expected value	0	0	

When expected monetary gain is used as a choice criterion, the decision maker would be indifferent between a_1 and a_2. Clearly, most people would not be indifferent, particularly if a \$10,000 gain or loss were large in relation to current wealth and if this choice were a nonrepeated decision. Evidently, in such a case, monetary values are not measuring accurately the real consequences of the gains or losses involved in the problem. Our aim in this chapter is to show how it is possible to derive a function that relates monetary values to another scale which measures the subjective value that the decision maker attaches to different levels of wealth. We call this subjective scale a utility scale and the function a utility function.

Suppose you had a utility function as shown in Figure 3.A (page 34), where wealth is measured along the horizontal axis and utility along the vertical axis. Your initial wealth is $15,000 at point M_2. If you take action a_1, you remain at point M_2 with your original holding intact. However, if you take action a_2, you could be, with probability $\frac{1}{2}$, at point M_1 with an increase in wealth of $10,000; or you could be, with probability $\frac{1}{2}$, at point M_3 with a decrease in wealth of $10,000. Your utilities at points M_1, M_2, and M_3 are 20, 55, and 70, respectively. Converting the payoff table above to utility we obtain:

States	a_1	a_2	$P(\theta_i)$
	Utility		
θ_1	55	70	$\frac{1}{2}$
θ_2	55	20	$\frac{1}{2}$
Expected utility	55	45	

Now we find the expected value (expected utility) for each action. The expected value for a_1 is $\frac{1}{2}(55) + \frac{1}{2}(55) = 55$ and for a_2 is $\frac{1}{2}(70) + \frac{1}{2}(20) = 45$. Given this particular utility function, you would choose a_1. Notice from Figure 3.A that the expected utility of the certain amount $15,000 occurs at M_2; and that the expected utility of the uncertain action a_2 occurs at M_4 which falls on a straight line between M_1 and M_3 at the expected gain of $15,000.

In obtaining the expected utility values in the above example, we see that the probabilities attached to the θ's apply to the monetary outcomes of each action. Thus each action transforms the random variable θ into two new random variables, that is, the monetary outcomes of actions a_1 and a_2. The utility function transforms the monetary scale into a utility scale. Since the monetary outcomes correspond to a random variable, the transformed utility outcomes correspond to another random variable. The original probability distribution applies directly to the utility outcomes in obtaining the expected value of utility.

FIGURE 3.A
UTILITY FUNCTION FOR WEALTH

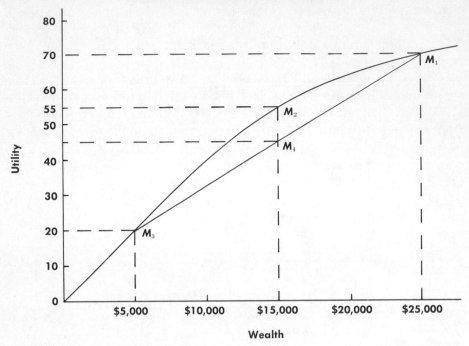

In contrast to the discrete case just discussed, some decision problems involve continuous probability distributions and payoff functions. In the continuous case, the transformations are not as straightforward as in the discrete situation. To provide an intuitive basis for making these same transformations in the continuous case, we illustrate them graphically in Figure 3.B. Where θ is a continuous function, it is necessary to find the probability distribution (usually also continuous) of the outcomes (payoffs) of each action individually. Case 1, Figure 3.B shows in the top diagram a continuous uniform distribution $P(\theta)$ over the range of θ from a to b; that is, each value of θ (state of nature) is equally likely. The second diagram under Case 1 represents the function showing the payoffs or outcomes (in money, M) of a selected action for any state of nature represented by the continuous variable, θ; this function is sometimes called the *response function*. The third diagram under Case 1 shows the resulting probability distribution of the outcomes (in money terms) which, in the case of a uniform $P(\theta)$ and linear response function, is itself uniform. In this case, the action results in a range of monetary outcomes in the range A to B, each of which is equally likely. The fourth diagram under Case 1 shows the utility function $U = f(M)$ with diminishing marginal utility

FIGURE 3.B
CONVERSION OF CONTINUOUS $P(\theta)$ INTO THE PROBABILITY DISTRIBUTION OF OUTCOMES FOR A GIVEN ACTION, WHERE OUTCOMES ARE EXPRESSED IN MONEY (M) OR UTILITY (U)

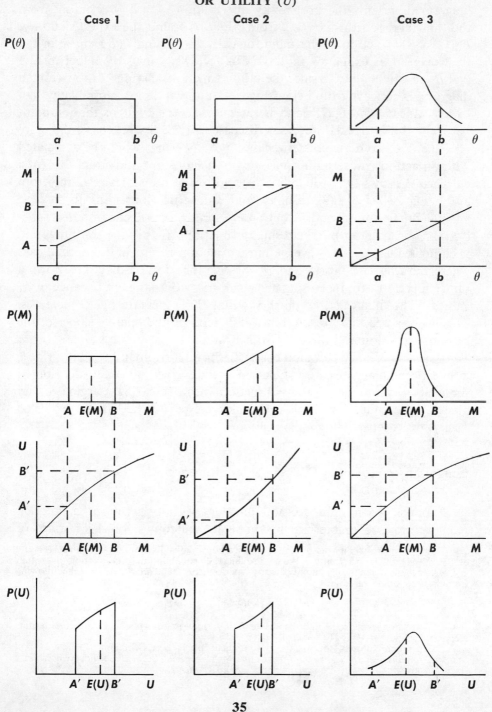

35

throughout, that is, utility increasing at a decreasing rate. This function relates the monetary outcomes with the utility scale selected. The final diagram represents the probability distribution of utility resulting from the third and fourth diagrams from which is found the expected utility, $E(U)$, of that action. The monotonically increasing $P(U)$ curve in the final diagram is explained intuitively as follows: values of M between A and B are equally likely; since the utility function relating U to M (fourth diagram) is concave from below, higher utility values are more likely than lower values. The $E(U)$ point is therefore to the right of the midpoint between A' and B'. However, as discussed in the discrete case of Figure 3.A, the $E(U)$ so derived is lower than the $E(U)$ that would be associated with an action whose monetary outcome is constant and equal to $E(M)$.

Case 2 shows the probability distribution of outcomes resulting from an alternative set of $P(\theta)$, response and utility functions. In this case we again assume a uniform distribution $P(\theta)$, but a non-linear response function (second diagram). The resulting function $P(M)$ in the third diagram need not be linear. However, a linear function results in our special case where the $P(\theta)$ is uniform and $M = \sqrt{\theta}$. The fourth diagram shows a utility function with increasing marginal utility over the entire range of M values. The final $P(U)$ graph shows that $P(U)$ increases as U increases. This is not a necessary result, but will depend on the relative slopes of the response function and the utility function.

Case 3 is a fairly common case. It shows a normal distribution of θ, a linear monetary response function, which gives normally distributed monetary outcomes.[1] A utility function with decreasing marginal utility gives a probability distribution of utility skewed to the left and expected utility to the left of the modal utility.

Converting a Complex Decision to a Standard Reference Contract[2]

Suppose we have a decision problem with two actions a_1 and a_2. Each action is characterized by monetary outcomes for three states of

---

[1] Let $f(\theta)$ = probability density function for a continuous distribution of θ, and $M = r(\theta)$ or $\theta = r^{-1}(M)$ for some action a_1. We wish to find the probability density function of M, that is $k(M)$. To transform the probability density function from $f(\theta)$ to $k(M)$, we need the following formula for a single variable:

$$k(M) = f[r^{-1}(M)]\frac{dr^{-1}(M)}{dM}.$$

In Case 3, the first term on the right-hand side of this equation is normal and the second term is a constant, hence, $k(M)$ is also normal.

[2] This section closely follows the development by Robert Schlaiffer, *Probability and Statistics for Business Decisions, An Introduction to Managerial Economics Under Uncertainty* (New York: McGraw-Hill Book Company, 1959), Chapter 2.

nature as shown in Table 3.1. In this case, the states of nature are defined differently for each action and hence a different probability distribution applies for each action. Calculation of the expected monetary value (EMV) for each action shows $2,400 for a_1 and $1,800 for a_2.

To analyze this problem further, let us introduce the idea of a "standard reference contract." To set up the reference contract, we look at the most favorable and least favorable monetary consequences in the problem, in our case, $8,000 and −$8,000. We then select two values at least as favorable and as unfavorable as these values, let us say, $10,000 and −$10,000. Using these latter values, we define a "reference contract" (Alternative A) as one in which there is a probability π of winning $10,000

TABLE 3.1
AN EXAMPLE DECISION PROBLEM

States	a_1	$P(\theta_i)$	States	a_2	$P(\theta_i)$
θ_1	$8,000	.3	θ_1'	$6,000	.4
θ_2	6,000	.4	θ_2'	0	.5
θ_3	−8,000	.3	θ_3'	−6,000	.1
EMV	$2,400		EMV	$1,800	

and a probability $(1 - \pi)$ of losing $10,000. We define another alternative (Alternative B) as receiving a given amount of money with complete certainty. The alternatives are then

Alternative A: A reference contract with $\begin{cases} \text{probability } \pi \text{ of winning} \\ \$10,000 \\ \text{probability } (1 - \pi) \text{ of losing} \\ \$10,000 \end{cases}$

Alternative B: A given amount of money with certainty ("certain cash").

The decision maker is then asked to indicate his preference between A and B for a series of different values of π and levels of "certain cash." This process can be clarified by considering Table 3.2. Alternative B (certain cash) is listed in the left-hand column. Alternative A, providing either $10,000 with probability π or −$10,000 with probability $(1 - \pi)$, is listed across the top. The decision maker is then asked to indicate for each cell in each column whether he prefers A or B or is indifferent. For example, start from the bottom of the first column of Table 3.2. Do you prefer $11,000 certain cash ($B$) or a reference contract (A) with probability 1.0 of winning $10,000 and probability 0 of losing $10,000? Alternative

TABLE 3.2

CHOICE TABLE FOR FINDING INDIFFERENCE POINTS BETWEEN CERTAIN CASH AND VARIOUS REFERENCE CONTRACTS

Certain Cash (Alternative B)	Reference Contract with Probability π (Alternative A)					
	$\pi = 1.0$	$\pi = .8$	$\pi = .6$	$\pi = .4$	$\pi = .2$	$\pi = 0$
Dollars						
−11,000	A	A	A	A	A	A
−10,000	.	.	.	.	.	Indifferent
−9,000	.	.	.	.	A	B
−8,000	.	.	.	.	Indifferent	.
−7,000	.	.	.	A	B	.
−6,000	.	.	.	Indifferent	.	.
−5,000	.	.	.	B	.	.
−4,000	.	.	A	.	.	.
−3,000	.	.	Indifferent	.	.	.
−2,000	.	.	B	.	.	.
−1,000	.	.	.	.	.	.
0	.	.	.	.	.	.
1,000	.	A	.	.	.	.
2,000	.	Indifferent	.	.	.	.
3,000	.	B	.	.	.	.
4,000	.	.	.	.	.	.
5,000	.	.	.	.	.	.
6,000	.	.	.	.	.	.
7,000	.	.	.	.	.	.
8,000	.	.	.	.	.	.
9,000	A	.	.	.	.	.
10,000	Indifferent	.	.	.	.	.
11,000	B	B	B	B	B	B

B is obviously preferred. Moving up to the next cell, ask a similar question: Do you prefer $10,000 certain cash (*B*) or a reference contract (*A*) with probability 1.0 of winning $10,000 and probability 0 of losing $10,000? These alternatives are obviously identical and we write "indifferent." Moving up to the next cell and asking a similar question, we find that *A* is clearly preferred and likewise for all cells in the remainder of the first column. The remainder of the table is filled out in similar fashion. However, considerable reflection and introspection will be required in finding the indifference cells in the other columns (try it!). Obviously, except for the first and last columns, we would expect different decision makers to select a different pattern of "indifference" points depending, for example, on their initial wealth position and their general attitude toward taking risks.

The indifference points obtained in Table 3.2 are now plotted in Figure 3.C and a free-hand curve drawn through the six points. Of course,

FIGURE 3.C
CERTAIN CASH VALUES EQUIVALENT TO ALTERNATIVE
REFERENCE CONTRACTS

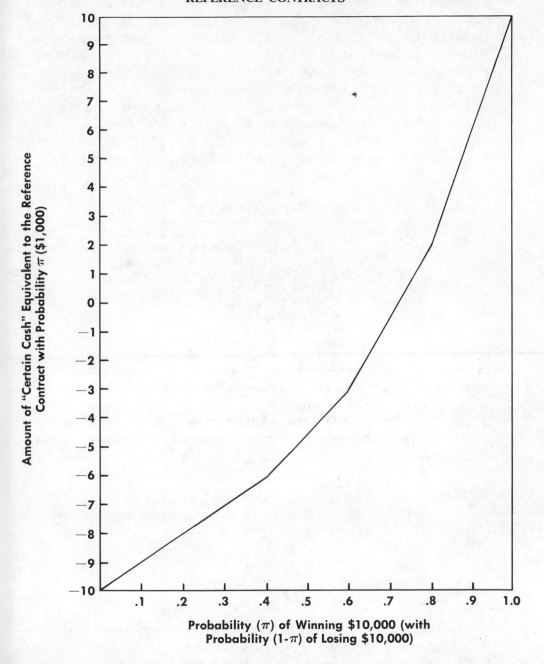

in practice, the curve might be constructed from more points (say, varying π in 0.1 intervals instead of 0.2 intervals). As a minimum, we should check other points on the curve shown in Figure 3.C to make sure that the decision maker is content with the values shown. Figure 3.C then shows what amount of certain cash is equivalent, in the decision maker's mind, to a reference contract in which he has a probability of winning $10,000 with probability π or losing $10,000 with probability $(1 - \pi)$.

Table 3.3 repeats the data for action a_1 in our original decision problem of Table 3.1. Reading from the curve in Figure 3.C, we see that the decision maker is indifferent between $8,000 "certain cash" and a reference contract with probability $\pi = .96$ of winning $10,000 (and probability $1 - \pi = .04$ of losing $10,000). The π values for a reference contract

TABLE 3.3
RESTATEMENT OF ACTION a_1

States	a_1	$P(\theta_i)$	π for a Reference Contract Equivalent to the Payoff ("Certain Cash") Value for Each θ_i
θ_1	$8,000	.3	.96
θ_2	6,000	.4	.91
θ_3	$-8,000	.3	.20

equivalent to $6,000 and $-$8,000 are .91 and .20, respectively, as also read from the curve in Figure 3.C. Thus, we might think of a new action $a_1{}^*$, which is equivalent to the original action a_1. The new action, $a_1{}^*$, has only two outcomes: $10,000 and $-$10,000. The question is: What are the probabilities associated with the two outcomes ($10,000 and $-$10,000) of the new action, $a_1{}^*$?

Let

$P_1 =$ probability of winning $10,000 for action $a_1{}^*$ and
$P_2 = 1 - P_1 =$ probability of losing $10,000 for action $a_1{}^*$,

then

$$P_1 = P(\theta_1)\pi(\theta_1) + P(\theta_2)\pi(\theta_2) + P(\theta_3)\pi(\theta_3)$$
$$= .3(.96) + .4(.91) + .3(.20)$$
$$= .71.$$

This result can be explained by referring to Table 3.3. The probability of obtaining $8,000 = P(\theta_1) = .3$. However, obtaining $8,000 is equivalent to a reference contract with $\pi = .96$ of winning $10,000. Therefore, the probability of θ_1 occurring and winning \$10,000 is $P(\theta_1)\pi(\theta_1) = .3(.96) = .288$. Similarly, the probability of θ_2 occurring and winning \$10,000 is $P(\theta_2)\pi(\theta_2) = .4(.91) = .364$, while the probability of θ_3 occurring and winning \$10,000 is $P(\theta_3)\pi(\theta_3) = .3(.20) = .06$. Since the three states of nature are mutually exclusive and exhaustive, the overall probability of winning \$10,000 is the sum of these three probabilities $= .71$. P_2, the probability of losing \$10,000 under the new action, $a_1{}^*$, is calculated similarly as follows:

$$P_2 = P(\theta_1)(1 - \pi)(\theta_1) + P(\theta_2)(1 - \pi)(\theta_2) + P(\theta_3)(1 - \pi)(\theta_3)$$
$$= .3(.04) + .4(.09) + .3(.80)$$
$$= .29.$$

We have thus replaced an action (a_1) with three outcomes by an action ($a_1{}^*$) with only two outcomes as shown in Table 3.5. This reduction of the

TABLE 3.4
Restatement of Action a_2

States	a_2	$P(\theta_i')$	π for a Reference Contract Equivalent to the Payoff ("Certain Cash") Value for Each θ_1'
θ_1'	\$6,000	.4	.91
θ_2'	0	.5	.72
θ_3'	−6,000	.1	.40

original problem to an equivalent problem with two outcomes is always possible, regardless of the number of outcomes in the original problem.

The other original action a_2 can now also be restated as an equivalent two-state action $a_2{}^*$ in a way analogous to that described above for transforming action a_1 to the equivalent two-state action, $a_1{}^*$. The relevant data are shown in Table 3.4.

Let

$P_1' =$ probability of winning \$10,000 for action $a_2{}^*$ and
$P_2' = 1 - P_1' =$ probability of losing \$10,000 for action $a_2{}^*$,

then

$$P_1' = P(\theta_1')\pi(\theta_1') + P(\theta_2')\pi(\theta_2') + P(\theta_3')\pi(\theta_3')$$
$$= .4(.91) + .5(.72) + .1(.40)$$
$$= .76 \text{ and}$$
$$P_2' = 1 - P_1' = .24.$$

We may now restate the original problem in terms of the modified two-state problem of Table 3.5. It is now clear that action $a_2{}^*$ (or its equivalent

a_2) is preferred to action a_1^* (equivalent to a_1), since a_2^* has the higher probability of winning \$10,000. Note that this decision reverses the choice between a_1 and a_2 in the original problem of Table 3.1 where expected monetary value was used as the decision criterion. This reversal is the result of allowing the decision maker's subjective feeling about risky situations, as expressed in Table 3.2, to affect the choice. The beauty of this procedure is that it can take any problem with many actions and states of nature and reduce it to a modified problem like that of Table 3.5 where each action has only two standard consequences.[3] However, applying this procedure to every separate decision problem facing a single decision

TABLE 3.5

**RESTATEMENT OF ORIGINAL DECISION
PROBLEM OF TABLE 3.1**

States	a_1^*	$P(S_i)$	States	a_2^*	$P(S_i')$
S_1	\$10,000	.71	S_1'	\$10,000	.76
S_2	−10,000	.29	S_2'	−10,000	.24

maker would be cumbersome and, in fact, as we shall see in the following section, unnecessary.

Utility Measurement

We hope that the steps taken in the preceding section appear to be reasonable as a way of accounting for subjective feelings toward risk in a decision problem. We now show that acceptance of the above procedure is equivalent to accepting a certain kind of "utility" and "utility function."

Suppose we arbitrarily select any two numbers to represent the utility of \$10,000 and −\$10,000 in the problem of the last section. For example, let

$$U(-\$10,000) = 0 \text{ and}$$
$$U(\$10,000) \;\;\; = 100.$$

Thus we have arbitrarily selected an origin and a scale for measuring utilities. A utility function so derived is a cardinal (rather than ordinal)

---

[3] It might also be noted that we could express our results in terms of a kind of "certainty equivalence." Since action a_1^* has a probability $P_1 = \pi = .71$ of winning \$10,000, we could read directly from the curve in Figure 3.C that this is equivalent to a "certain cash" payment of −\$400. Action a_2^* with $P_1' = \pi = .76$, however, has a "certain cash" payment of \$1,000. If we accept the assumptions made throughout the procedure used in this section, we can say that the "certainty equivalent" of the original risky action a_1 is −\$400 and that of a_2 is \$1,000. Clearly action a_2 is preferred.

function in a very restricted sense. Specifically, a monotonic linear transformation of the original utility function is itself a utility function that,
when applied to particular choice problems, results in the same decision as
the original function. We cannot, however, say that if the utility of
$A(U_A) = 10$ and $(U_B) = 60$ that the decision maker prefers B "6 times as
much" as A. Because the scale is arbitrary, we might have chosen another
scale such that, for example, $U_A = 10$ and $U_B = 600$. However, the
relative magnitudes of differences between utility numbers are meaningful
in that these do not change by a linear transformation. For example, sup-
pose $U_A - U_B > U_C - U_D$. Choose a linear transformation $U = aU^* + b, a > 0$. Substituting this transformation in the above inequality
we obtain:

$$(aU_A{}^* + b) - (aU_B{}^* + b) > (aU_C{}^* + b) - (aU_D{}^* + b)$$

or

$$U_A{}^* - U_B{}^* > U_C{}^* - U_D{}^*.$$

Thus, the relative utility differences are invariant under a linear transformation. Because of this characteristic, the general shape of the utility
function is not dependent on the origin and scale chosen (that is, the second
derivative of the utility function is invariant under a linear transformation).

Let us return to our particular example where we have arbitrarily selected $U(-\$10,000) = 0$ and $U(\$10,000) = 100$. We can then calculate
the expected utility (weighted average utility) for any reference contract
having probability π of winning $10,000 (and $1 - \pi$ of losing $10,000).
This expected utility is equal to the utility of the "certain cash" amount
because the "certain cash" amount is equivalent to that reference contract. For example, suppose we want to find the utility of a "certain
cash" value of $-\$6,000$. Figure 3.C shows that this is equivalent to a
reference contract with probability $\pi = .4$; therefore, the utilities of these
two equivalent choices are also equal. Thus

$$\begin{aligned} U(-\$6,000) &= U(\$10,000)\pi + U(-\$10,000)(1 - \pi) \\ &= 100(.4) + (0)(.6) \\ &= 40. \end{aligned}$$

Utilities for other "certain cash" values are calculated similarly. For
example,

$$\begin{aligned} U(\$8,000) &= U(\$10,000)\pi + U(-\$10,000)(1 - \pi) \\ &= 100(.96) + (0)(.04) \\ &= 96. \end{aligned}$$

FIGURE 3.D
THE UTILITY FUNCTION, USING DATA OF FIGURE 3.C

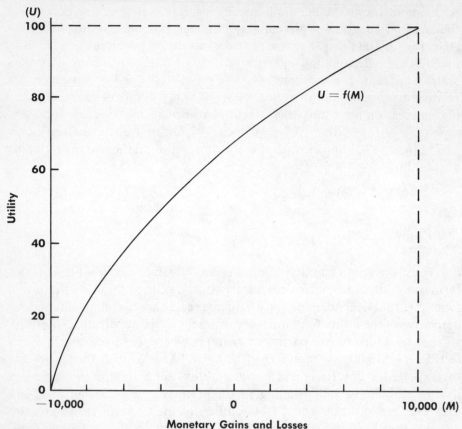

The utility function $U = f(M)$ derived from calculating such points is shown in Figure 3.D.

We can now read the utility values from the utility function of Figure 3.D corresponding to the monetary values in the original problem of Table 3.1 and solve directly for expected utilities of actions a_1 and a_2. These steps are set out in Table 3.6. The careful reader will note that the utility function of Figure 3.D is the same curve as that shown earlier in Figure 3.C with axes reversed and the probability axis rescaled to utility values. The numerical correspondence is obtained by choosing $U(-\$10{,}000) = 0$ and $U(\$10{,}000) = 100$. (However, regardless of the two arbitrary values chosen, the curve would have the same general shape as that of Figure 3.D.) Further, note that the utility values which appear in Table 3.6 correspond to the π values appearing in Tables 3.3 and 3.4, and, finally, that the expected utilities of the two actions in Table 3.6 correspond to the probabilities of winning $10,000 in Table 3.5. It is easy to see that defining a utility function as we have in this section and maximizing expected utility is equivalent to the procedure in the previous section where we reduced all complex actions to a set of standard two-state actions and selected that one with the highest probability of the more favorable consequence. Thus, the simplified procedure is to obtain a utility function from a two-state standard reference contract and apply the function to problems with many states and many actions.

TABLE 3.6
PRESENTATION OF ORIGINAL PROBLEM IN TERMS OF UTILITY VALUES

States	a_1	$P(\theta_1)$	States	a_2	$P(\theta_i')$
	Utility			Utility	
θ_1	96	.3	θ_1'	91	.4
θ_2	91	.4	θ_2'	72	.5
θ_3	20	.3	θ_3'	40	.1
Expected utility 71				76	

Types of Utility Functions

Within a given range of outcomes, the utility function can have three general shapes as shown in Figure 3.E. All three functions increase monotonically throughout, i.e., $dU/dM > 0$, showing that all three individuals prefer more money to less. However, the marginal utility of an additional dollar of gain varies among the three cases. Individual I has a constant marginal utility of money, i.e., $d^2U/d^2M = 0$, indicating that he values an additional dollar of income just as highly regardless of whether it is the first dollar of gain or the 10,000th dollar of gain. Individual II has a decreasing marginal utility of money, i.e., $d^2U/d^2M < 0$, indicating that as dollar gains increase, they become subjectively less valuable. Conversely, Individual III subjectively values each dollar of gain more highly, i.e., $d^2U/d^2M > 0$; he is a person who will sometimes take an "unfair" bet in the sense that he will take an action for which the expected monetary value of the outcomes is negative.

To illustrate more clearly the effect of alternative shapes of utility functions, consider the problem set out in Table 3.7. The initial problem at the left is in terms of dollar payoffs, showing both actions with the same expected monetary value (EMV).   When the same problem is solved with a linear utility function (Individual I's utility function from Figure 3.E), we find expected utility (*EU*) equal for the two actions.   Thus, when the

FIGURE 3.E
THREE POSSIBLE SHAPES OF UTILITY FUNCTIONS

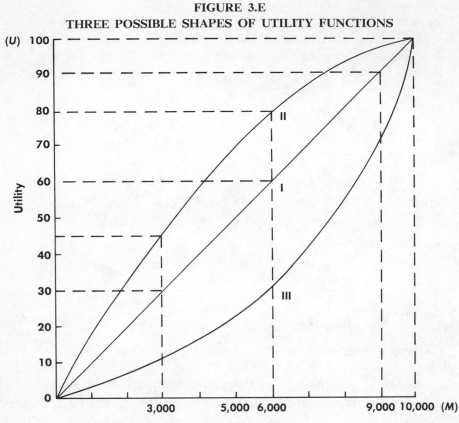

Monetary Gains

utility function is linear, maximizing expected monetary value will also maximize expected utility.   If we now solve the same problem, Table 3.7, with a utility function showing diminishing marginal utility (Individual II), we find that action a_1 provides higher expected utility. This is in line with our intuition: Individual II is "conservative" in the sense that in a risky situation he prefers the action with lower variability, even though both have the same expected monetary value.   Individual III, on the other hand, is a "risk taker" or "gambler" in the sense that he will pick the action with greater variability even though both have the same expected monetary value. His utility function shows that he values very highly the small chance of very large gains.

It should be stressed that there is nothing "irrational" in the behavior of either of these individuals. For example, if the "risk taker" (Individual III) is offered two actions with the same two possible monetary outcomes, he will choose the action that has the higher probability of the more favorable outcome. Hence, even a risk taker prefers less risk to more risk — given the same monetary outcomes. This comparison of decision behavior

TABLE 3.7

PRESENTATION OF A DECISION PROBLEM WITH THE THREE KINDS OF UTILITY FUNCTIONS SHOWN IN FIGURE 3.E

				Problem with Different Types of Marginal Utility (MU)					
Initial Problem				Constant MU (Individual I)		Decreasing MU (Individual II)		Increasing MU (Individual III)	
$P(\theta_i)$	States	a_1	a_2	a_1	a_2	a_1	a_2	a_1	a_2
		Dollars		Utility					
$\frac{1}{3}$	θ_1	6,000	3,000	60	30	80	45	30	10
$\frac{1}{3}$	θ_2	6,000	6,000	60	60	80	80	30	30
$\frac{1}{3}$	θ_3	6,000	9,000	60	90	80	95	30	70
EMV		6,000	6,000	EU 60	60	EU 80	$73\frac{1}{3}$	30	$36\frac{2}{3}$

(risk taking) between individuals is not an interpersonal comparison of utility. The fallacy of interpersonal comparisons of utility will be discussed below.

Figure 3.F shows another shape for the utility function $U = f(M)$ that has received much attention in the literature.[4] It shows, for example, why an individual might simultaneously (1) buy fire insurance when the cost of the premium is greater than the expected monetary value of the loss and (2) buy a lottery ticket when the cost of the ticket is greater than the expected monetary value of the lottery. In the first instance, the individual is comparing a small dollar outlay to the small probability of some very large loss, therefore, he is operating on the "conservative" portion of his utility curve to the left of his initial position in Figure 3.F.

[4] Milton Friedman and L. J. Savage, "The Expected Utility Hypothesis and the Measurability of Utility," *Journal of Political Economy*, Vol. 60 (December, 1952), pp. 463–474.

In the second instance, he is comparing a small dollar outlay to the small probability of a very large gain; therefore, he is operating mainly on the "gambler" portion of his utility curve to the right of his initial position.

To clarify this point, consider an individual at an initial point, 0, who has the choice of (1) buying an insurance policy with premium $0A$ or (2) not buying the policy and running the probability p of a loss $0B$ (with probability $1 - p$ of no loss and remaining at point 0). Suppose, for purposes of illustration, that this is a "fair" insurance policy in the sense that the expected value of the loss equals the premium cost. We can now read off the utility of the two possibilities. The utility associated with paying the premium $0A$ is read at point A' on the utility function, or utility level D. The utility associated with not paying the premium is read off the chord $0B'$ at point A'', or utility level E. The chord $0B'$ represents the expected utility of the noninsurance alternative, which has two possible monetary outcomes: $0B$ with probability p, and 0 with probability $1 - p$. Probability p then represents the proportion of the total distance $0B$, at which to read off the utility from chord $0B$. For example, if the probability p of loss $0B$ is $\frac{1}{4}$, and $0A$ is $\frac{1}{4}$ the distance from 0 to B, then the expected utility of not taking out insurance is found $\frac{1}{4}$ the distance from 0 to B', or point A'', corresponding to utility level E. Also, $0E = \frac{1}{4} \, 0F$; i.e., $0E$ is the weighted average of the two utilities 0, and $0F$. Since the expected utility (D) of paying the premium is greater than the expected utility (E) of not buying the policy, this individual buys insurance.

Suppose now that this same individual has the opportunity to participate in a "fair" lottery where the cost of the lottery ticket is $0A$ and there is a probability p of winning $0C$. Again, there are two alternatives: (1) if he does not buy the lottery ticket, he remains at point 0; and (2) if he buys the ticket, he ends up with a loss $0A$ if he does not win or with a gain $0C$ if he does. By an argument analogous to that above, the expected utility of not buying the ticket is 0, while the expected utility of buying the ticket is $0'$ on chord $A'C'$. Again, $0'$ is the weighted average utility of $0D$ and $0G$. Clearly, he should buy the ticket according to his utility function.

Thus, a person may maximize expected utility by simultaneously engaging in insurance and in lotteries. The argument does not depend on the use of "fair" insurance and lotteries, although we have used this case to simplify the exposition. It is left to the student to demonstrate to his own satisfaction that a person with the shape of utility function in Figure 3.F may simultaneously engage in insurance and lotteries (or similar types of situations) with "unfair" odds.[5]

[5] Milton Friedman and L. J. Savage, "The Utility Analysis of Choices Involving Risk," *Journal of Political Economy*, Vol. 56 (August, 1948), pp. 279–304.

FIGURE 3.F
UTILITY FUNCTION SHOWING RANGES OF BOTH
DECREASING AND INCREASING
MARGINAL UTILITY

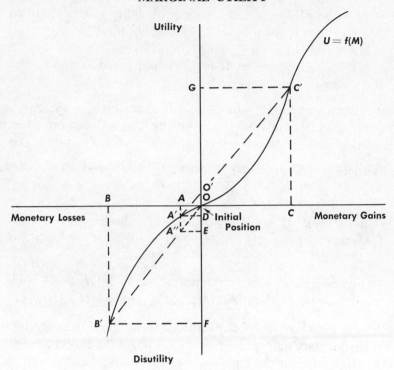

Properties of a Utility Function

We may now attempt to summarize more formally the properties of the utility function derived. Recall that a function is a rule which associates the elements of one set with the elements of another set. In the case of a utility function, we are looking for a rule (function) that will associate or assign numbers, $U(M)$, from the set of all numbers, to the set of monetary outcomes (M), or as we shall call them here, wealth prospects. We use the term *wealth* to reflect the fact that a person is initially at some wealth or net worth position; monetary gains or losses simply add to or decrease this wealth position. For example, in Figure 3.F, point 0 is the initial wealth position and the horizontal axis could be rescaled from monetary gains and losses to wealth by adding a constant at all points equal to initial wealth. To each wealth prospect, M, there corresponds a number $u(M)$, which is called the utility of the prospect. This function has the following properties:

1. $u(M_1) > u(M_2)$, if the individual prefers M_1 to M_2;
2. if M is the prospect where, with probability p the individual faces M_1, and with probability $1 - p$ faces M_2, then
    $u(M) = p\,u(M_1) + (1 - p)\,u(M_2)$ or
    $u(M) = E[u(M)]$, where M is a random variable; and
3. the utility function is bounded, i.e., $u(M) \neq +\infty$.

The existence of a utility function with the above properties implies that the decision maker satisfies the following four assumptions concerning his preferences among the prospects. [6]

1. (Ordering of alternatives). Either $M_1 > M_2$ (read M_1 is preferred to M_2), $M_1 = M_2$ or $M_2 > M_1$.
2. (Transitivity). If $M_1 \geq M_2$ and $M_2 \geq M_3$, then $M_1 \geq M_3$.
3. (Continuity). If $M_1 > M_2 > M_3$, then there exist probabilities p for which the prospect $[M_1, M_3; p, (1 - p)] > M_2$ or $M_2 > [M_1, M_3; p, (1 - p)]$. [7]
4. (Independence of irrelevant alternatives). If $M_1 > M_2$ and M_3 is another prospect, then $[M_1, M_3; p, (1 - p)] > [M_2, M_3; p, (1 - p)]$.

Although the above rules constitute a technique for assigning utility numbers to monetary outcomes, they do not prove the existence of a utility function. However, for the remainder of this book, we shall assume that such a function exists and can be specified for individual decision makers. A summary of empirical studies of utility functions for farm managers is given in the appendix to the chapter. Use of specific utility functions will also be illustrated in the empirical studies of decision making under uncertainty in the later chapters of this book.

Because there can be misunderstandings of the concept of utility, let us enumerate some common fallacies that frequently surround discussions of utility measurement.[8]

Fallacy 1
$[M_1, M_3; p, (1 - p)] > M_2$ because

---

[6] This set of assumptions follows Herman Chernoff and Lincoln E. Moses, *Elementary Decision Theory* (New York: John Wiley and Sons, Inc., 1959). Another set is given by R. Duncan Luce and Howard Raiffa, *Games and Decisions, Introduction, and Critical Survey* (New York: John Wiley and Sons, Inc., 1957) pp. 25–29.

[7] $[M_1, M_3; p, (1 - p)]$ is read "prospect M_1 with probability p and prospect M_3 with probability $(1 - p)$."

[8] R. Duncan Luce and Howard Raiffa, *op. cit.*, pp. 31–34.

the utility of the first is greater than the second. This is false because the preferences among the prospects are logically prior to the utility function.

Fallacy 2
If $M_1 > M_2 > M_3 > M_4$, and the utilities are
$u(M_1) + u(M_4) = u(M_2) + u(M_3)$, then
$[M_2, M_3; \frac{1}{2}, \frac{1}{2}] > [M_1, M_4; \frac{1}{2}, \frac{1}{2}]$ since the variance of

the first is less than the second. This statement again is false because it denies that preference comes first, that is, the expected utility numbers have already accounted for variance in the original preferences.

Fallacy 3
If $M_1 > M_2 > M_3 > M_4$ and the function shows that
$u(M_1) - u(M_2)$ is greater than $u(M_3) - u(M_4)$, then a change

from M_2 to M_1 is more preferred than from M_4 to M_3. This also is false, since utility functions are constructed from preference between pairs, not between pairs of pairs.

A simple example will aid in interpreting this fallacy. Suppose a decision maker says he is indifferent between Option 1 and Option 2 for the following gains tables:

Probability	State	Option 1 (Certain Cash)	Option 2 (Reference Contract)	Probability	State	Option 1 (Certain Cash)	Option 2 (Reference Contract)
$\frac{1}{2}$	θ_1	$1,600	$ 0	$\frac{1}{2}$	θ_1	$1,400	$ 0
$\frac{1}{2}$	θ_2	$1,600	$3,000	$\frac{1}{2}$	θ_2	$1,400	$1,600

Making the assignments $u(\$0) = 0$ and $u(\$3,000) = 1$, then from the first set of preferences we get $u(\$1,600) = \frac{1}{2}$ and from the second set $u(\$1,400) = \frac{1}{4}$.[9]

As an example of a decision involving change in position versus actual gains, let us now consider the following decision problem and the choices implied by the utility points derived above.

Probability		a_1	a_2
$\frac{1}{2}$	θ_1	no change	change from $1,600 to $3,000
$\frac{1}{2}$	θ_2	change from $0 to $1,400	no change

---

[9] Since $\frac{1}{2} u(3000) + \frac{1}{2} u(0) = u(1600) = \frac{1}{2}$ and $\frac{1}{2} u(0) + \frac{1}{2} u(1600) = u(1400) = \frac{1}{4}$.

If each action were evaluated using the derived utility points, one might suppose (incorrectly) that:

$$u(a_1) = \tfrac{1}{2}u(\$0) + \tfrac{1}{2}[u(\$1,400) - u(\$0)] = \tfrac{1}{8}$$
$$u(a_2) = \tfrac{1}{2}[u(\$3,000) - u(\$1,600)] + \tfrac{1}{2}u(\$0) = \tfrac{1}{4},$$

which implies that a_2 would be chosen over a_1. However, in terms of the actual gains involved, the decision maker is faced with the following choice

Probability		a_1	a_2
$\tfrac{1}{2}$	θ_1	$\$ \quad 0$	$\$1,400$
$\tfrac{1}{2}$	θ_2	$\$1,400$	$\$ \quad 0$

But clearly, in this case, the decision maker would be indifferent between a_1 and a_2. The fallacy is in assuming that the difference in utility between the pair of pairs, [\$0 to \$1,400] and [\$1,600 to \$3,000] is given by the utility function that was derived using only preferences between two options (one pair). Of course, a utility function could be derived using two options involving changes between two positions. But a utility function obtained by the theory of this chapter is not that kind of a function. Therefore, out utility function allows the comparison between two positions along the curve, but does not allow the comparison between the differences between two pairs of positions.

Fallacy 4

Interpersonal comparisons of utility are possible. The following discussion illustrates that this is a fallacy.

The index suggested above for the measurement of utility says nothing about the amount of "satisfaction" that is experienced by an individual as a result of obtaining money. We should be careful to distinguish between the "actual" measurability of utility (referring to the inner satisfaction which derives from possession) and the "substitute",measurability of utility which merely implies that a uniquely measurable quantity can be associated with utility. However, this distinction appears to be quite unnecessary if one considers that most quantitative measurements which can be found or which are conceivable in either scientific or applied work, are "substitute" measurements. To illustrate, if I would choose to sit down on a hot stove whose plate had a temperature of, let us say, 300 degrees, then a thermometer attached to this plate measures in no way the unpleasant sensation I will have experienced, although I would, and next time undoubtedly will, associate these two otherwise unrelated quantities.

Consequently, the "utility" we have measured represents a concept to be used in the formulation of a scientific theory of individual decision making. It has no immediate relevance for welfare economics.[10]

Maximizing Expected Values

At the beginning of this chapter we said that maximizing expected utility is the general choice criterion. We have shown how a decision maker's preferences among risky prospects can be converted into utility numbers, and thus a utility function for monetary gains can be derived. Given the utility function, we can then solve decision problems by maximizing expected utility. Thus, expected utility is an index that any decision maker will maximize if he is to remain consistent with his preferences among risky prospects. Having derived the utility function for a decision maker, he can retain his preferences for risky prospects in more complex decision problems by using his utility function to solve them, that is, by maximizing expected utility.

There are, however, two special cases in which maximizing expected monetary value is equivalent to maximizing expected utility. The first case has been illustrated in Table 3.7 where it was shown that maximizing expected monetary value leads to the same choice of action as does maximizing expected utility when the utility function is linear. The second case is that of repeated decision, that is, decisions in which the opportunity for decision is recurring and the decision maker is financially able to participate repeatedly. Obviously, this is a limiting case of a continuum of decisions; a decision made only once is one extreme and a decision repeated continuously is the limiting case. In this limiting case, the decision maker has a preference among monetary outcomes independent of the risk involved with each action. Maximizing expected monetary value provides a choice among actions that is consistent with those preferences. Maximizing expected monetary value in each decision will result in the largest monetary sum over all decisions.[11] Thus, in the long run, the decision maker would also maximize utility, since if $M_1 > M_2$, then the utility of M_1 is greater than the utility of M_2.

Therefore, we conclude that whether a decision is made once or whether it is made many times, the criterion that is consistent with the decision maker's preferences is utility maximization. Furthermore, when a

[10] Milton Friedman and L. J. Savage, "The Expected Utility Hypothesis and the Measurability of Utility," *Journal of Political Economy*, Vol. 60 (December, 1952), pp. 463–474.
[11] The truth of this statement is based upon the law of large numbers from statistical theory. William T. Morris, *The Analysis of Management Decisions* (Homewood, Illinois: Richard D. Irwin, Inc., 1964), Appendix C, pp. 527–528.

decision maker's preferences can be represented by a utility function, then he is behaving (making choices) as if he were a maximizer of expected utility.

Lexicographic Utility Functions

A possible alternative to the use of a continuous utility function for gains and losses is a lexicographic utility function. Application of this utility function to decision problems of the firm has been suggested by Encarnación and elaborated further by Ferguson.[12] They argue that the typical entrepreneur has multiple goals or objectives, and that a multidimensional utility function is required to characterize the relationship among these objectives. Specifically, they propose that the entrepreneur has a lexicographic utility function that ranks a hierarchy of objectives in which goal Z_1 is "more important than Z_2," Z_2 is "more important than Z_3," and so forth. Assume an entrepreneur with n goals $(Z_1, Z_2, \ldots, Z_n)$. Consider two alternative actions Z^0 and Z^1 which provide the following levels of attainment of each of the goals:

$$Z^0 = (Z_1^0, Z_2^0, \ldots, Z_n^0)$$
$$Z^1 = (Z_1^1, Z_2^1, \ldots, Z_n^1)$$

Then by lexicographic ordering, $U(Z^0) > U(Z^1)$ if $Z_1^0 > Z_1^1$, irrespective of the relationship between Z_i^0 and Z_i^1 for $i > 1$. If $Z_1^0 = Z_1^1$, then the choice between Z^0 and Z^1 is based on the relative value of the second components, Z_2^0 versus Z_2^1. If $Z_2^0 = Z_2^1$, the choice is made by reference to the third component, and so on. Now let Z_i^* be a "satisfactory level" or "saturation point" for objective Z_i.[13] That is, assume $\dfrac{\partial U}{\partial Z_i}\bigg] Z_i > Z_i^* = 0$, or, in words, that the marginal utility of overachievement of goal Z_i is zero. Applying this argument to the two-goal case, let:

$$Z^0 = (Z_1^0, Z_2^0)$$
$$Z^1 = (Z_1^1, Z_2^1).$$

---

[12] Jose Encarnación, Jr., "Constraints and the Firm Utility Function," *Review of Economic Studies*, Vol. 31 (April, 1964) pp. 113–120, and C. E. Ferguson, "Theory of Multidimensional Utility Functions in Business: A Synthesis," *Southern Economic Journal*, Vol. 46 (October, 1965).

[13] Encarnación and Ferguson point out that many recent formulations of the theory of the firm emphasize multiple goals, such as various "satisficing" behavior models, and that these fit in the framework of lexicographic utility ordering. Reder's suggestion that firms maximize net worth subject to control of the firm and Baumol's dynamic model suggesting maximization of the growth of sales subject to a "satisfactory" profit rate and dividend policy, both can be cast in the lexicographic utility framework. See: M. W. Reder, "A Reconsideration of the Marginal Productivity Theory," *Journal of Political Economy*, Vol. LV (October 1947), pp. 450–458, and W. J. Baumol, *Business Behavior, Value, and Growth* (New York: Macmillan Company, 1959).

If $Z_1{}^0 \geq Z_1{}^*$ and $Z_1{}^1 \geq Z_1{}^*$, then the decision is made by reference to the maximum value of Z_2. That is, find the plan that maximizes the value of Z_2 subject to $Z_1 \geq Z_1{}^*$. Extending the argument to n goals, the objective is to maximize the least important goal, subject to satisfactory levels for all other goals. That is:

$$\max Z_n$$
$$\text{subject to } Z_i \geq Z_i{}^* \text{ for } i = 1, \ldots, n-1.$$

If no feasible solution exists, drop goal Z_n and formulate a new problem:

$$\max Z_{n-1}$$
$$\text{subject to } Z_i \geq Z_i{}^* \text{ for } i = 1, \ldots, n-2.$$

Proceed in this way until a feasible solution is reached.[14] The result will be consistent with the lexicographic utility function specified.

The lexicographic utility formulation is probably closely akin to actual decision processes. It appears likely that in many cases the decision maker can list his goals in order of priority and attach to them satisfactory levels of attainment. If we restrict his goals to those dealing with income variability, it can be shown that lexicographic ordering may sometimes be a practical alternative to the more rigorous formulation of a continuous utility function.

To illustrate one form of lexicographic utility in a problem of decision making under risk and uncertainty, assume a lexicographic utility function with two goals:

$$Z = (Z_1, Z_2)$$

where Z_1 = a risk aversion goal, or firm survival goal. The satisfactory level of Z_1 is designated as $Z_1{}^*$, stating that income in any year must be $\geq \$M_0$ with probability p, and

Z_2 = a profit maximizing goal, defined as maximum expected income.

Suppose that the decision maker feels that an income of less than $\$M_0$ is a serious threat to firm survival. Suppose further that he is willing to run the risk of an income less than $\$M_0$ with probability 0.10. Goal $Z_1{}^*$ is then defined as: probability of income $\geq \$M_0$ must be ≥ 0.90.

[14] The logic of this procedure can be simply demonstrated by reference to Baumol's hypothesis of sales maximization subject to a minimum profit constraint. Here the lexicographic utility function is a two-component vector (Z_1, Z_2) where Z_1 is profit and Z_2 sales. Let $Z_1{}^*$ be the minimum satisfactory profit. We then maximize sales (Z_2), subject to $Z_1 > Z_1{}^*$. In complex cases this might be done by linear programming. If there is no plan that permits a level of profits equal to or greater than $Z_1{}^*$, the goal of sales maximization is dropped and the firm acts as a profit maximizer.

FIGURE 3.G
GRAPHIC REPRESENTATION OF A PARTICULAR
LEXICOGRAPHIC UTILITY FUNCTION

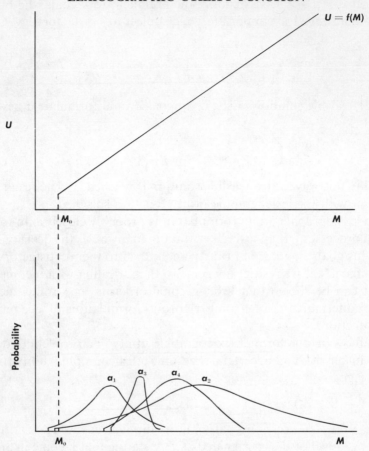

This lexicographic utility can be related to the conventional utility function for gains and losses as shown in Figure 3.G. A critical absolute monetary value M_0 is selected. The utility function is then assumed to be linear down to this critical minimum income level with lower incomes assigned a value of negative infinity as shown in the upper portion of Figure 3.G. The critical probability level (10 percent) has also been selected. The lower tail of the probability distribution of income for each action is then truncated at this critical (10 percent) point as shown in the lower portion of Figure 3.G. The expected utility of any action whose truncated probability distribution of income contains points to the left of M_0 is then negative infinity (such as for a_1 and a_2, Figure 3.G). Since the utility function is linear above M_0, the optimal action will be that one, from among those actions whose truncated distributions lie wholly to the right of M_0, which has maximum expected monetary value (that is, a_4 is picked over a_3 in Figure 3.G).[15] The rationale for using lexicographic utility is that it may provide an acceptable approximation to the conventional utility function in many cases, and has the possibility for being derived quickly by asking only for the "disaster" income level and the probability with which the individual is willing to risk it. However, it is recognized that the conventional utility function is a more rigorous and theoretically satisfactory formulation if time and circumstances permit its derivation.

SUMMARY

This chapter has shown how a utility function can be defined and measured in such a way that it can be used in practical decision-making problems. Utility numbers in the utility function can be found from the basic relation that:

$$u(M) = pu(M_1) + (1 - p)u(M_2)$$

after making an arbitrary assignment of the origin and a unit of measure. The various possible shapes for utility functions were seen to be those showing increasing or decreasing marginal utility, separately or in combination. Four common fallacies surrounding utility measurement were discussed; the most important from the standpoint of decision theory and human behavior being the one concerned with interpersonal comparisons of utility. It was argued that maximizing expected utility insures the decision maker that he will be consistent with his preferences for money in risky situations in either the short run or the long run.

Lexicographic utility functions were discussed and shown to be a simple approximation to a portion of the conventional utility function. In subsequent chapters we accept the conclusion that utility is measurable and proceed to show how to solve decision problems under uncertainty using utility as the subjective measure of value.

FURTHER READINGS

Chernoff, Herman, and Lincoln E. Moses. *Elementary Decision Theory*. New York: John Wiley and Sons, Inc., 1959, Chapter 4.

Friedman, Milton, and L. J. Savage. "The Utility Analysis of Choices Involving Risk," *Journal of Political Economy*, Vol. 56 (August 1948), pp. 279–304. Reprinted, with

[15] For this statement to be correct, the mean for each action must be based on the entire probability distribution, even though the lower tail is truncated.

a correction, in *Readings in Price Theory*, G. J. Stigler, and K. E. Boulding (ed.), Chicago: Richard D. Irwin, 1952.

Halter, Albert N., and Christoph Beringer. "Cardinal Utility Functions and Managerial Behavior," *Journal of Farm Economics*, Vol. 42 (February, 1960), pp. 118–132.

Luce, R. Duncan, and Howard Raiffa. *Games and Decisions*. New York: John Wiley and Sons, Inc., 1958, Chapter 2.

EXERCISES

1. An individual faced with two alternatives will be able to order them by preference or indifference. Further, for an individual for whom $A_1 > A_2$ and $A_2 > A_3$ we conclude that $A_1 > A_3$.
   a) By what rule do we conclude this?
   b) Give an example that denies the rule.
2. For an individual who prefers M_1 to M_2 to M_3 there is a mixture of M_1 and M_3 that is preferred to M_2, and there is a mixture of M_1 and M_3 over which M_2 is preferred.
   a) State the relation that is derived from this assumption and leads to the utility function.
   b) Give an example that might deny the assumption.
   c) What can be said in defense of the assumption?
3. If an individual prefers p_1 to p_2 and p_x is another prospect, then the individual will prefer a mixture of p_1 and p_x to the same mixture of p_2 and p_x.
   a) What might this assumption be called?
   b) This assumption is used in proving which property of the utility function?
4. Mr. Decision Reckoner's utility function is given by: $u \leq m^3$ where u = utility and m = money. Which of the following statements are true or false and explain why.
   _____ a) He will accept all fair bets.
   _____ b) Suppose he has $20 and is offered a bet yielding a gain of $10 with probability $11/20$ and a possible loss of $15 with probability $9/20$. Will he accept the bet?
   _____ c) The bet in b) is a fair bet.
   _____ d) He prefers $100 to $90 since $(100)^3 > (90)^3$.
   _____ e) The function $u' = 2m^3 + 9$ will do just as well as $u = m^3$ for making his decisions.
   _____ f) Suppose when he is "broke" he can make a choice between the options

p.d.f.		Option 1	Option 2
$\frac{1}{2}$	θ_1	$10	$11
$\frac{1}{2}$	θ_2	$45.40	$12

   He will accept Option 2.
   _____ g) His utility function will provide decisions for bets involving all values of positive m.
   _____ h) He has $2 left in his pocket and is offered a bet that would yield him $10 with probability p at a cost of $1. The value of p that would make him indifferent is less than $7/1000$.
   _____ i) The utility function $u \leq m^2$ is a subset of his function $u \leq m^3$. (Hint: Show the utility function with all the attainable points.)
   _____ j) The utility function $u = 10m - m^2$ intersects his function for values of $m \leq 10$. ´
   _____ k) The union of his utility function and $u = 10m - m^2$ is concave from below.

5. Derive your utility function for grades by answering the following set of questions: Suppose that you had the following choice to make in determining your grade for a course in your major area of interest.

You can take a C for certain or pick your grade from a hat that contains ten D's and ten B's.

Would you take the C for certain or pick from the hat?

Now in each of the following situations indicate your choice (check the alternative you prefer):

Take C for Certain   *Pick from a Hat of*

_____ ____18 D's and 2 B's
_____ ____16 D's and 4 B's
_____ ____14 D's and 6 B's
_____ ____12 D's and 8 B's
_____ ____10 D's and 10 B's
_____ ____ 8 D's and 12 B's
_____ ____ 6 D's and 14 B's
_____ ____ 4 D's and 16 B's
_____ ____ 2 D's and 18 B's

Take B for Certain   *Pick from a Hat of*

_____ ____18 C's and 2 A's
_____ ____16 C's and 4 A's
_____ ____14 C's and 6 A's
_____ ____12 C's and 8 A's
_____ ____10 C's and 10 A's
_____ ____ 8 C's and 12 A's
_____ ____ 6 C's and 14 A's
_____ ____ 4 C's and 16 A's
_____ ____ 2 C's and 18 A's

Take C for Certain   *Pick from a Hat of*

_____ ____18 D's and 2 A's
_____ ____16 D's and 4 A's
_____ ____14 D's and 6 A's
_____ ____12 D's and 8 A's
_____ ____10 D's and 10 A's
_____ ____ 8 D's and 12 A's
_____ ____ 6 D's and 14 A's
_____ ____ 4 D's and 16 A's
_____ ____ 2 D's and 18 A's

APPENDIX TO CHAPTER III

This appendix reports three tests of the approach to derivation of utility functions discussed in Chapter III. The first section shows the derivation of utility functions for three individuals, the part-owner manager of a large California ranch emphasizing orchard production, a part-owner manager of a large grain operation, and a college professor. The second section reports some results of an extensive survey of midwestern farmers in which utility functions were derived and related to managerial behavior. The third section reports the results from an empirical study in Australia involving derivations of farmers' utility functions and the accuracy of these functions in predicting practical decisions.

DERIVATION OF INDIVIDUAL UTILITY FUNCTIONS

One approach to utility function derivation is indicated in Table 3.1 and the accompanying general comments and instructions. Alternative A (certain dollars) is listed in the left-hand column. Alternative B, providing either $100,000 or − $50,000 with specified probabilities is listed across the top. (For ease of presentation to decision makers, the probabilities were not specified directly. Instead, the two possibilities under alternative B were described as having an occurrence of so many years out of ten.) The decision maker is then asked to go down each column and indicate for each cell in that column whether he prefers A or B or is indifferent. Taking one column at a time, the entire table is completed. Presenting the options in this way allows the decision maker to check as he goes along for internal consistency. For example, if the pattern of indifferent points is not monotonically increasing or is wildly erratic, this is immediately apparent to the decision maker. In several cases, the decision maker modified his initial choice in a particular column after deciding on his choice in another.

In completing Table 3.1, the grain farmer indicated his indifference point at − $15,000 in the column where $p = 0.9$. To illustrate the assignment of utility values to dollar values, we assumed that $U(\$100,000) = 100$

and $U(\$0) = 0$. The utility value at $-\$15,000$ was derived as follows, using $U(-\$50,000) = -185.7$.[16]

$$U(-\$15,000) = pU(-\$50,000) + (1\text{-}p)\ U(\$100,000)$$
$$U(-\$15,000) = 0.9(-185.7) + 0.1(100)$$
$$U(-\$15,000) = -157.1$$

Utilities for the other indifference points are calculated similarly and plotted as the grain farmer's utility function in Figure 3.A. The overall shape is intuitively quite reasonable, except perhaps for the section for dollar values below $-\$15,000$ where utility seems to level out. This shape says that losses below $-\$20,000$ are viewed as having about equal disutility. Perhaps $-\$20,000$ is viewed as so disastrous that heavier losses are not regarded as significantly more serious. However, this interpretation does not seem too likely, given prior knowledge of the operator's financial position. The remaining portions of the function look quite reasonable. Gains of up to about $35,000 show slightly diminishing marginal utility, followed by a section of increasing marginal utility, and then a section of sharply decreasing marginal utility. The shape of this particular function can be related to the decision maker's view of his financial position. The first portion of incremental losses or gains is quite critical for the operator in order to service debts, pay for normal family consumption expenditures, etc. Thus, increasing losses up to about $-\$15,000$ have increasing marginal disutility and increasing gains up to about $35,000 have slightly diminishing marginal utility. Gains of around $35,000 take care of the critical needs of the operator. Beyond this amount for a certain range, he is willing to gamble against unfavorable odds for the possibility of a windfall gain. However, this range is rather narrow (about $35,000 to $55,000), and beyond this level additional gains have very little additional marginal subjective value.

The orchard farmer's utility function was linear over the entire range of gains and losses specified. Apparently, gains and losses within this range were not viewed as serious in view of his financial position. He clearly stated that he was taking the long-run view of the problem, and that incomes would "average out" over time.

The college professor's utility function shows diminishing marginal

---

[16] $U(-\$50,000) = -185.7$ was derived as follows:

$$U(\$0) = pU(-\$50,000) + (1 - p)\ U(\$100,000).$$

The value of p from the grain farmer's completed choice table was 0.35. Thus, $0 = 0.35U(-\$50,000) + 0.65(100)$.
Solving for $U(-\$50,000)$,

$$U(-\$50,000) = -185.7$$

TABLE 3.1

CHOICE TABLE FOR FINDING INDIFFERENCE POINTS FOR THE DERIVATION OF UTILITY FUNCTION.[a]

Certain Dollars (A) (e.g., Cash Rent)	Possible Owner Incomes	Years Out of Ten That Owner Income Will Be $100,000 or −$50,000 (Probabilities)										
	$100,000 −$50,000	0 10	1 9	2 8	3 7	4 6	5 5	6 4	7 3	8 2	9 1	10 0
$110,000		A	X									A
100,000		A										indiff.
90,000		A										B
80,000		A										B
70,000		A										B
60,000		A										B
50,000		A										B
40,000		A										B
30,000		A										B
20,000		A										B
10,000		A										B
0		A										B
−10,000		A										B
−20,000		A										B
−30,000		A										B
−40,000		A										B
−50,000	indiff.											B
−60,000	B											B

[a] *General Explanation of Table 3.1*

1. You will be given a series of choices where:
   (A) = an income of $X with complete certainty
   (B) = an income of $Y with probability p
   (continued on next page)

utility over almost the entire range of the function. Gains up to around $30,000 have nearly constant marginal utility, with rapidly decreasing marginal utility beyond that point. When confronted with the S-shaped portion of the utility function (in the loss region), the professor explained that in his financial position losses of $20,000 to $30,000 would be quite disastrous, and that larger losses would not be viewed as proportionately more serious.

Difficulties and Evaluation

The three individuals were asked for their reactions to the procedures followed, and to indicate difficulties, questions, or reservations they experienced in filling out the choice table. The orchard farmer had difficulty visualizing the problem as a "one shot" decision for a single year, and stated that he could not avoid the reasoning that over a ten-year period each choice B would yield a predictable total. Perhaps the particular empirical example used to illustrate the A and B choices—cash rent versus owner operation—suggested a repeated annual decision through time, despite instructions to regard it as a one-time decision. When the grain farmer's results were explained to him, he stated that they seemed reasonable, but that he wasn't really sure whether the utility function derived revealed his true degree of conservatism.

None of the respondents had any real difficulty in understanding the method of filling out the table. All, however, expressed some doubts about whether the results were valid for other decisions. Both farmers pointed out that their utility function would depend on their financial position at a particular point in time, stressing the constantly changing nature of the utility function and need for periodic reappraisal if the utility function were to be used in either recommending or predicting behavior. An inter-

---

or
an income of Z with probability $(1 - p)$.
You should indicate whether you prefer A, prefer B, or are indifferent between A and B.
2. Try to think of this as farm income possibilities for next year.
  Alternative (A) might be to lease out the farm for cash rent—no uncertainty.
  Alternative (B) might be to operate the farm yourself—considerable uncertainty.
3. Make the decision, taking into account your current financial position. Try to think of this as a deal you would really have to take for next year, once you make it.
4. There are no "correct" answers. Just try to respond as realistically as possible.
5. Take as long as you wish to make your decisions, and use pencil and paper if you wish.

Specific Instructions for Completing Table 3.1
  Fill out the table with A, B, or indiff. (indifferent). For example, to fill cell X, ask yourself: "Which do I prefer, $110,000 certain income (A), or an uncertain income alternative (B) consisting of $100,000 with probability 1 in 10 and $-$50,000 with probability 9 in 10?" Obviously, (A) is preferred, so (A) is marked in cell X. Continue this procedure for that column until you find a point where you are "indifferent" between (A) and (B). Proceed in the same fashion to find indifference points in each of the columns.

FIGURE 3.A
UTILITY FUNCTIONS FOR THREE INDIVIDUALS

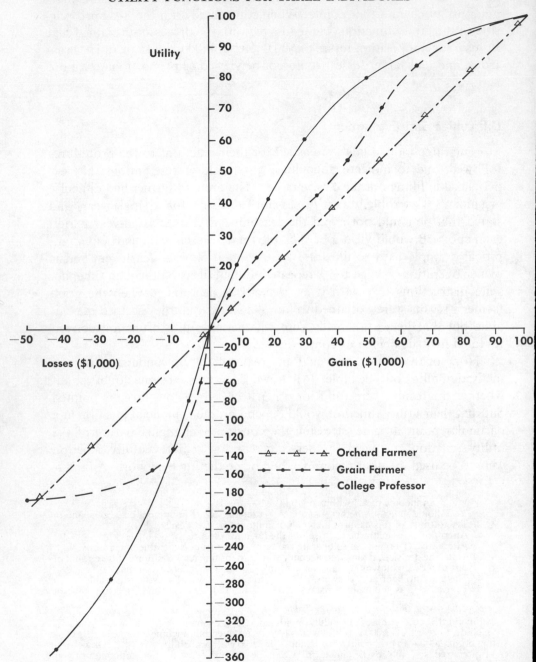

esting follow-up would be to present several specific realistic decision problems to the respondents and see to what extent their choices conform to the predicted choice that could be made, using the derived utility functions. The following section reports a more extensive study in which utility functions derived for a large sample of farmers were related to their managerial behavior.

COMPARISON OF UTILITY FUNCTIONS WITH BEHAVIOR

In 1954 a survey of 1,075 farm managers was made in North Dakota, Iowa, Kansas, Kentucky, Indiana, Ohio, and Michigan to obtain information relevant to a better understanding of the decision-making process.[17] About half of the farmers included in the survey were asked to answer a set of questions involving hypothetical gains and losses from which utility functions were constructed. The hypothetical gain and loss situations used for the estimation of utility functions are shown in Table 3.2. The various bets and insurance schemes listed in Table 3.2 were presented to farm managers in the form illustrated below. By phrasing the questions in this way it was hoped to avoid the connotation of "roulette wheel gambling," an attempt that turned out to be not completely successful.

Example of the type of questions asked in obtaining farmers' responses to hypothetical gain and loss situations:

Losses

If you were in a group of 1,500 people in which you knew one person would have to bear a loss of $10,000, would you be willing to pay $10 in order to get out of the group and thus avoid the risk of having to bear the loss?

Here is a group of similar situations. Please fill in your answer to show whether or not you would be willing to pay these costs to get out of groups in which one person has to bear a loss.

Number of people in group . 1,000   Number of people in group . . 1,000
Amount of loss . . . . $25,000   Amount of loss $50,000
Cost of getting out of group . $ 25   Cost of getting out of group . $ 25
Yes____   No____   Yes____   No____

Gains

If you knew that one person out of a group of 1,400 would get a piece of property worth $15,000, at no further cost to him, would you be willing to pay $15 out of your present income to become a member of that group?

Here is another group of situations that are similar to this one. Please fill in your answer to show whether or not you would be willing to pay these costs to get into a group in which one person would get the gain.

[17] Glenn L. Johnson *et. al.*, *A Study of Managerial Processes of Midwestern Farmers* (Ames, Iowa: Iowa State University Press, 1961).

Number of people in group. .	40	Number of people in group. .	200
Value of property gained. . . .	$1,000	Value of property gained. . . .	$5,000
Amount you pay to get in. . .	$ 25	Amount you pay to get in. . . .	$ 25
Yes____ No____		Yes____ No____	

Those responses that were classified as consistent between odds were used to derive individual utility functions. The location of the indifference points was the basis of estimating utility values. As was shown in Chapter III, a number was derived that could be attached to the gain or loss which

TABLE 3.2

HYPOTHETICAL GAIN AND LOSS SITUATIONS USED FOR THE ESTIMATION OF UTILITY FUNCTIONS

Situation Number	Amount of Possible Gain or Loss	Probability of Gain or Loss Occurring[a]	Amount of Payment and Types of Odds[bc]		
			MF	F	UF
Gain Situations					
	Dollars		Dollars		
1	500	1/20	10	25	40
2	1,000	1/40	10	25	40
3	5,000	1/200	10	25	40
4	10,000	1/400	10	25	40
5	25,000	1/1000	10	25	40
6	50,000	1/2000	10	25	40
Loss Situations					
7	100	1/4	10	25	40
8	500	1/20	10	25	40
9	1,000	1/40	10	25	40
10	10,000	1/400	10	25	40
11	25,000	1/1000	10	25	40
12	50,000	1/2000	10	25	40

    [a] The range of objective probabilities from 1/2000 to 1/20 for the gain situations and 1/2000 to 1/4 for the loss situations was kept to a minimum to try to avoid the possible confounding effects of the utility attached to probability distributions. Cf. W. Edwards, *Experiments on Economic Decision Making in Gambling Situations* (Seminar Notes, University of Michigan, November, 1952).
    [b] The range of payment or stakes from 10 to 40 dollars for both sets of situations was intended to avoid the possible offsetting disutility of this loss. Thus, it was assumed that the disutility of the payment was constant over that range. Cf. E. W. Thrall, C. H. Combs, and R. L. Davis, *Decision Processes*, New York.
    [c] The three subcolumns under this heading correspond respectively to more than fair, just fair, and unfair odds. All 10 dollar payments are MF; 25 dollar payments, F; and 40 dollar payments, UF. Variations in the size of the payment rather than manipulation of the probabilities as such was considered to be a more easily comprehended method of varying the effective probabilities of winning (losing).

occurred for an indifference point. Thus, for each respondent, depending upon the number of indifference points present "between odds" in his answers, a point or a number of points were obtained, indicating the nature of his utility function.[18]

Out of the 529 farm managers interviewed, approximately 67 percent gave answers that could be used for purposes of utility function estimation. The others were inadequate for various reasons.[19] In addition, it was found that the questions concerning losses were answered consistently in more cases than with the gains questions. A likely explanation for this is that more individuals are familiar with insurance taking than they are with chance taking for gains in property.

Another part of the analysis, after the utility function estimation, was directed toward finding empirical relationships between the estimates of numerical utility and the character, disposition, and behavior of farm managers. The first step was to divide the total group of consistent answers into types based upon the relative marginal utility differentiated from the individual's estimated utility function. This classification was based upon the hypothesis that individuals who attach approximately similar marginal utility to wealth at different amounts of gains and losses will have similar characteristics and behavior.

Types of Individual Behavior

The type of individual who answered "Yes" to all the losses and the gains made up a sizable group with rather distinguishing characteristics. They were the oldest individuals of those interviewed and had the most farming experience and the fewest dependents. On the average they had a high net worth and low debt positions, relative to the other types. Their other behavior was commensurate with this type of individual; however, the fact that they accepted all the unfair insurance schemes and the unfair risk situations is surprising. This fact may reflect more heavily upon the technique than upon the disposition of the individual. Contrary to the conclusion that they attach an extremely high marginal utility to wealth, may be their feeling that it made no difference to them what they answered. Thus, the technique and interviewing procedures may be ineffective with this type of individual.

The second type of individual, which did not appear in significant numbers on the losses question, was one who would not accept a fair bet on

[18] For further details of procedure, see *ibid.* Chapter 7.
[19] Albert N. Halter, "Measuring Utility of Wealth Among Farm Managers," (Doctoral dissertation, Michigan State University, 1956).

gains.   Like the type just described, these individuals have a high net worth but, by way of contrast, have the highest debt position of any of the consistent groups.   This result suggests that these individuals may have a positive preference for certain odds, aside from either the probabilities involved or the utility of the gain.   An hypothesis to this effect could be tested by a more extensive schedule of more-than-fair odds and fair odds.   The fact that for the individuals who were consistent on both gains and losses, the size of gain necessary to induce acceptance of an unfair risk was, at most, 26 times as large as the size of loss necessary to induce acceptance of an insurance scheme, substantiates the contention that the range of gains needs to be more extensive.

In those cases where an estimate of utility was derived from a fitted equation, two of the most meaningful variables found related to marginal utility for gains were the amount of debt and the type of farming engaged in by the respondent.

Marginal Utility for Monetary Gains.   Due to yield and price variability, it is generally considered that farmers specializing in either cash crops or fat-stock feeding are specializing in more risky undertakings than those engaged in other types of farming.   Consequently, we were interested in determining whether or not a farm manager's marginal utility for monetary gains was related to his preference for risky enterprises.   It can be seen from a study of the first five lines of Table 3.3 that large proportions of farmers in those groups having relatively high marginal utility per dollar of wealth were also those who specialized in the more risky enterprises.[20]   Those farmers who were intermediate in marginal utility were combining fat stock and cash crops, or were in dairying or tobacco farming.   Those who were lowest in respect to marginal utility per dollar of gain had a higher proportion in general farming than those with higher marginal utility.   Further support is given to the relation between marginal utility and taking "risky" actions by the fact that farmers with high marginal utility for monetary gains were also more likely to incur greater debts than persons with a low marginal utility per dollar of wealth.   These results indicate that the technique and the procedures followed for ascertaining utility functions does provide, for at least some individuals, numerical utility estimates useful in predicting managerial behavior.

---

[20] High marginal utility means relatively higher than another group.   This does not infer interpersonal comparisons of utility nor intensity of satisfaction from carrying on risky enterprises.

TABLE 3.3

PROPORTION OF RESPONDENTS IN VARIOUS TYPES OF FARMING BY DERIVED MARGINAL UTILITY GROUPS FOR THE $30,000 GAIN AND LOSS SITUATIONS[a]

Marginal Utility (Disutility) Groups	Number	Type of Farming							
		Dairy	Fat Stock	Cash Crops	General	Fat Stock—Cash Crops	Tobacco	Other	Total
		Gain Situations (percent)							
.14 or .26[b]	61	9.8	26.1	27.9	9.8	8.2	3.3	4.9	100.0
0 – .30[c]	38	15.8	23.7	28.9	18.4	2.6	5.3	5.3	100.0
.31 – 1.00	62	24.2	17.8	35.5	1.6	9.7	6.5	4.8	100.0
> 1.00	34	5.9	32.4	41.2	11.8	5.9	2.9	0.	100.0
1.56[d]	32	15.6	15.6	28.1	3.1	15.6	15.6	6.3	100.0
Number	227	34	58	73	19	19	14	10	
		Loss Situations (percent)							
0 – .40[c]	44	9.3	39.5	32.5	4.6	4.6	7.0	2.3	100.0
.41 – 1.00	69	10.4	26.9	44.8	3.0	4.5	7.5	3.0	100.0
1.01 – 2.00	60	26.6	26.6	26.6	9.4	6.3	3.1	1.6	100.0
1.56[d]	70	10.3	45.6	13.2	4.4	11.8	8.8	5.9	100.0
> 2.00	58	10.5	19.3	36.8	12.3	12.3	1.8	7.0	100.0
Number	299	41	94	91	20	24	17	12	

[a] Chi-square significant at 10 percent for gains and 1 percent for losses.
[b] Marginal utility estimated for respondents who answered all "No" to fair (.14) or to unfair odds (.26); no utility function was fitted.
[c] The groups specified by an interval were defined by the derivative of the fitted utility function at $30,000 gain or loss.
[d] Marginal utility and disutility estimated for respondents who answered "Yes" to all odds (1.56); no utility function was fitted.

Marginal Disutility for Losses. The marginal disutility of losses was derived in a way analogous to that used to derive the marginal utility of gains. Again, it was found that the type of farming variable was positively correlated with the shape of the utility function. Farmers who showed a relatively large marginal disutility for losses of wealth engaged in relatively low-risk enterprises, namely general farming and a combination of fat-stock/cash-crop farming, while farmers who have a relatively smaller marginal disutility for losses were found in cash-crop farming similar to that prevalent in Iowa, Kansas, and North Dakota. The proportions in each type of farming category are shown in the lower half of Table 3.3.

There was also some indication that farmers who had low net worths and low gross incomes showed a greater marginal disutility per dollar of loss than did farmers who had higher incomes and net worths. A possible explanation for this association is that, although engaged in enterprises with a high probability of loss (or with a low probability of large monetary gain), individuals with a low marginal disutility for losses have participated in these situations and have been successful.

The questionnaire also included an appropriately worded question from which it could be determined whether the respondent was more concerned about committing a Type 1 or a Type 2 error. A comparison of the answers obtained with the estimates of marginal disutility revealed that individuals who have a high marginal disutility for losses, which is in part indicated by their willingness to participate in unfair insurance schemes, are also more concerned about not taking action when they should. This comparison is shown in Table 3.4.

ACCURACY OF UTILITY FUNCTIONS IN PREDICTING PRACTICAL DECISIONS

In May, 1965, a questionnaire was mailed to 72 wool producers in northern New South Wales, Australia — a region which at the time was experiencing its worst recorded drought. One question was an open-ended one asking what the farmers thought would be their most difficult problem in coping with the drought. Almost without exception, the answers given by the 45 farmers who completed the questionnaire raised the problem of how to make decisions under the uncertain conditions that prevailed. The 45 farms were stratified into six categories on the basis of property size and stocking rate. One farmer from each of these categories was randomly selected and asked to participate in a more detailed study of "how farmers make decisions."

Utility functions were derived for each of these six farmers and tested

TABLE 3.4
CONCERN FOR THE TWO TYPES OF ERRORS
BY DERIVED TYPES FOR THE $30,000
LOSS SITUATIONS[a]

Marginal Disutility Groups[b]	Number	Proportion Concerned			
		First[c]	Second[d]	Both[e]	Total
		percent			
0 − .40	43	27.9	27.9	44.2	100.0
.41 − 1.00	65	16.9	28.5	44.6	100.0
1.01 − 2.00	63	27.0	39.7	33.3	100.0
1.56	64	35.9	23.4	40.6	100.0
2.01 − 20.00 +	56	28.6	39.3	32.1	100.0
Number	291	79	99	113	

[a] Chi-square significant at 30 percent.
[b] See footnotes to Table 3.2.
[c] More concerned about taking action when they should not.
[d] More concerned about not taking action when they should.
[e] Equally concerned about both types of error.

against decisions that they made for an operational decision problem.[21] To encourage farmers to take this operational decision problem seriously, the problem was cast in the framework of one of the most pressing problems raised by farmers during the drought, namely the amount of fodder reserve that should be carried. By keeping the number of participants small and by casting the study in a realistic and important decision context, it was possible to evaluate the hypotheses of the study in greater depth.

The main hypothesis of the study was that farmers' operational decisions are more consistent with a criterion of minimizing expected disutility (maximizing expected utility) than with the criterion of minimizing expected costs (maximizing expected returns). A subsidiary hypothesis was that useful utility functions could be derived under field conditions. Three alternative models were used to derive the utility functions and thus permit a comparison of the relative feasibility and suitability of these models under field conditions.

Another hypothesis of the study was that, if utility functions are to serve as a guide to the decision maker, they must be derived at each point in time at which decisions are made. For this reason, the study was conducted in two stages, approximately a year apart, thus providing an oppor-

[21] Reported in R. R. Officer, "*Decision Making Under Risk: A Brief Examination of the Bayesian Approach and an Empirical Study of Utility Analysis in Agriculture*," (Master's thesis, University of New England, Armidale, Australia, 1967).

tunity to observe the effect of time on farmers' decisions and their utility functions.

Fodder Reserve Model

The fodder reserve problem is described by a simple inventory model developed by Officer and Dillon, which generates expected costs and the standard deviations of costs for discrete amounts of reserve.[22]   During the first visit to each of the subjects, the fodder reserve model and its advantages were explained.   Values for the parameters of the model were collected from each subject and a fodder reserve program was determined for each of the subjects' farms.   Together with these farms, fourteen other farm situations were programmed for fodder reserves.   An example of these fodder programs is given in Table 3.4.   Each of the six farmers was

TABLE 3.4
SAMPLE FODDER RESERVE PROGRAM AS PRESENTED TO FARMERS

Months of Fodder Reserve	Expected Cost of This Reserve[a]	The Actual Cost of the Reserve Will Fall in This Range 70 Percent of the Time[b]
0	£899	£372–1,426
1	812	285–1,339
2	859	390–1,328
.	.	.
.	.	.
.	.	.
12	1,631	1,236–2,208

[a] The expected cost of the reserve is comprised of the following components: acquisition cost, penalty cost due to a feed shortage, salvage value, opportunity cost of funds, and the probabilities of a feed shortage.   £ Australian is approximately $2.25 U.S.
[b] The range represents about one standard deviation above the mean for a normal distribution.

confronted with the programmed situations and asked to make a decision on the level of reserve that he would keep in each case.[23]

[22] R. R. Officer and John L. Dillon, *Calculating the Best-Bet Fodder Reserve*, Farm Management Guidebook 1 (Armidale, Australia: University of New England, 1965).
[23] Each farmer faced between 10 and 19 fodder reserve programs.   As the first stage of the study progressed, fodder programs which gave a better test of farmers' decisions were developed, so that not all farmers encountered the same programs.   In the second stage, the best 10 programs were selected and all farmers made decisions on the same set of programs.

Estimation of Utility Functions

Subsequent to the presentation of the fodder reserve programs, two evenings, approximately a week apart, were spent with each of the six subjects, determining utilities. Utility functions were derived for each subject, using the von Neumann-Morgenstern (*N-M*) model, a modified version of the von Neumann-Morgenstern (modified *N-M*) model, and the Ramsey model.[24]

An equation was fitted to each set of utilities derived by each model, with monetary outcomes as the independent variables. The form of function was determined, first, by graphing the utilities for various money outcomes and drawing a freehand curve through the observations and, second, by using linear, quadratic, and cubic functions fitted to the observations by regression analysis. The form of the function chosen was initially based on the freehand curve, and then evaluated further by using F ratios, error sums of squares, and R^2 values. The method used selected the form of function that was most suitable in terms of the subject's choices, rather than that which was desirable on statistical grounds alone, although the two are not incompatible.

Predicted Versus Actual Decisions

Using the utility function for each farmer derived above, the expected utility of each possible act (level of fodder reserve) was estimated and the act with the maximum expected utility[25] was the predicted decision. When the individual's utility function was a quadratic, the expected utility of each act was estimated by use of the equation:

$$E(U) = bE(x) + cV + c[E(x)]^2$$

where $b > 0$ and $c < 0$ are constants, $E(x)$ is the expected outcome, and V is the variance.[26]

When the decision maker's utility function is cubic[27] the expected

---

[24] For details, see R. R. Officer and A. N. Halter, "Utility Analysis in a Practical Setting," *American Journal of Agricultural Economics*, Vol. 50, No. 2 (May, 1968).

[25] The fodder reserves were stated in terms of costs; the utilities were estimated for costs; that is, disutility was estimated as a function of costs. Therefore, the actual criterion of decision is minimization of expected disutility. However, for ease of exposition, we will discuss the criterion in terms of expected utility.

[26] For details of derivation, see Chapter IV, section on maximizing expected values.

[27] In the derivation of $E(U)$ for a cubic utility function, the third moment about the mean, skewness, enters the expression. However, because the variance of the expected cost of a level of fodder reserve was expressed for a normal distribution, the degree of skewness is zero and hence can be dropped from the $E(U)$ equation.

utility of an investment that has an expected return $E(x)$ with a variance V is given by the following equation:

$$E(U) = bE(x) + cV + c[E(x)]^2 + d\{3V \cdot E(x) + [E(x)]^3\}.$$

In each of the fodder programs, it was specified that there were 13 permissible levels of reserve (investment), numbered 0 through 12, indicating the number of months of fodder reserve. For each of these levels, the expected cost and standard deviation were specified. These parameters are substituted in the expected utility equations for each type of utility function, and the criterion of maximizing utility chooses that level of reserve that has the minimum expected disutility, since the programs were framed in terms of costs. The relationship between the *E-V* indifference system for costs and the investment opportunity set for a fodder reserve program is shown in Figure 3.B.

FIGURE 3.B
A GAMBLER'S (E-V) INDIFFERENCE SYSTEM FOR COSTS AND AN INVESTMENT OPPORTUNITY SET FOR A FODDER RESERVE PROGRAM

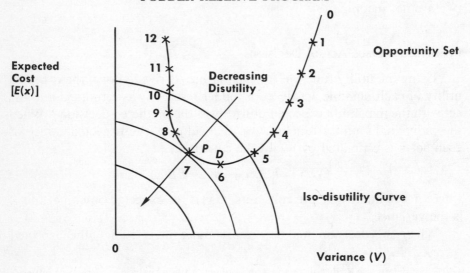

RESULTS

The complete study consisted of two stages separated by a year. Some of the findings of the first stage were used as a basis for the second stage. A time lapse of a year was allowed so that the effect of time on both the farmers' decisions and their utility functions could be studied. Because farmers make their decisions on fodder reserves annually, the two stages of the study were conducted at a time when the farmers would first be considering the next year's fodder requirements.

The utility functions derived for each subject, by use of the three models, are shown in Table 3.5.

The figures in Table 3.6 give the average units of error between the farmers' actual decisions on fodder reserves and the predicted results from using the alternative of (a) minimizing expected cost and (b) minimizing expected disutility with three different models. In general, the criterion of minimizing expected disutility, where the utilities were derived by method 2 (modified *N-M* model), was superior to the criterion of minimizing expected cost.

The utility function of each subject, as implied by his actual decisions on fodder reserves, had increasing marginal disutility. All subjects were

TABLE 3.5

THE SUBJECTS' UTILITY FUNCTIONS

Subject and Model[a]	Utility Functions[b]	R^2
11	$DU = 1.3466118x - 0.0005616x^2 - 0.0000001x^3$	0.997
12	$DU = 0.6780515x + 0.0001214x^2$	0.998
13	$DU = 0.52047663x - 0.00004608x^2$	0.998
21	$DU = $ linear function[c]	0.999
22	$DU = $ linear function	0.971
23	$DU = 0.40865088x - 0.00005451x^2$	0.984
31	$DU = 1.09494028x - 0.00062713x^2$	0.998
32	$DU = 1.3707371x - 0.0000657x^2$	0.998
33	$DU = 0.60085112x - 0.00015136x^2 + 0.0000004x^3$	— —
41	$DU = 1.9351493x - 0.00003186x^2$	0.996
42	$DU = 0.8179823x + 0.0000604x^2$	0.998
43	$DU = 0.52427426x - 0.00005757x^2$	0.998
51	$DU = 1.12629762x - 0.0005337x^2 + 0.0000001x^3$	0.996
52	$DU = 1.486854x + 0.002904x^2$	0.992
53	$DU = 2.9968986x + 0.0008333x^2$	0.997

[a] The first digit indicates the subject; the second indicates the method used to derive utilities, where 1 is the *N-M* model, 2 is the modified *N-M* model, and 3 is the Ramsey model. Thus, 12 indicates the utility function derived for the first subject by use of the modified *N-M* model.

[b] The utility functions were derived for a range of costs from approximately 0 to £3,500. DU is the amount of disutility; that is, $DU = -U$; the x's represent the size of the costs. Approximately 10 observations were taken to derive each function.

[c] The disutilities in functions 21 and 22 were linearly related to costs, so that the criterion of minimizing expected costs is equivalent to minimizing expected disutility —risk plays no part in the decisions implied by these functions.

TABLE 3.6
DECISION ACCURACY OF THE MODELS[a]

| Subject | Minimizing Expected Cost | Minimizing Expected Disutility with Three Models | | |
		N-M	Modified N-M	Ramsey
1	0.684	1.211	0.316	1.000
2	0.286	0.286	0.286	0.927
3	0.167	0.167	0.250	0.167
4	0.154	1.231	0.000	0.385
5	1.850	2.300	1.000	1.200
Average error	0.628	1.039	0.390	0.726

[a] The figures in the body of the table are average units of error per fodder reserve program, a unit being one month's supply of fodder.

therefore to a greater or lesser degree risk averters. The criterion of minimizing expected cost, if not coincident with the farmers' actual decision on fodder reserves, always selected a plan with a greater variance than that selected by the farmers. Therefore, if the assumption is true that farmers made their best decisions for the fodder reserve programs, then the utility function of money over the range of costs involved in fodder reserves should show increasing marginal disutility throughout. The utility functions derived by use of the modified N-M model for subjects 1, 4, and 5 were consistent with the type implied by their actual decisions on fodder reserves. On the other hand, the function for subject 2 was linear, while subject 3's utility function (that is, 32) showed decreasing marginal disutility, which implies a risk preference over the range. However, the rate of decreasing marginal disutility for subject 3 was slight, hence the small number of errors. Contributing to the few errors made by this function were the types of fodder reserve programs shown to subject 3. This subject was the first tested, and at that stage the sensitivity of the plans in some of the programs to risk was not high, a feature that was corrected for tests on the other subjects.

The N-M model gave the poorest predictions of all the methods. This suggests that the subjects had difficulty in correctly using probabilities, even though the probabilities were expressed as frequencies in this study. It is difficult to determine precisely what factors contribute to this apparent misuse of probabilities. It could have been due to probability preferences and/or the inability of subjects to use basic elements of probability calculus. The time required for teaching subjects how to handle probabilities correctly encourages the use of other models in field studies.

The same five farmers were involved in the second stage of the study.

The aims of this second stage were to make another comparison between the criteria of utility maximization (minimization of expected disutility) and profit maximization (minimization of expected costs). Two methods were used to determine utilities—the Ramsey model and the modified N-M model, both with ethically neutral probabilities. The results of the two methods were compared to determine whether one model was clearly superior to the other. The effect of time on the subjects' utility functions, in particular the degree of risk aversion, was also examined.

Fodder Reserve Decisions

Ten fodder reserve programs, each representing a different farm situation, were selected from 19 programs used in the first stage. The meaning of the programs was explained in the same manner as in the first stage. The farmers were asked to decide on a particular plan for each program as though they were making the decision for their own farms.

Utility Functions and Predictions

The utility functions derived for the subjects, by use of both the modified N-M model and the Ramsey model, are shown in Table 3.7.

TABLE 3.7
Utility Functions for Subjects

Subjects and Model	Function	R^2
12	$DU = 4.651592x + 0.0044781x^2 - 0.0000009x^3$	0.999
13	$DU = 0.77160942x + 0.00013491x^2$	0.998
22	$DU = $ linear	0.999
23	$DU = 0.78333569x + 0.00010586x^2$	0.999
32	$DU = 0.6944732x + 0.200463x^2$	...[a]
33	$DU = 0.2094875x + 0.0038317x^2$	0.998
42	$DU = $ linear	0.997
43	$DU = 1.01909165x - 0.00006392x^2$	0.998
52	$DU = 3.1197489x + 0.0040217x^2$	0.988
53	$DU = 0.4708493x + 0.00032314x^2$	0.998

[a] It was difficult to get a function to fit accurately a section of the observations of utility for 32. This lack of fit caused large errors. To solve the problem, additional observations were interpolated from the freehand curve in the region of poor fit.

The decisions made by the farmers, together with the best prediction (the one closest to their decision) made by utility analysis, were marked on the fodder reserve programs and mailed to the farmers for their further consideration.   Returning the results allowed the subjects to reflect on their initial decisions in their own time and negated any influence that the experimenter might have had on their decisions.

The accuracy of utility functions in predicting the farmers' decisions before the decisions were reconsidered is shown in Table 3.8, and their accuracy after these decisions were reconsidered is shown in Table 3.9.

TABLE 3.8

ABSOLUTE ERRORS BEFORE RECONSIDERATION OF DECISIONS[a]

Subject	Minimized Expected Cost	Modified *N-M* Model	Ramsey Model
1	7	14	5
2	8	8	9
3	6	8	7
4	8	8	5
5	12	8	6
Errors per Model	41	46	32
Average Error[b]	0.82	0.92	0.64

[a] The figures in the table are units of error.

[b] Average error is the error per subject per fodder reserve program.   There were ten programs.

TABLE 3.9

ABSOLUTE ERRORS AFTER RECONSIDERATION OF DECISIONS[a]

Subject	Minimized Expected Cost	Modified *N-M* Model	Ramsey Model
1	4	13	2
2	3.5[b]	4	4
3	10	4	3
4	4	4	1
5	14	5	3
Errors per Model	35.5	30	13
Average Error	0.71	0.60	0.26

[a] See footnotes to Table 3.5.

[b] A decision indicated by this criterion was indifferent between two levels of fodder reserve; since the subject chose one of these levels, the error was taken as half of one unit.

After comparing the results given in Tables 3.8 and 3.9, it was concluded that many of the apparent errors made by the utility models in the first stage of the study may have been due to inconsistencies in the subjects' decisions on the fodder reserve programs. The importance of being able to have some check on a subject's decisions, even for comparatively simple problems, is demonstrated, although in this stage of the study none of the corrections made by the subjects to their initial decisions were great. Utility analysis with the Ramsey model was superior to that with the modified N-M model. Subjects appeared to find it easier to make choices for the questions used in the Ramsey model. However, the Ramsey model requires more work on the part of the experimenter than the modified N-M model in deriving utilities.

Utility analysis with either model was superior to the criterion of minimizing expected cost. In fact, utility analysis with the Ramsey model gave accurate predictions 76 percent of the time. The criterion of minimizing expected cost gave accurate predictions only 58 percent of the time. Also, when the latter criterion gave a wrong decision, the wrong decision had a greater degree of error than a wrong decision given by utility analysis.

Comparisons of Utility Functions and Decisions over a Period of Time

A utility function is a summary of an individual's Gambler's (E-V) indifference system. The significance of this system is that it describes the way in which a decision maker discounts expected outcomes for the risk involved in those outcomes (Figure 3.B). The slope of an E-V indifference curve (iso-utility curve) provides an index of the decision maker's risk aversion. For positive sums of money, the greater the slope, the greater the degree of risk aversion at that point (local risk aversion). The slope of an E-V indifference curve derived from a quadratic utility function is

$$dE(x)/dV = c/[b + 2cE(x)].$$

The measure permits interpersonal comparisons of risk aversion, that is, comparisons between individuals of predictable behavior, and also comparison of an individual's risk aversion — and his utility function — over two time periods. Table 3.10 gives the local risk aversion for the two stages of the study at about £800.

These estimates of risk aversion were based on the utility functions derived by the modified N-M model for the first stage and the Ramsey for the second stage. Subject 3's risk aversion is not shown because the modi-

TABLE 3.10
LOCAL RISK AVERSION AT £800 IN THE
TWO STAGES OF THE STUDY[a]

Subject	First Stage	Second Stage
1	0.139	0.137
2	0.000	0.111
3	—	0.605
4	0.066	−0.076
5	0.474	0.327

[a] The negative sign is dropped from the slope.   The
figures in the table are from the original calculations multiplied by 1,000.

fied N-M model gave a completely misleading utility function for the subject in this stage.

By comparing the changes in decisions made on those fodder reserve
programs which appeared in both stages of the study with those made by
the utility functions, we found that the utility functions accurately reflected the direction of change in the subject's attitude to risk on fodder
reserves.   As one would expect, these changes in attitude towards risk are
demonstrated by the degree of risk aversion given in Table 3.10.   The
magnitude of change was not accurately reflected by the utility functions.

Conclusions

The study showed that even for the small amounts of money involved
in the operational decisions of fodder reserves, farmers had nonlinear
utility functions.   The usefulness of utility analysis as a decision-making
aid was clearly demonstrated in the second stage of the study.   The advantage of having a reference decision based on farmers' utility functions
(preferences) was illustrated by the number of decisions that the subjects
changed when confronted with their original decisions and those made by
utility analysis.   Where the two decisions were different, subjects invari-
ably changed, for apparently rational reasons, to the decision made by
utility analysis.   Thus, even for simple decisions such as level of fodder reserve, farmers can be inconsistent and utility analysis may permit detection
of these inconsistencies.   The predictive accuracy of utility analysis
in the simple decisions, where there is a high probability that subjects
reveal the correct ordering of their preferences, suggests that utility analysis
can be used for complex decisions where there is no other check on the
correct ordering of preferences: thus, we are in a position to make tentative

recommendations for the use of utility analysis as an aid to complex decision making.

Over a period of a year, it was found that farmers' decisions on fodder reserves, as well as their utility functions, did not change radically. The same situation may not exist for decisions involving larger amounts of money. One subject (subject 4) changed from risk aversion to risk preference, which was explained by his going into debt to such an extent that his equity decreased by 20 percent over the period of the drought.

CHAPTER IV

Three Classes of Decision Problems

In the previous chapter it was shown how finding the expected value (utility) of each act for a decision-making problem under uncertainty could lead to a solution by maximizing utility over the set of actions in the problem. It was assumed that the probability density function over the states of nature was known. We would now like to place this particular type of problem into perspective by considering three general classes of decision problems. These correspond to: (1) no prior distribution on the states of nature; (2) a prior distribution on the states; and (3) a posterior distribution on the states.

DECISION PROBLEMS WITH NO PRIOR DISTRIBUTION

This type of decision-making problem is characterized by complete ignorance of any probability distribution on the states of nature. While one might argue that this situation is somewhat rare in a real situation, various scholars of decision making under uncertainty have proposed decision criteria to solve such problems.[1]

Maximin or Minimax Criterion

Wald suggests that we examine the minimum gain associated with each action and then take the action that maximizes the minimum gain. This is a pessimistic criterion that directs attention to the worst outcomes and then makes the worst outcome as desirable as possible. It is called the *maximin criterion*. If the outcomes of the action are stated in terms of loss or disutility then one minimizes the maximum loss; that is, he minimaxes.

In the "wet-dry" example used in Chapter I, recall that a grape grower was faced with a decision among three alternative actions:

---

[1] These criteria are discussed further in Luce and Raiffa, *op. cit.*, Chapter 13. Detailed references to relevant literature in this area are provided by their extensive bibliography.

a_1 = allocate all of the acreage for raisins
a_2 = allocate all of the acreage for wine crush
a_3 = allocate half of the acreage to each use.

The states of nature involved both drying weather and relative prices. The gains table for this problem is given in Table 1.7. The maximin solution to this decision-making problem is action a_2, since it provides the largest gain, $14.80, among the smallest gains for each action, $-$23.20, $14.80, and $5.18.

A possible objection to the maximin criterion can be shown by the following example:

	a_1	a_2
θ_1	5	10
θ_2	8	2
minimum gain	5	2
maximin	5	

In this case the maximin action is a_1 since 5 is the maximum of the minimums (5, 2).

Now suppose that the decision maker found that he had made an error in calculating the gain for θ_2 and upon recalculating found that he would gain an additional 6 units of utility from either action in the event that θ_2 occurred. His utility table would be altered as follows:

	a_1	a_2
θ_1	5	10
θ_2	14	8
minimum gain	5	8
maximin		8

The maximin action in this case is a_2 since 8 is now the maximun of the minimums (5, 8). However, since the error had the same effect on each action, it is amazing that it should change the decision maker's action completely. One would not have expected that making a constant calculation error for each action would have changed the decision maker's mind. From this kind of simple illustration it is said that the maximin criterion does not possess the property of "row linearity."

Minimax Regret

Savage has suggested that a transformation of the gains table to a regret table and then the application of the minimax criterion is an im-

provement over the maximin gain or utility criterion just discussed. If
the decision maker takes an action and the state of nature occurs for which
the gain is largest for this act, then he will have no regret. However, if he
takes an action for which the gain is not the largest, and that same state of
nature occurs, then he will have a regret of the difference between the largest
gain and that which he receives.

To convert the gains table to a regret table, pick out the largest gain
for every state of nature. Now subtract each of the entries in the same row
(state) from the largest and enter them in a new table. You should have a
zero in the cell where the largest gain had appeared before. All the other
entries are regrets, or opportunity losses. One then applies the minimax
criterion to the regrets. In the event that the original table was in terms
of losses, then one picks out the smallest loss for each state and subtracts
it from each row entry. Each entry in the regret table is now the opportunity loss associated with a state-action combination. The cells where the
smallest loss appeared before, now show zeros. Here the minimax criterion is applied just as you would in the original problem.

To illustrate the minimax regret criterion, consider the following gains
table:

	a_1	a_2	a_3	a_4	maximum gain
θ_1	0	4	8	20	20
θ_2	30	26	18	0	30

Following the instructions above, we obtain the following regret table:

	a_1	a_2	a_3	a_4
θ_1	20− 0=20	20− 4=16	20− 8=12	20−20= 0
θ_2	30−30= 0	30−26= 4	30−18=12	30− 0=30
maximum	20	16	12	30
minimax			12	

In addition to the objections raised against the maximin gain criterion,
the minimax regret criterion has a number of additional ones that can be
raised against it. One objection is that it violates the property of "independence of irrelevant alternatives." Let us consider the example from
above. In this case action a_3 is the minimax regret action. Now suppose
that a_4 is found to be irrelevant to our decision maker; for example, he may
have found that a_4 is illegal and he discards a_4. In that case we would transform the regret table into a new table, getting a zero in the first row and
third column. Our new regret table would be:

	a_1	a_2	a_3
θ_1	8	4	0
θ_2	0	4	12
maximum	8	4	12
minimax		4	

In this case action a_2 is the minimax regret action, and we see that a_4 was not an irrelevant alternative when one is applying the minimax regret criterion.

The second objection arises when the gains or losses table is stated in terms of utility. The utility functions that we discussed in Chapter III do not allow one to subtract utility numbers and conclude something about the differences.[2] In other words, it is not possible to say that the regret of going from a utility of 5 utils to a utility of 3 utils is half as dissatisfying as going from a utility of 11 utils to a utility of 7 utils. This is also true of temperature measurement, that is, we have no basis for saying that an increase in temperature from 80 to 85 degrees is half as uncomfortable as going from 80 to 90 degrees. Thus, it is doubtful that differences in utility as we have defined it reflect regrets in the same sense as differences in monetary gains.

Hurwicz α Index

Hurwicz (perhaps with tongue in cheek) suggests that we examine some weighted combination of the maximum and minimum gain and then take the action which has the most desirable weighted value. The weights α and $1 - \alpha$ are numbers between zero and one, hence the name α index.

For each act t of the "wet-dry" example used in Chapter I, pick out the minimum m_t and maximum M_t gain. Assume we have the fixed number $\alpha = \frac{2}{3}$, then for each act compute the index $\alpha m_t + (1 - \alpha)M_t$. Of all the acts, the one with the highest index is preferred. If the outcomes were stated in terms of losses, then one would prefer the act with the smallest index. In our example the Hurwicz solution is action a_2. (For a_1: $\frac{2}{3}(-23.20) + \frac{1}{3}(60.20) = 4.60$; for a_2: $\frac{2}{3}(14.80) + \frac{1}{3}(41.96) = 23.85$; for a_3: $\frac{2}{3}(5.18) + \frac{1}{3}(39.35) = 16.57$).

Obtaining the Value of α. To carry the fable one step backward, let us suppose that we could obtain the value of α by answering a simple question about the following gains table:

[2] See Fallacy 3, pp. 51–52.

	a_1	a_2
θ_1	0	x
θ_2	1	x

What value of x would make you indifferent between taking action a_1 and a_2? Suppose you answered $\frac{1}{3}$. Since you are indifferent between a_1 and a_2, then you could supposedly solve for your α from the relation:

$$\alpha(0) + (1 - \alpha)1 = \alpha(\frac{1}{3}) + (1 - \alpha)\frac{1}{3}$$
$$\alpha = \frac{2}{3}.$$

No one has suggested empirically doing this sort of thing with decision makers; but if someone feels that the Hurwicz index characterizes his criterion, the burden of proof is upon him.

Objections to Hurwicz' α Index. One objection to the Hurwicz criterion is the same as we found for the maximin, that is, the criterion does not possess the property of row linearity. Consider the following gains table and let $\alpha = \frac{3}{4}$.

	a_1	a_2
θ_1	5	10
θ_2	8	2
α index	$(\frac{3}{4})5 + (\frac{1}{4})8 =$ $5\frac{3}{4}$	$(\frac{3}{4})2 + (\frac{1}{4})10 =$ 4

In this case a_1 would be the choice. Now add 5 to each act of θ_2

	a_1	a_2
θ_1	5	10
θ_2	13	7
α index	$(\frac{3}{4})5 + (\frac{1}{4})13 =$ 7	$(\frac{3}{4})7 + (\frac{1}{4})10 =$ $7\frac{3}{4}$

Now a_2 would be the choice and the property of row-linearity is shown not to hold.

"Convexity" is another property that the Hurwicz criterion does not possess. *Convexity* means that any act which is a randomized combination of equal acts should not alter the action chosen. Consider the gains table:

	a_1	a_2
θ_1	0	1
θ_2	1	0
θ_3	0	0

Regardless of what value α may have, the decision maker would be indifferent between the two acts, since the α index is the same. Adopt the rule that a coin will be flipped to decide the optimal act. Then $\frac{1}{2}$ of the time a_1 would be chosen and $\frac{1}{2}$ the time a_2 would be chosen. This constitutes a new act with gains equal to the average of the gains from a_1 and a_2 for each state. This act is added to the previous gains table to form the following array:

	a_1	a_2	a_3
θ_1	0	1	$\frac{1}{2}$
θ_2	1	0	$\frac{1}{2}$
θ_3	0	0	0

$$\tfrac{5}{8}(\tfrac{1}{2}) + \tfrac{3}{8}(0) =$$

α index $\frac{5}{8}$ $\qquad \frac{5}{8} \qquad \frac{5}{16}$

Using $\alpha = \frac{3}{8}$, a_3 has a smaller α index than either a_1 or a_2, in spite of the fact that we were indifferent between them. When a new act that is a random combination of two or more optimal acts is not optimal, then we say the convexity property is violated.

Laplace—Principle of Insufficient Reason

If we are completely ignorant of which state might occur, then we could behave as though the states were equally likely, that is, assign each state the same probability, calculate the expected gain for each act, and take the act with the largest expected gain. Thus we would treat the problem as though we had a uniform probability density function over the states and, if the gains were stated in terms of utility, solve the problem as was suggested in Chapter III by finding that act which maximized the expected value.

This criterion has the following difficulties:

1. It requires a mutually exclusive and exhaustive listing of the states.
2. It violates the property of row duplication.

The first difficulty is self-explanatory. The second means that if two or more states have the same gain and we collapse these states into one, then the optimal act may not remain the same as for the original problem.

To illustrate, consider the following gains tables and the uniform probability density function over the states.

Original Problem

$P(\theta_i)$		a_1	a_2
$\frac{1}{4}$	θ_1	6	0
$\frac{1}{4}$	θ_2	2	5
$\frac{1}{4}$	θ_3	2	5
$\frac{1}{4}$	θ_4	2	5

Expected gain
$$\frac{\frac{6}{4} + \frac{2}{4} + \frac{2}{4} + \frac{2}{4} = \frac{5}{4} + \frac{5}{4} =}{3 \qquad\qquad 3\frac{3}{4}}$$

$$\begin{array}{c|c}
\frac{6}{4} + \frac{2}{4} + & 0 + \frac{5}{4} + \\
\frac{2}{4} + \frac{2}{4} = & \frac{5}{4} + \frac{5}{4} = \\
3 & 3\frac{3}{4}
\end{array}$$

Collapsed Problem 1

$P(\theta_i)$		a_1	a_2
$\frac{1}{4}$	θ_1	6	0
$\frac{3}{4}$	θ_2'	2	5

Expected gain
$$\begin{array}{c|c}
\frac{6}{4} + \frac{6}{4} = & \frac{15}{4} = \\
3 & 3\frac{3}{4}
\end{array}$$

Collapsed Problem 2

$P(\theta_i)$		a_1	a_2
$\frac{1}{2}$	θ_1'	6	0
$\frac{1}{2}$	θ_2''	2	5

Expected gain
$$\begin{array}{c|c}
3 + 1 = & \frac{5}{2} = \\
4 & 2\frac{1}{2}
\end{array}$$

The optimal act for the original problem is a_2. Act a_2 is also optimal for the first collapsed problem, where θ_2, θ_3 and θ_4 are collapsed into a new state θ_2' with probability $\frac{3}{4}$. However, a_1 is optimal for the second collapsed problem where θ_2, θ_3, θ_4 are collapsed into a new state θ_2'' with probability $\frac{1}{2}$. The question that can be raised is, which of the two collapsed problems is identical to the original problem? If you say the first, then this implies that you are not completely ignorant of the states, since θ_2' is now said to be three times as likely as θ_1. If you are completely ignorant, then you would still assign equal probabilities to each state. Thus, the second collapsed problem must be equivalent to the original problem. Whoever would be that ignorant?

Row linearity, Convexity, and Independence of Irrelevant Alternatives. It is of interest to note how the Laplace criterion holds up against the properties that the other criteria violated. To test row linearity, we add 6 to each act for state θ_2 in the following gain table.

$P(\theta_i)$		a_1	a_2
$\frac{1}{2}$	θ_1	5	10
$\frac{1}{2}$	θ_2	8	2
Expected gain		$6\frac{1}{2}$	6
Maximin		5	2

We now obtain:

$\mathbf{P}(\theta_i)$		$\mathbf{a}_1$	$\mathbf{a}_2$
½	θ_1	5	10
½	θ_2	14	8
Expected gain		9½	9
Maximin		5	8

While the optimal act changed for the maximin criterion, it remained the›
same for the Laplace criterion.

To test for convexity, we add a new act that is a randomization of two
acts with equal expected gains in the following gain table:

Original Problem				Randomized Problem				
$\mathbf{P}(\theta_i)$		$\mathbf{a}_1$	$\mathbf{a}_2$	$\mathbf{P}(\theta_i)$		$\mathbf{a}_1$	$\mathbf{a}_2$	$\mathbf{a}_3$
⅓	θ_1	0	1	⅓	θ_1	0	1	½
⅓	θ_2	1	0	⅓	θ_2	1	0	½
⅓	θ_3	0	0	⅓	θ_3	0	0	0
Expected gain		⅓	⅓			⅓	⅓	⅙ + ⅙ = ⅓

The new randomized act a_3 has the same expected gain as the original
problem and hence, if a_1 and a_2 were optimal, then a_3 is also.

Consider the same example we used for showing that the property of
independence of irrelevant alternatives did not hold for the minimax regret
criterion.

$\mathbf{P}(\theta_i)$		$\mathbf{a}_1$	$\mathbf{a}_2$	$\mathbf{a}_3$	$\mathbf{a}_4$
½	θ_1	20	16	12	0
½	θ_2	0	6	12	30
Minimax regret				12	
Expected regret minimum		10	11	12	15

After deleting a_4 we obtain:

$\mathbf{P}(\theta_i)$		$\mathbf{a}_1$	$\mathbf{a}_2$	$\mathbf{a}_3$
½	θ_1	8	4	0
½	θ_2	0	6	12
Minimax regret			6	
Expected regret minimum		4	5	6

In this one example the Laplace criterion does not fail; this demonstration is not a proof that it will hold for all such cases. However, as we shall

see later, it is true that the Laplace criterion does have the property that
it is independent of irrelevant alternatives.

Criteria of a Criterion

We have examined four decision criteria that have been proposed for
solving decision-making problems characterized by complete ignorance
of any probability distribution over the states of nature. We saw that
each of the criteria had certain characteristics which might be a difficulty
if one were to adopt the criterion and use it indiscriminately. Thus, at
this point the logical question that can be raised is, just how does one
choose a decision criterion? In other words, what are the criteria of a
criterion? In answering this question we turn the solving of the no prior
distribution problem around and suggest some desirable properties that a
criterion of choice should possess, and then see what this tells us about
approaching the complete ignorance problem. In a somewhat abbrevi-
ated and modified way, the following list of criteria of a criterion is taken
from Luce and Raiffa.

Most of the properties have already been illustrated by counter-
examples. The additional properties are included for completeness and
are mainly self-explanatory. The proof of the theorems presented later
are beyond the scope of this book. However, the significance of the
theorems to decision-making theory is too great to be ignored. The following notational conventions and definitions will be used:

$a' \smile a''$, equivalent acts, i.e., a' and a'' yield the same utility for each
   state

$a' > a''$, strongly dominates, i.e., act a' is the act preferred to a''
   for each state

$a' \gtrsim a''$, weakly dominates, i.e., act a' is preferred to a'' for at least
   one state and a'' is never preferred to a'

A,   set of all acts

(A,θ,u), characterization of a decision-making problem with a set
   of acts A, a set of states θ, and a utility function u.

$\hat{A}$,   optimal subset of all acts

Definition. A decision criterion associates to each (A,θ,u) a subset $\hat{A}$
relative to the criterion.

List of criteria of a criterion:

1. *Ordering.* For any (A,θ,u) the set $\hat{A}$ is not empty, i.e., every problem
   can be resolved.

2. *Symmetry in respect to acts.* The set $\hat{A}$ is invariant under the labeling of acts, i.e., the act singled out as optimal does not depend upon the arbitrary labeling of acts.

3. *Strong domination.* If a' belongs to $\hat{A}$ and $a'' \gtrsim a'$ or $a'' \frown a'$ then a'' belongs to $\hat{A}$ and furthermore, if a' belongs to $\hat{A}$ then a' is admissible, i.e., there is no a such that $a \gtrsim a'$.

4. *Column adjunction or independence of irrelevant alternatives.* The addition of new acts does not transform an old, originally non-optimal act into an optimal one and it can change an old, originally optimal act into a non-optimal one only if at least one of the new acts is optimal.

5. *Row linearity.* The addition of a constant to each entry of a row in the gains table does not alter the optimal set.

6. *Convexity.* If a' and a'' are both optimal, then a probability mixture is also optimal, i.e., the optimal set is convex.

Using the above statements, it has been shown deductively that: to each criterion which resolves (A, θ, u) there is an appropriate prior probability distribution over the states of nature that is independent of any new acts which might be added, such that an act is optimal only if it is best against this prior distribution. This result implies that our first step in solving the decision-making problem is to search for a suitable prior distribution which depends upon the information that we possess concerning the states of nature. As we have already noticed, the maximin gain, minimax regret, and Hurwicz α index criteria were eliminated by statements 4, 5, and 6.

7. *Symmetry in respect to states.* For any decision problem the optimal set should not depend upon the labeling of the states of nature. The conjunction of statements 1 through 6, the theorem stated above, and statement 7 says that an act is optimal if and only if it yields the highest average utility — the average being taken over all n utilities associated with the act and where each state is given the weight $\frac{1}{n}$, that is, each state is equally likely. Thus, up until now the only criterion to qualify for further consideration is Laplace — principle of insufficient reason.

8. *Row duplication.* If a repetitious state of nature is dropped, then the optimal set is not altered. As we have noted above, the Laplace criterion violates this property. Thus, no criteria that has been suggested satisfies all statements in this list. However, if we admit that a subjective probability distribution over the states can be specified,

then the criterion of maximizing the expected utility would satisfy property 8, as well as properties 1–7.

Criteria Equivalent to Expressing Subjective Probability

In this section we argue that any decision-making problem under uncertainty can be viewed as including a probability distribution, at least a subjective probability distribution as defined in Chapter II. In the notation of the previous section we argue that $(A, \theta, \bar{P}, u)$ characterizes every decision-making problem with a set of acts A, a set of states θ, a subjective probability distribution $\bar{P}$, and a utility function u.

Let us consider each of the criteria discussed above and note how each is equivalent to expressing a subjective probability distribution over the states of nature and then maximizing the expected value.

The maximin criterion expresses the belief that the probability of the possible states depends on which action is chosen, that is, for any action the worst possible state will occur with probability one. In the example below, if the maximin criterion is applied, the decision maker is saying that "if I take action a_1 then θ_1 will occur with probability 1 and θ_2 with probability 0. Whereas if I take action a_2 then θ_2 will occur with probability 1."

	$\bar{P}(\theta_i)_1$	a_1	$\bar{P}(\theta_i)_2$	a_2
θ_1	1	5	0	10
θ_2	0	8	1	2
Minimum gain		5		2
Maximin		5		
Maximum expected gain		$\boxed{5}$		2

In this case the maximin action is a_1. By calculating the expected values of each act using the associated $\bar{P}(\theta_i)$ as the probability distribution, we find that maximizing the expected gain leads to the choice of the same act, a_1.

A similar conclusion can be drawn for the Savage minimax regret and the Hurwicz α criteria. In the case of Hurwicz α it may not be as clear as for the minimax regret. Let us consider the same example as a way of illustrating the idea for the Hurwicz α criterion.

We saw above that if $\alpha = \frac{3}{4}$, then the α index for a_1 was $5\frac{3}{4}$ and 4 for a_2, and the decision maker would choose a_1. The α index expresses the belief that the probability of the possible states again depends upon which action is chosen, that is, the subjective probabilities in this example are as listed under $\bar{P}(\theta_i)_1$ and $\bar{P}(\theta_i)_2$.

	$\bar{P}(\theta_i)_1$	a_1	$\bar{P}(\theta_i)_2$	a_2
θ_1	$\frac{3}{4}$	5	$\frac{1}{4}$	10
θ_2	$\frac{1}{4}$	8	$\frac{3}{4}$	2
α index		$5\frac{3}{4}$		4
Maximum α index		$5\frac{3}{4}$		
Maximum expected gain		$\boxed{5\frac{3}{4}}$		4

Taking the expected value for each action and choosing the maximum leads to the same result as the Hurwicz procedure with $\alpha = \frac{3}{4}$.

Applying the Laplace criterion is obviously equivalent to assuming a uniform subjective probability distribution over the possible states of nature.

Each of the criteria has been shown to be equivalent to expressing a subjective probability distribution over the states of nature. Thus, if we admit subjective probability then we need only consider the criterion of maximizing expected value. Furthermore, we believe that no decision maker is so ignorant of his domain of interest that he cannot propose a subjective probability distribution. In other words, we believe that every decision maker can characterize his decision problems as $(A,\theta,\bar{P},u)$. The criterion that satisfies all of the criteria listed above (1–8) is maximizing expected value (gain, loss, or utility).

We will assume that the decision maker has sufficient resources to define the relevant states of nature, obtain the values associated with each action, and attach a subjective probability distribution to the states. The subjective probability distribution can be derived by the procedures of Chapter II. Realistic examples in later chapters will show how states of nature can be defined and values associated with each action-state combination.

DECISION PROBLEMS WITH PRIOR DISTRIBUTION

In the previous section we have, in effect, said that every decision problem can be viewed as one having a prior distribution, admitting subjective probability as the element that keeps us in the realm of uncertainty. In this section we want to allow for other types of probability distributions. Although the method of solution to the decision maker's problem is the same regardless of the type of probability distribution, we want to place in perspective the various types of decision-making situations.

We will say that decision problems with a prior probability distribution are characterized by the decision maker having either partial or complete knowledge of the probability distribution on the states of nature. If the decision maker has some knowledge of his decision-making environment, we say he has "partial knowledge" and, hence, the circumstances are at least present for his attaching a subjective probability distribution to the states of nature.   Following Johnson we could call this case the subjective risk knowledge situation.[3]   If the decision maker has sufficient knowledge to derive a frequency probability distribution, we say he is in the risk-knowledge situation.   Of course, it is difficult to say just where the subjective risk case leaves off and the risk situation begins.   If the decision maker has sufficient knowledge that on prior grounds he can establish an objective probability distribution on the states of nature, then we say he is in the objective risk knowledge situation; an example is where the number of states is small and the logical possibilities can be deduced, like the outcomes of the toss of a die.

Many times in a decision-making problem it is possible to obtain some observations from an experiment before making the decision.   Other times it is not feasible, or is too costly, to experiment.   The first case we call the "data" problem, and the second the "no data" problem.   We want to consider the "no data" problem in this section, and then introduce the "data" problem in the next section.   The entire next chapter will be concerned with Bayesian decision making in the context of the "data" problem.

No Data Problem

Our Wet or Dry example in Chapter I is a classic case of the "no data" problem.   The possible outcomes of each action depend primarily on weather conditions and prices, neither of which is known at the time the decision must be made.   Prices are difficult to forecast, even by sophisticated techniques, because events during the raisin-drying period can alter the market forces and cause actual prices to deviate wildly from the predictions.   Also, it is extremely difficult to predict the small changes in weather conditions that may affect the quality of the raisin crop.   At today's stage of prediction technology probably the best that one could hope for is a prior frequency probability distribution based upon past history and modified by each decision maker according to his own subjective feelings.

We saw in Chapter I that, given the prior frequency probability dis-

---

[3] Glenn L. Johnson and Curtiss F. Lard, "Knowledge Situations" in *A Study of Managerial Processes of Midwestern Farmers* (edited by) Glenn L. Johnson et al (Ames, Iowa: Iowa State University Press, 1961), Chapter 14.

tribution used there, the decision maker would take action a_1 if he were maximizing expected monetary value. In a problem like this one, the decision maker's subjective probability distribution probably reflects his local conditions better than a prior frequency distribution provided by an analyst. In such a case it may be helpful to the decision maker to know how small the probability of a specific state would have to be in order that the preferred action associated with that state would still remain the preferred action. We have outlined the largest gains associated with each state in the Wet or Dry problem in Table 4.1. Thus, we see that action a_1 would be preferred action if the decision maker knew for certain that either θ_1 or θ_2 would occur, and that a_2 would be preferred if he knew that either θ_3, θ_4, θ_5, or θ_6 would occur with certainty.

TABLE 4.1
GAINS TABLE FOR WET OR DRY
PROBLEM

State of Nature	Actions		
	a_1	a_2	a_3
θ_1	60.20	18.50	39.35
θ_2	44.00	18.50	31.25
θ_3	−3.88	14.80	5.46
θ_4	28.00	41.96	34.98
θ_5	16.20	41.96	29.08
θ_6	−23.20	33.57	5.18

A question of interest is: How small would the probability of θ_1 have to be before the decision maker would prefer another action other than a_1? A similar question can be asked about each of the other five states and the associated preferred actions. We now outline the four steps in the calculation of these minimum probability values and illustrate their application with the Wet or Dry problem of Table 4.1.

Step 1. Subtract from each element of the preferred action the elements for the same states under each of the other actions. These we shall call d_{ij} where i stands for the row and j stands for the column.

Step 2. Find the minimum of d_{ij} over the rows (i) for each column (j). These we shall call d_{mj}.

Step 3. Solve the formula:

$$P_k = \frac{-d_{mk}}{d_{hk} - d_{mk}}$$

where k takes on the same numbers as j except the number of the preferred action, and h takes on only the number of the state of nature for which the probability is being calculated.

Step 4. Find the maximum of the P_k for Step 3. This is $\bar{P}(\theta_h)$, the probability that will make the preferred action the optimal action when the hth state of nature is being considered. Any prior probability on θ_h that is equal to or greater than $\bar{P}(\theta_h)$ will make the preferred action optimal.

We now illustrate this procedure with reference to the Wet-Dry problem in Table 4.1.

Steps 1 and 2. The d_{ij} calculated from Table 4.1 are shown below when a_1 and a_2 are the preferred actions. The minimums in each column are shown in the last row.

d_{ij} **When a_1 Is Preferred**

Row	Column 2	Column 3
1	41.70	20.85
2	25.50	12.75
3	−18.68	− 9.34
4	−13.96	− 6.98
5	−25.76	−12.88
6	−56.77	−28.38
Minimum	−56.77	−28.38

d_{ij} **When a_2 Is Preferred**

Row	Column 2	Column 3
1	−41.70	−20.85
2	−25.50	−12.75
3	18.68	9.34
4	13.96	6.98
5	25.76	12.88
6	56.77	28.39
Minimum	−41.70	−20.85

Steps 3 and 4. The P_k calculated, using the formula $P_k = \dfrac{-d_{mk}}{d_{hk} - d_{mk}}$ are shown in Table 4.2. The maximums of the P_k in each row are shown in the last column.

To understand the interpretation of the $\bar{P}(\theta_h)$, let us consider the one calculated for θ_6, i.e., $\bar{P}(\theta_6) = .42348$. Any prior probability larger than this value assigned to θ_6 by the decision maker will leave a_2 the preferred action. For example, assume that our decision maker assigns the probability 0.5 to θ_1 and 0.5 to θ_6. Since $P(\theta_6) = .5$ exceeds the critical value of $\bar{P}(\theta_6) = .42348$ calculated in Table 4.2, action a_2 is optimal. As a check, the expected values calculated for each action are:

$$E(a_1) = 18.50,$$
$$E(a_2) = 26.03, \text{ and}$$
$$E(a_3) = 22.26,$$

TABLE 4.2
CALCULATION OF P_k AND $\bar{P}(\theta_h)$

	1	2	3	Maximum Over $k = \bar{P}(\theta_h)$
θ_1		$\dfrac{56.77}{41.70 + 56.77} = .57652$	$\dfrac{28.38}{20.85 + 28.38} = .57648$	.57652
θ_2		$\dfrac{56.77}{25.50 + 56.77} = .69004$	$\dfrac{28.38}{12.75 + 28.38} = .69001$	.69004
θ_3	$\dfrac{41.70}{18.68 + 41.70} = .69063$		$\dfrac{20.85}{9.34 + 20.85} = .69063$	.69063
θ_4	$\dfrac{41.70}{13.96 + 41.70} = .74919$		$\dfrac{20.85}{6.96 + 20.85} = .74973$	.74973
θ_5	$\dfrac{41.70}{25.76 + 41.70} = .61814$		$\dfrac{20.85}{12.88 + 20.85} = .61814$	.61814
θ_6	$\dfrac{41.70}{56.77 + 41.70} = .42348$		$\dfrac{20.85}{28.39 + 20.85} = .42348$	.42348

leaving a_2 the preferred action. However, if the decision maker assigned the probability 0.6 to θ_1 and 0.4 to θ_6, then $P(\theta_1) = .6$ exceeds the critical value of $\bar{P}(\theta_1) = .57652$ and action a_1 is optimal. The expected values calculated in this case are:

$$E(a_1) = 26.84,$$
$$E(a_2) = 24.52, \text{ and}$$
$$E(a_3) = 25.68,$$

which means that a_1 is the preferred action. Note that this change in preferred action would not have occurred if we were considering assigning the probabilities 0.6 and 0.4 to θ_4 and θ_6 respectively. Our procedure will find a minimum probability that will change the preferred action in comparison to at least one other state of nature, not necessarily against all other states of nature.

DECISION PROBLEMS WITH POSTERIOR DISTRIBUTION

This type of decision-making problem is characterized by the possibility of obtaining additional information or data before a decision is rendered. We called this the "data" problem in the previous section. If we were to characterize this problem in the notation used above, we would have $(A,\theta,\bar{P},u,Z)$ where the Z stands for the experiment or any other device for getting evidence about the likelihood of the various states of nature. In Chapter I we saw an example of a decision that involved looking at a fire danger meter before the decision was made. Many decisions in agriculture, business, and our daily lives are made after we have considered or searched for some additional information about the likelihood of the states of nature. Many times the information we get is not perfect in regard to predicting which state of nature will occur. Thus the outstanding characteristic of information or data from our observation, experimentation, and sampling is that it comes from some probability distribution. In particular, we said in Chapter I that the probability distribution was interpreted as providing the probability of an observation given the state of nature. Thus, in Table 4.3 the probabilities in any row are read as the probability of z given θ_i. In Chapter II we called such probabilities "conditional probabilities." Furthermore, we saw in Chapter II how these conditional probabilities are used in Bayes' formula to revise the prior probability distribution.

Let us consider the forest fire example from Chapter I again. We assumed the states of nature had a prior distribution of $P(\theta_1) = .5$, $P(\theta_2) = .3$, and $P(\theta_3) = .2$. In the notation of Chapter II this is $P(A_i)$ where $A_i = \theta_i$.

TABLE 4.3
FIRE DANGER METER READINGS

	Low	Medium	High
	z_1	z_2	z_3
θ_1	.7	.2	.1
θ_2	.5	.3	.2
θ_3	.1	.5	.4

In the notation of Chapter II any element of this table is $P(E|A_i)$ where E stands for any element of the set of meter readings (Low, Medium, High) and $A_i = \theta_i$. Bayes' formula as given in Chapter II,

$$P(A_i|E) = \frac{P(A_i)\,P(E|A_i)}{P(A_1)\,P(E|A_1) + P(A_2)\,P(E|A_2) + \cdots}$$

can be rewritten in terms of θ_i and z_k if we let z_k stand for any element of E

$$P(\theta_i|z_k) = \frac{P(\theta_i)\,P(z_k|\theta_i)}{P(\theta_1)\,P(z_k|\theta_1) + P(\theta_2)\,P(z_k|\theta_2) + \cdots}.$$

Thus, suppose a medium meter reading (z_2) was made; then the new distribution or posterior probability distribution would be:

$$P(\theta_1|z_2) = \frac{(.5)(.2)}{(.5)(.2) + (.3)(.3) + (.2)(.5)}$$

$$= \frac{.10}{.29} = .345$$

$$P(\theta_2|z_2) = \frac{.09}{.29} = .310$$

$$P(\theta_3|z_2) = \frac{.10}{.29} = .345$$

Note that observing data has modified the prior probabilities to a considerable extent: $P(\theta_1)$ from .5 to .345, $P(\theta_2)$ from .3 to .310, and $P(\theta_3)$ from .2 to .345. The posterior probabilities add to one just as did the prior probabilities. The decision is made between the available actions by finding the expected value for each act, using the posterior probabilities and selecting the largest. This is the procedure regardless of whether the outcomes are stated in terms of money or utility. In the next chapter a convenient tabular presentation will be given for finding the posterior distributions as well as the expected values.

Maximizing Expected Values

We have seen in Chapter III, and again in this chapter, how to find expected values when there are a number of discrete states of nature. The criterion of decision in case a prior probability distribution is known is to maximize the expected value from the available actions. Expected values can be found, whether or not the outcomes are stated in terms of money or in terms of utility. In many decision problems the states of nature cannot be easily categoized into discrete states, and the expected value of an action must be found for a more or less continuous variable (or set of variables). Thus, when θ is a continuous random variable, an action transforms the random variable θ into another random variable X, which represents the continuous outcomes from the action.[4] Let us denote $u(X)$ as the utility of any action "*a*" and show how to derive the expected utility of *a*.

The function $u(X)$ can be expanded to a function in powers of $(X\text{-}c)$ where X is a random variable and c is a fixed value.[5] In particular, the Taylor series expansion of $u(X)$ is:

$$u(X) = u(c) + (X\text{-}c)\frac{du(c)}{dX} + \frac{1}{2}(X\text{-}c)^2 \frac{d^2u(c)}{dX^2}$$

$$+ \frac{1}{3!}(X\text{-}c)^3 \frac{d^3u(c)}{dX^3} + \frac{1}{4!}(X\text{-}c)^4 \frac{d^4u(c)}{dX^4} + \cdots$$

Letting $c = E(X)$, expected gain for any action, we obtain

$$u(X) = u[E(X)] + [X - E(X)]\frac{du[E(X)]}{dX} + \frac{1}{2}[X - E(X)]^2 \frac{d^2u[E(X)]}{dX^2}$$

$$+ \frac{1}{3!}[X - E(X)]^3 \frac{d^3u[E(X)]}{dX^3} + \frac{1}{4!}[X - E(X)]^4 \frac{d^4u[E(x)]}{dX^4} + \cdots$$

Taking the expectation of each side of this equation, we obtain the expected utility of action *a*:

$$u(a) = Eu(X) = u[E(X)] + \frac{1}{2}\sigma^2 \frac{d^2u[E(X)]}{dX^2} + \frac{1}{3!}g_1 \frac{d^3u[E(X)]}{dX^3}$$

$$+ \frac{1}{4!}g_2 \frac{d^4u[E(X)]}{dX^4} + \cdots \text{ where}$$

the expectation of the constant $E(X) = E(X)$,
the expectation of $X - E(X) = 0$,

---

[4] For example, see Case 3, Figure 3.B.
[5] R. G. D. Allen, *Mathematical Analysis for Economists* (London: Macmillan & Co., 1953), p. 449.

the expectation of $[X - E(X)]^2 = \sigma^2$ i.e., the variance of the distribution of X,

the expectation of $[X - E(X)]^3 = g_1$, i.e., the skewness of the distribution of X,

and the expectation of $[X - E(X)]^4 = g_2$, i.e., the kurtosis of the distribution of X.

The equation for $u(a)$ gives the expected utility for any probability distribution over the monetary gains of an action in terms of (1) the moments of the distribution, that is, mean, variance, skewness, and kurtosis, and (2) the first four derivatives of the utility function. Thus, the number of terms that are used to calculate the expected utility for any action depends upon: (1) the number of moments that describe the distribution, and (2) the number of derivatives that can be taken from the utility function. For example, a normal distribution has only two moments, the mean and variance; and thus if the outcomes of an action are distributed normally, only the first two terms are used to obtain the expected utility regardless of how many derivatives the utility function may have beyond two. In the event that the distribution of outcomes has more than two moments, for example it may be skewed, then it depends upon the number of derivatives that the utility function has as to the number of terms used to obtain the expected utility. If the utility function is described by a quadratic equation, then only the first two derivatives are non-zero, and the expected utility is derived using only the first two terms.

The relationship between the expected utility and the moments of the distribution can be shown on a two-dimensional diagram, provided the probability distribution is described by two moments, the mean and variance. In Figure 4.A the mean, μ, is measured along the horizontal axis, and the variance σ^2 along the vertical axis. The level of utility is shown by an indifference curve which connects the combinations of μ and σ^2 to which the decision maker is indifferent. Higher levels of indifference (utility) are labeled on curves from left to right ($I_1 < I_2 < I_3 < I_4 < I_5$). Any action can also be represented on the diagram by a point that illustrates the mean and variance of the monetary outcomes of the action. In this manner, each of the points labeled a_i, $i = 1, \cdots, 7$ in Figure 4.A represents a risky action. Among the actions, the one labeled a_3 would be chosen by the decision maker, since it is on his highest indifference curve and provides the maximum expected utility. The characterization of the decision problem in this geometric picture is known as the gambler's indifference curve analysis, or E-V analysis.

Suppose we use as our utility function $u = -.04x^3 + .48x^2 + 1.04x$. Since this function exhibits a range of increasing marginal utility and then

FIGURE 4.A

**HYPOTHETICAL GAMBLERS INDIFFERENCE CURVES
AND SEVEN POSSIBLE ACTIONS**

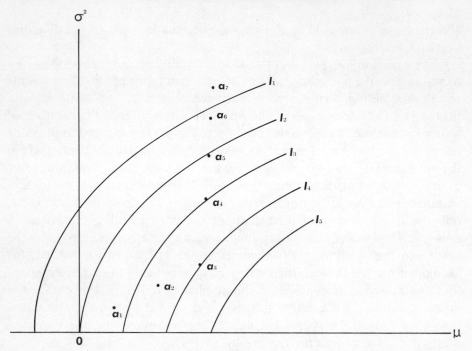

a range of decreasing marginal utility, we will be able to show the shape of the gambler's indifference surface for both ranges in one diagram. Substituting into the expression for $u(a)$ we obtain:

$$u(a) = (-.04\mu^3 + .48\mu^2 + 1.04\mu) + \tfrac{1}{2}\,\sigma^2(-.24\mu + .96) \text{ where } \mu \text{ is } E(x)$$

and $(.24\mu + .96)$ is the second derivative of the utility function with respect to x evaluated at μ. Since we are assuming that the distribution of outcomes has only a mean and variance, the third term of $u(a)$ is zero. Solving the above expression for σ^2 as a function of μ we obtain:

$$\sigma^2 = \frac{u(a) + .04\mu^3 - .48\mu^2 - 1.04\mu}{.5\,(-.24\mu + .96)}$$

Setting $u(a)$ equal to a constant, we can plot σ^2 as a function of μ on a graph. The gambler's indifference curves for various values of $u(a)$ are plotted in Figure 4.B.

For the range in which the utility function is increasing at an increasing rate, the gambler's indifference curves show that the decision maker would obtain more utility at the same level of μ with alternatives that have more variance associated with them. For the range in which the utility function is increasing at a decreasing rate, the gambler's indifference curves show that the decision maker would obtain more utility at the same level of μ only if his alternatives have less variance associated with them. The curve labeled $u(a) = 9.28$ is the point of inflexion on the utility function. If the distribution contained more than two moments, we would need a three-dimensional diagram to show the gambler's indifference curves.

FIGURE 4.B

GAMBLERS INDIFFERENCE CURVES FOR UTILITY FUNCTION
$$u = -.04x^3 + .48x^2 + 1.04x.$$

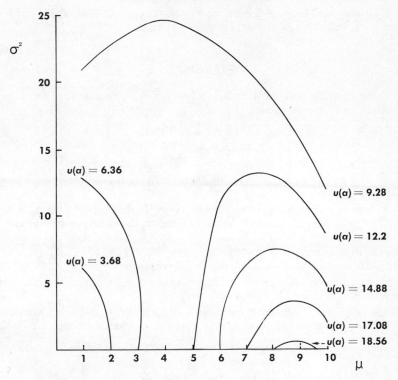

SUMMARY

This chapter has traced out an introduction to decision making under uncertainty. We characterized decision problems as (1) those having no prior probability distribution, (A,θ,u), (2) those with a prior distribution but no data, $(A,\theta,u,\bar{P})$, and (3) those with a prior distribution and data giving posterior distribution, $(A,\theta,u,\bar{P},Z)$. We saw how various decision criteria could be applied and that choosing the maximum or minimum expected value was the most consistent of the criteria for a reasonable decision maker to use.

The elements of a Bayesian decision-making approach have now been given. The next chapter will bring together what we shall call Bayesian decision making in the context of the third type of decision-making problem, that is, one with a posterior probability distribution.

FURTHER READINGS

Chernoff, Herman, and Lincoln Moses. *Elementary Decision Theory*. New York: John Wiley and Sons, Inc., 1959, Chapter 5.

Luce, R. Duncan, and Howard Raiffa. *Games and Decisions*. New York: John Wiley and Sons, Inc., 1958, Chapter 13.

EXERCISES

1. Mr. Choicemaker is faced with the following monetary outcomes for a decision which he can make only once:

	a_1	a_2
θ_1	+ \$2,000	0
θ_2	− \$2,000	0

At present he has \$4,000 and a utility of 25. His utility of \$6,000 is 65 while the utility of \$2,000 is 7.5.
a) For what probabilities on θ would he be indifferent between taking a_1 and a_2?
b) If he could repeat this decision many times at the same probabilities as in a), which action would he take?

2. For the utility function $u = -.02x^3 + .18x^2 + x$, express σ^2 as a function of $E(X)$ and $u(a)$, and then plot the gambler's indifference curves.

3. Construct a numerical example to illustrate the difficulty of applying the minimax regret criterion to a utility gains table.

4. Using the (dis) utility function for losses $u = 1.48685x + .002904x^2$, what decision would you predict the decision maker would make among the following alternatives:

Alternative	$E(X)$	σ^2
0	−795	270,400
1	−384	260,100
2	−308	150,544
3	−274	81,796
4	−283	52,441
5	−292	30,976
6	−301	16,384
7	−319	16,384

5. In an individual decision-making problem under uncertainty, actions a_1, a_2, a_3 belong to the optimal set $\hat{A}$. Does a_4 belong to $\hat{A}$ if $a_4 \sim a_3$?

6. Actions a_1, a_2, and a_3 make up the set A, the class of all acts. Now, $a_1 > a_3$ and $a_2 > a_3$. Which acts are admissible?

7. Actions a_1, a_2, and a_3 belong to the set A, only a_1, and a_2 belong to $\hat{A}$. Now a_4 is added to A. Under what condition would a_4 belong to $\hat{A}$ and not a_2?

8. Under the assumption of complete ignorance, if a_1 belongs to $\hat{A}$, and if the utilities for a_2 over three states of nature are (6, 4, 3) and for a_1 are (3, 6, 4), then what can you say about a_2?

9. What specific desirable criteria do each of the following criteria for solving a decision-making problem under complete ignorance violate?
   a) minimax regret
   b) Laplace
   c) Hurwicz index
   Illustrate each contradiction with a simple numerical example.

10. Consider the Forest Fire Problem given in Table 1.1 as a no data problem and find the minimum probabilities for each state of nature which will leave the preferred action optimal.

11. Two six-sided dice are thrown, one of which is visible to you, the other is hidden under a box so you can't see it. The states of nature are the sum of the dots on the faces of the two dice; specifically (1) the sum is equal to or less than 4, (2) the sum is greater than 4 and less than or equal to 8, (3) the sum is 9 or more. Using the visible die as observations, let the following three observations be possible: (1) a 1 or 2, (2) a 3 or 4, (3) a 5 or 6. Construct the $P(Z|\theta)$ distribution of the observable data for the various states of nature. Suppose on one throw of the dice a 6 is observed on your visible die, calculate the posterior probability of the second state of nature

CHAPTER V

Bayesian Decision Making

Chapter I demonstrated how a table of average utilities could be calculated for each strategy s_t and each state of nature θ_i. It was tentatively suggested there that a selection from many strategies might be made on the basis of maximum expected value, given some probability distribution of θ. Chapter IV has shown that the tentative suggestion was sound: maximization of expected utility is the only criterion satisfying the 8 desirable characteristics of a decision criterion. Chapter IV also demonstrated how posterior probabilities for a "data" problem could be generated, and a decision made on the basis of maximizing expected utility. In this chapter we bring together the concept of a strategy from Chapter I with the concept of posterior distributions from Chapter IV to formulate an efficient decision procedure for the "data" problem.

Let us assume we have two states of nature, eight strategies, and the average utilities shown in Table 5.1. We will call the strategies like those in the table "pure strategies" because they involve only one action for each possible observation or z_i.

TABLE 5.1
AVERAGE UTILITY FOR EIGHT STRATEGIES

	s_1	s_2	s_3	s_4	s_5	s_6	s_7	s_8
θ_1	3	4	3	3.4	4.8	1	2	1.4
θ_2	1	.6	4	2	2	5	4	3

Notice that s_1, s_2, and s_4 are dominated by s_5, and s_7 and s_8 dominated by s_3. Letting the average utility for θ_1 and any strategy be denoted by $G_1 = G(\theta_1, s)$ and the average utility for θ_2 and any strategy be $G_2 = G(\theta_2, s)$, we say that s dominates s^* if $G(\theta_1, s) \geq G(\theta_1, s^*)$ and $G(\theta_2, s) \geq G(\theta_2, s^*)$. A strategy s is said to be admissible if it is not dominated by any other strategy. Hence, pure strategies, s_3, s_5, and s_6 are admissible. We will show that every admissible strategy is a Bayes strategy.

Average utilities G_1 and G_2 can be shown as ordinates of a point on a graph with $G(\theta_1, s)$ plotted on the horizontal axis and $G(\theta_2, s)$ plotted on the vertical axis. In Figure 5.A, each pure strategy is presented as a point on a

FIGURE 5.A
SET S OF STRATEGIES OF A DECISION-MAKING PROBLEM

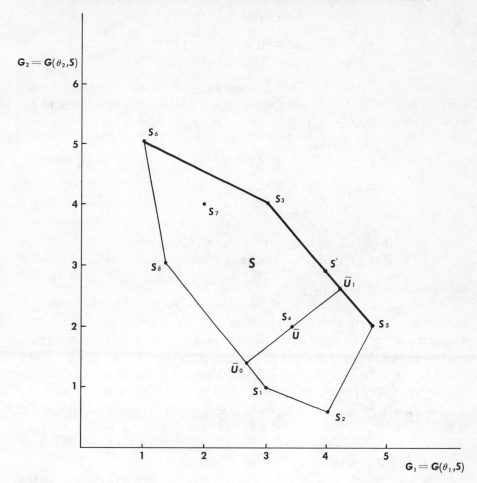

graph. Strategies s_3, s_5, and s_6 are seen to lie to the right and/or above the other points.

What about the points lying on a straight line connecting two admissible strategies, say, s_3 and s_5? These points correspond to so-called mixed strategies of the pure strategies s_3 and s_5. A mixed or randomized strategy s is one of two pure strategies where the choice between them is made with a random device.

Let us consider a randomized strategy of s_3 and s_5. Let s' stand for the mixed strategy and let $(1 - W)$ and W be the weights or probabilities generated by the random device and associated with s_3 and s_5 respectively. Then the expected utility for s' is:

$$G(\theta_1, s') = (1 - W) \, G(\theta_1, s_3) + WG(\theta_1, s_5)$$
$$G(\theta_2, s') = (1 - W) \, G(\theta_2, s_3) + WG(\theta_2, s_5)$$

or

$$G(\theta_1, s') = (1 - W)(3) + W(4.8)$$
$$G(\theta_2, s') = (1 - W)(4) + W(2)$$

If $W = \frac{1}{2}$, then $G(\theta_1, s') = 3.9$ and $G(\theta_2, s') = 3.0$. In fact, for any weights $0 \le W \le 1$ the mixed strategy would fall on a straight line segment between s_3 and s_5. These mixed strategies are also said to be admissible.

The line segment between two points can be represented as the set:

$$\{ \bar{U} : \bar{U} = (1 - W) \, \bar{U}_0 + W\bar{U}_1 \}$$

where $\bar{U}_0$, $\bar{U}_1$, and $\bar{U}$ represent the points

$[G(\theta_1, s_3), \, G(\theta_2, s_3)], \, [G(\theta_1, s_5), \, G(\theta_2, s_5)]$ and
$[G(\theta_1, s'), \, G(\theta_2, s')]$ respectively. The weights W and $(1 - W)$

are non-negative and add to 1.

Consider other points on the graph of Figure 5.A corresponding to pure strategies. As above, these points can be connected by a straight line segment. Points corresponding to any randomized or mixed strategy can also be connected by a straight line segment. For example, s_4 is a member of a set where $\bar{U}_0$ is on the line segment between s_1 and s_8, and $\bar{U}_1$ is on the line segment between s_3 and s_5. A set of points which has the property that $\bar{U}_0$ and $\bar{U}_1$ are points of the set and the line segment connecting $\bar{U}_0$ and $\bar{U}_1$ is contained in the set, is called a convex set. In other words, a set S is convex if, when $\bar{U}_0$ is contained in S and $\bar{U}_1$ is contained in S, then $[(1 - W) \bar{U}_0 + W\bar{U}_1)]$ is contained in S for all W between 0 and 1.

The convex set S shown in Figure 5.A is the smallest convex set that contains the points corresponding to strategies s_1, s_2, s_3, s_5, s_6, and s_8. It is clear that this set contains all the strategies of the problem, both pure and randomized. Hence, S is the convex set generated by the points representing the pure strategies.

Recall that strategy s_t is admissible if it is not dominated by any other strategy. Hence, the class of admissible strategies correspond to a portion of the boundary of the convex set. That is, the admissible strategies are the pure strategies s_3, s_5, and s_6, plus the randomized strategies that fall on the straight line segments connecting these pairs of points. These strategies constitute the admissible part of the boundary shown as the extra dark line in Figure 5.A. No matter how we decide on a strategy, it should be clear that we need consider only those on the boundary. In this way we have cut down the number of strategies that need be considered.

GEOMETRICAL INTERPRETATION OF DECISION CRITERIA

The decision criteria discussed in the previous chapter can be given a geometrical interpretation by placing them on a graph similar to Figure 5.A.

Maximin Criterion

The maximin criterion specifies that the minimum utility is found for any strategy and then the maximum of those minimums is determined. Thus to show this graphically for two states of nature, all minimums in respect to θ_1 can be represented by a vertical line and all minimums in respect to θ_2 by a horizontal line. When considering both states of nature, the two lines will intersect at a common minimum value. Several such lines are drawn in the graph of Figure 5.B. The one labeled c_1 represents the minimum values (c, c) for both θ_1 and θ_2 that could be obtained from any strategy that might fall on the line.

We can conceive of these two intersecting lines as an indifference curve of a "right angle" shape, that is, any strategy that provides a gain of c when θ_1 occurs is indifferent to one that provides a gain of c when θ_2 occurs. All points on an indifference curve such as c_2 are equally desirable and are preferred to all points on c_1, that is, indifference curves more distant from the origin are preferred. To locate the maximum of these minimums we must find a point in set S that touches the highest indifference curve. Thus, the mixed strategy s^* is optimal using the maximin criterion because it allows us to reach the highest indifference curve c_0.

More formally, the sets of points (G_1, G_2) for which the smaller of the two coordinates is four, is designated by the set

$$\{(G_1, G_2):\min (G_1, G_2) = 4\}$$

and is the set of points on two intersecting half-lines. One is a horizontal line for which $G_2 = 4$ and $G_1 \geq 4$. The other is a vertical line for which $G_1 = 4$ and $G_2 \geq 4$. The graph of the two half-lines is shown as indifference curve c_2 in Figure 5.B. The set of points for which min $(G_1, G_2) = c$ is similar except that the intersection point is at (c, c) on indifference curve c_1. As c decreases, the intersecting lines move downward and to the left along a 45° line through the origin. The points where the intersecting lines touch the admissible part of the boundary of S is the point corresponding to the maximin expected utility strategy. A line drawn from the

FIGURE 5.B
GEOMETRIC INTERPRETATION OF MAXIMIN STRATEGY

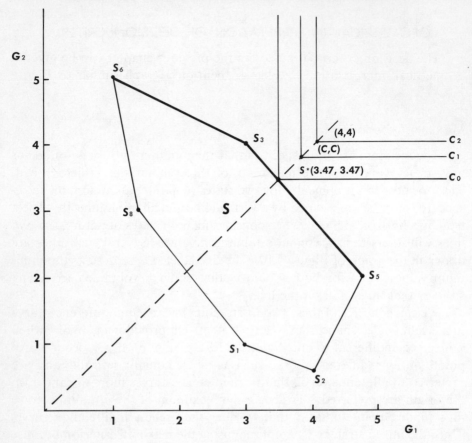

origin through the points of intersection to the admissible part of the boundary will locate the maximin strategy, provided that the set S is in the path of the line.

The equation of the line between s_3 and s_5 is $2G_1 + 1.8G_2 = 13.2$, and the equation of the line from the origin is $G_2 = G_1$.[1] Thus, the maximin point on the admissible boundary is $(3.47, 3.47)$.[2] This point corresponds to a mixed strategy of s_3 and s_5 with weights .74 and .26 respectively.[3]

[1] The equation $aG_1 + bG_2 = c$ can be found from the coordinates of the points at s_3 and s_5. If the coordinates of s_3 are (G_1^0, G_2^0) and of s_5 are (G_1', G_2'), then $a = (G_2' - G_2^0)$, $b = (G_1^0 - G_1')$, and $c = (G_1^0 G_2' - G_2^0 G_1')$.
[2] Found by solving the two equations simultaneously.
[3] Found by solving the expected utility equation.

$$G(\theta_1, s^*) = (1 - W) G(\theta_1, s_3) + WG(\theta_1, s_5)$$
$$3.47 = 3(1 - W) + 4.8W.$$
$$W = \text{approximately .26}$$
$$1 - W = \text{approximately .74}$$

This means that for the decision maker to make a choice between s_3 and s_5, he might draw a slip of paper at random from a hat containing 74 slips of paper with s_3 written on them and 26 slips of paper with s_5 written on them. Whichever one he draws would be the strategy that he would follow.

Minimax Regret Criterion

Let us see how converting the utilities to regrets changes the position of the convex set S.[4] Recall that to convert the utilities to regrets we subtract from the largest utility for each state all the entries in the same (state) row. For Table 5.1 this gives the regrets of Table 5.2.

TABLE 5.2

EXPECTED REGRETS FOR EIGHT STRATEGIES

	s_1	s_2	s_3	s_4	s_5	s_6	s_7	s_8
θ_1	1.8	.8	1.8	1.4	0	3.8	2.8	3.4
θ_2	4	4.4	1	3	3	0	1	2

Plotting these points on a graph gives the convex set S as shown in Figure 5.C. We can notice that the convex set S is the same one that we had in Figure 5.A, except that (1) the admissible part of the boundary is now closest to the origin, and (2) the set touches the axes. The minimum expected regrets appear along the admissible part of the boundary (heavy dark line in Figures 5.A and 5.C). We want to find the maximum of these. A straight line from the origin at a 45° angle with the G_1 axis locates the minimax expected regret strategy. In this case it is a mixed strategy corresponding to the point (1.42, 1.42). The mixed strategy s^* is a mixture of s_3 and s_5 with weights approximately .82 and .18 respectively.

Hurwicz α Index

The Hurwicz α index criterion can also be shown geometrically in two dimensions. Recall that this criterion says to take that action or, in this case strategy, which maximizes the index $\alpha\, m_t + (1 - \alpha)M_t$, where m_t is the smallest utility and M_t is the largest utility for any strategy s_t. Now the strategies for which G_2 is the largest and G_1 the smallest are those that are

---

[4] If the gains are stated in terms of utility, it is doubtful that differences in utility can be called regret. It is not clear, and is probably a fallacy, to say that the regret of going from a point on the utility function corresponding to 5 utils to a point of 3 utils is equivalent to going from a point of 11 utils to 9 utils.

FIGURE 5.C

GEOMETRIC INTERPRETATION OF MINIMAX REGRET STRATEGY

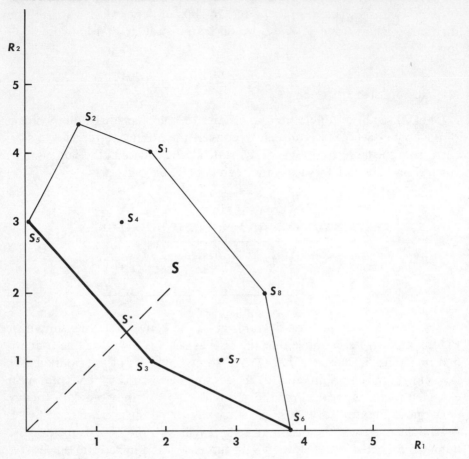

above a 45° line on a graph of the strategies. Since $H_\alpha = \alpha\, m_t + (1 - \alpha)M_t$

is an equation of a straight line with a slope of $-\dfrac{\alpha}{1 - \alpha}$ above the line and

$-\dfrac{1 - \alpha}{\alpha}$ below the line, we can draw a wedge on the graph such as line c_1,

to represent the α index. The set of strategies we have been using in this chapter are reproduced in Figure 5.D, and the wedge representing $\alpha = \frac{3}{4}$ is drawn above the convex set. Points such as α', and α'' on the line, represent combinations of G_1 and G_2 that provide the same level of H_α when $\alpha = \frac{3}{4}$. Moving the wedge downward and to the left like line c_0 until it touches the convex set S locates the admissible strategy s^* that maximizes

FIGURE 5.D
HURWICZ α INDEX AND MAXIMUM α INDEX STRATEGY

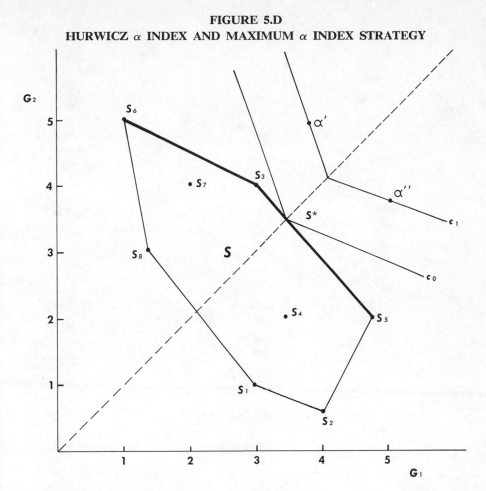

the value of the α index when $\alpha = \frac{3}{4}$.[5] In this case the α index is a maximum for a mixed strategy that is identical to the maximin strategy. The maximin strategy is not always equal to the maximum α index strategy, as is shown in Figure 5.E.

Laplace Criterion

According to the Laplace criterion, we assign equal probabilities to each state and find the strategy that has the maximum expected value. The

---

[5] The reader should notice that the maximin criterion is a special case of the Hurwicz α index, where above the 45° line the slope of H_α is ∞, and below the line the slope is 0 for $\alpha = 1$ and $1 - \alpha = 0$.

FIGURE 5.E
MAXIMIN AND MAXIMUM α INDEX STRATEGIES

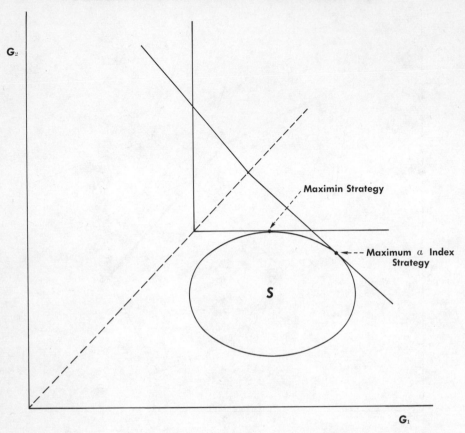

expected value, for the two state case that we have been considering, is given by

$$E(u) = \tfrac{1}{2}\, G_1 + \tfrac{1}{2}\, G_2.$$

This is the equation of a straight line of slope -1 that can be plotted on a graph, as in Figure 5.F, above the convex set S. When this line is moved downward parallel to itself, until it touches the convex set S, it locates the maximum expected value strategy according to the Laplace criterion. In this case, s_3 is the strategy that maximizes the expected value, for any other line lower and to the left of the one through s_3 would provide a smaller expected utility. Thus, at s_3, $E(u) = \tfrac{1}{2}(3) + \tfrac{1}{2}(4) = 3.5$ and at s_5 $E(u) = \tfrac{1}{2}(4.8) + \tfrac{1}{2}(2) = 3.4$. Notice that in this case the strategy that satisfies the Laplace criterion is a pure strategy.

FIGURE 5.F
LAPLACE CRITERION AND THE MAXIMUM EXPECTED
UTILITY STRATEGY

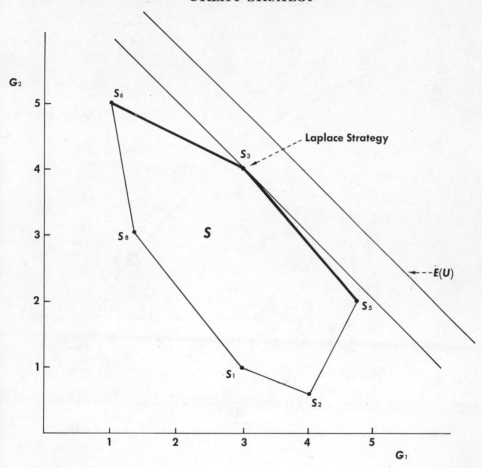

Locating Bayesian Strategies

A Bayesian strategy for two states of nature is a strategy that maximizes $G(s) = (1 - w)G_1 + wG_2$ where $1 - w$ and w are any prior probabilities. To locate such a strategy on a graph we plot a straight line with a slope
of $-\dfrac{(1 - w)}{w}$ above the convex set S. Then by moving a line of this slope
parallel to itself until it touches S, we can find the Bayesian strategy for any
prior probabilities. For example, let $w = \frac{1}{3}$ and $1 - w = \frac{2}{3}$. The line
with slope of -2 labeled $G(s)$ that touches S at s_5 in Figure 5.G locates the
maximum expected value for prior probabilities $\frac{2}{3}$ for θ_1 and $\frac{1}{3}$ for θ_2.

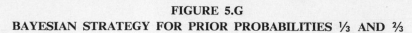

FIGURE 5.G
BAYESIAN STRATEGY FOR PRIOR PROBABILITIES ⅓ AND ⅔

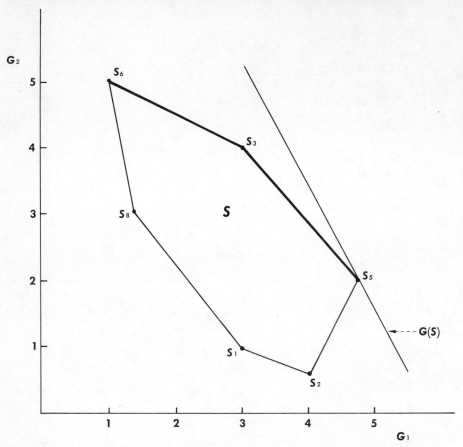

The prior probabilities are probabilities that are known in some sense before the observation of the outcome of the experiment which led to the setting up of the set of strategies. These probabilities can be any of the three types that we discussed in Chapter III, that is, logical, empirical, or subjective.[6]

FUNDAMENTAL THEOREMS OF BAYESIAN DECISION MAKING

The fundamental theorem of Bayesian decision making states that every admissible strategy is a Bayesian strategy for some prior probabili-

[6] Note that the Laplace criterion is a special case of the Bayesian strategy with equal probabilities attached to each state.

ties $1 - w$ and w. A partial converse is that if $1 - w$ and w are positive prior probabilities, the corresponding Bayesian strategies are admissible. To show a geometric proof of these theorems, a number of properties of convex sets and lines need to be given.

Properties of Convex Sets and Lines

Let us consider the convex set S shown in Figure 5.H. The properties are:

1. A line is called a supporting line of a set S at the boundary point $\bar{U}$ if $\bar{U}$ is a boundary point of S and (1) the line passes through $\bar{U}$ and (2) S is completely on one side of the line (S may touch the line).
2. A set is bounded, so to speak, if it can be completely enclosed in a sufficiently large circle.
3. If S is a bounded set and L is a line, it is possible to make L a supporting line at some boundary point (or points) of S by moving the line parallel to itself toward the convex set.
4. Given any boundary point $\bar{U}$ of a convex set S, there is a supporting line of S at $\bar{U}$.

Suppose the line $L = \{(G_1, G_2): aG_1 + bG_2 = c\}$ supports S at $\bar{U}$. Since S is on one side of the line, it follows that either:

$$aG_1 + bG_2 \geq c \text{ for all } (G_1, G_2) \text{ in } S$$

or

$$aG_1 + bG_2 \leq c \text{ for all } (G_1, G_2) \text{ in } S$$

and since $\bar{U}$ is on the line

$$aG_1^0 + bG_2^0 = c \text{ where } (G_1^0, G_2^0) = \bar{U}.$$

5. If two convex sets have no points in common, a line can be drawn separating them in the sense that all points of one set lie on one side of the line and all points of the other set lie on the other side of the line.

Demonstration of Fundamental Theorems

Definition: A Bayesian strategy corresponding to the prior probabilities $1 - w$ and w is a strategy s that maximizes $G(s) = (1 - w)G(\theta_1, s) + wG(\theta_2, s)$.

Theorem: Every admissible strategy is a Bayesian strategy for some prior probabilities $1 - w$ and w.

1. Let s_0 be an admissible strategy represented by a point $\bar{U}$ in Figure 5.I.

2. Then no point of S lies in the convex set T, which is the interior of the rectangle ($\bar{U}$ is on the boundary of T but is not in the convex set T).
3. Any line separating S and T must go through $\bar{U}$ and hence is a supporting line of S and T at $\bar{U}$.
4. The supporting line of T must have a negative $\left(-\dfrac{a}{b}\right)$, vertical ($a = 0$), or horizontal ($b = 0$) slope and hence a and b in the equation of line L do not have different signs and do not sum to zero.
5. Divide the coefficients of the equation of line L by $a + b$. The equation becomes $a'G_1 + b'G_2 = c'$ where $a' = \dfrac{a}{a+b}$, $b' = \dfrac{b}{a+b}$, $c' = \dfrac{c}{a+b}$, and a' and b' are non-negative and add to 1.
6. Now, let $a' = 1 - w$ and $b' = w$ where $1 - w$ and w are weights between 0 and 1. Then for any admissible strategy s_0 represented by $\bar{U}$ there is a pair of weights $1 - w$ and w so that $(1 - w)G_1 + wG_2 = c'$, which supports S at $\bar{U}$.

FIGURE 5.H
SUPPORTING LINE L OF CONVEX SET S

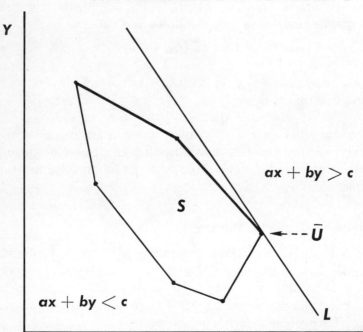

FIGURE 5.I
GEOMETRIC INTERPRETATION OF EVERY ADMISSIBLE STRATEGY
IS A BAYESIAN STRATEGY

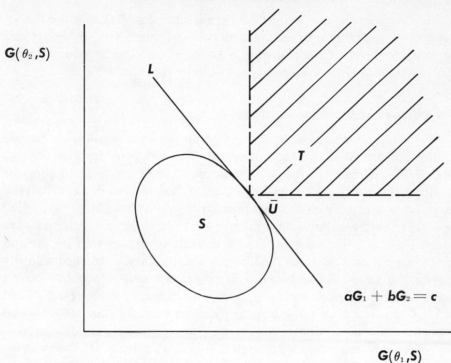

7. Furthermore, since T is above and to the right of the line L, S is below and to the left of the line L, $(1 - w)G_1 + wG_2 \leq c'$ for all points of S and $(1 - w)G_1 + wG_2 = c'$ at $\bar{U}$. But this means s_0 is the Bayesian strategy corresponding to the prior probabilities $(1 - w)$ and w since s_0 maximizes $G(s) = (1 - w)G_1 + wG_2$.

Theorem: If $(1 - w)$ and w are positive prior probabilities, the corresponding Bayesian strategies are admissible.

1. For a strategy s_0 represented by $\bar{U}$ to be Bayesian, $\bar{U}$ must be a point of S that maximizes $(1 - w)G_1 + wG_2$.

2. Draw a line $(1 - w)G_1 + wG_2 = c$ above S. Decrease c, thereby moving the line downward parallel to itself until it touches S.

3. The points where the line $(1 - w)G_1 + wG_2 = c$ supports S are the Bayesian strategies corresponding to the prior probabilities $1 - w$ and w. Since all points of S are below the line and all points that dominate a point of support are above the line, no point of S can dominate a point of support.

4. This means that no strategy can dominate one of these Bayesian strategies, that is, each Bayesian strategy corresponding to positive prior probabilities is admissible.

In the case where $w = 0$ or 1, there is the possibility that the line of support representing a Bayesian strategy could touch S along the vertical or horizontal part of the boundary. In either case the Bayesian strategy that maximized G_1 or G_2 separately would be the admissible strategy.

Advantages of Bayesian Strategy

Bayesian strategies corresponding to all possible sets of prior probabilities contain all admissible strategies. This fact provides that one can reasonably restrict attention to only the Bayesian strategies in looking for an optimal strategy. A second advantage of Bayesian strategies is that the Bayesian strategy can always be a pure strategy. Although the supporting line representing a Bayesian strategy for some prior probabilities may touch S along a line segment, the pure strategies represented by the end points are the only ones that need be considered, if one is satisfied with any Bayesian strategy. Since there are many decision-making problems with a finite number of pure strategies, but with infinitely many randomized strategies, it is a clear advantage to focus only on the pure strategies, at least from a computational standpoint.

Although we have shown that all admissible strategies are Bayesian for a problem with two states of nature, the same results can be obtained for n states of nature.[7] The prior probabilities over the states must sum to one. Then for any such set of probabilities it follows that only pure strategies need be considered.

A third advantage of Bayesian strategies is that they are relatively easy to obtain computationally. How a Bayesian strategy is obtained computationally is the subject of the next section.

COMPUTATION OF BAYESIAN STRATEGIES

In Chapter I and in this chapter we have approached the decision problem as though the decision maker who has some data has calculated expected utilities for every strategy of his decision problem. Listing all of the strategies and their average utilities can be impractical in problems where there is a large number of possible outcomes of an experiment. The number of strategies, as noted in Chapter I, is the number of pure

---

[7] David Blackwell and M. A. Girshick, *Theory of Games and Statistical Decisions* (New York: John Wiley and Sons, Inc., 1954).

actions raised to the power of the number of observations. However, recall from Chapter IV that we can revise prior probabilities to obtain posterior probabilities using Bayes' formula. Using the posterior probabilities as though we were solving a no-data problem, we can find the expected value of each action and, upon choosing the largest, find an optimal act. If this procedure is carried out for every possible observation from the experiment, we can locate a Bayesian strategy and calculate the expected value of that strategy.

The computations to obtain a Bayesian strategy for the forest fire example presented in Chapter I are shown in Table 5.3.[8]

TABLE 5.3

COMPUTATION OF THE BAYESIAN STRATEGY FOR THE FOREST FIRE PROBLEM OF CHAPTER I

	$P(Z\vert\theta_i)$					z_1 Low	z_2 Medium	z_3 High
	z_1	z_2	z_3	$P(\theta_i)$				
θ_1	.7	.2	.1	.5	$P(\theta_1)P(Z\vert\theta_1)$	.35	.10	.05
θ_2	.5	.3	.2	.3	$P(\theta_2)P(Z\vert\theta_2)$	.15	.09	.06
θ_3	.1	.5	.4	.2	$P(\theta_3)P(Z\vert\theta_3)$	.02	.10	.08
Utility Table, $u(\theta_i, a)$				$P(Z)$		.52	.29	.19
	a_1	a_2	a_3	$P(\theta_i\vert Z)$				
θ_1	50	40	20	p_1		$\dfrac{.35}{.52} = .673$	$\dfrac{.10}{.29} = .345$	$\dfrac{.05}{.19} = .263$
θ_2	30	50	30	p_2		$\dfrac{.15}{.52} = .288$	$\dfrac{.09}{.29} = .310$	$\dfrac{.06}{.19} = .316$
θ_3	10	20	60	p_3		$\dfrac{.02}{.52} = .039$	$\dfrac{.10}{.29} = .345$	$\dfrac{.08}{.19} = .421$
				$G[P(\theta_i\vert Z),A]$		$a_1 = 42.68$ $a_2 = 42.10$ $a_3 = 24.44$	$a_1 = 30.00$ $a_2 = 36.20$ $a_3 = 36.90$	$a_1 = 26.84$ $a_2 = 34.74$ $a_3 = 40.00$
				Maximizing Action		a_1	a_3	a_3
				$B[P(\theta_i\vert Z)]$		42.68	36.90	40.00

Weighted Average Utility Corresponding to Bayesian Strategy

$$(.52)(42.68) + (.29)(36.90) + (.19)(40.00) = 40.49$$

[8] This tabular form for the computation of Bayesian strategies is from Herman Chernoff and Lincoln Moses, *Elementary Decision Theory* (New York: John Wiley and Sons, Inc., 1959).

First, each element of the columns headed $P(Z|\theta_i)$ is multiplied by each element of the column headed $P(\theta_i)$ to give the three columns on the right-hand side of the table.

Second, these columns are summed to give the row labeled $P(Z)$.

Third, each element in these same columns is divided by the $P(Z)$ row to give the rows labeled p_i. These numbers are the $P(\theta_i|Z)$, or posterior probabilities as provided by Bayes' formula. The remainder of the table shows the calculation of the expected value for each action and finally the expected value associated with the Bayesian strategy.

The row labeled $G[P(\theta_i|Z),A]$ is obtained by multiplying posterior probabilities of each column by the utilities under each action column of the utility table on the left-hand side of Table 5.3. These are the expected values of each action given the prior distribution assumed by the decision maker and given that some z_k, $(k = 1,2,3)$, had been observed. Maximizing over the a_j, $(j = 1,2,3)$, under each z_k, $(k = 1,2,3)$, gives the optimal action, provided that the particular z_k is observed, in the row labeled "maximizing action." By the definition of a strategy, that is, a recipe for action given the observation of an event, (a_1, a_3, a_3) is a strategy. We call it the Bayesian strategy for the prior probability distribution of the problem. The row labeled $B[P(\theta_i|Z)]$ is the expected value of each action. The final row is the weighted expected utility of the Bayesian strategy obtained by multiplying each action's expected value by the corresponding element in the $P(Z)$ row. This value corresponds to the expected value of the Bayesian strategy that was obtained by evaluating every strategy against the given prior distribution in Table 1.5. Completing the computations of Table 5.3 means that there is no need to evaluate the other strategies.

The Bayesian strategy calculated by the above procedure is the same one as would be obtained had we applied the prior probabilities to each strategy and searched for the maximum, that is, the expected value of the Bayesian strategy would be the maximum obtained from

$$G(S) = w_1\, G(\theta_1, s) + w_2\, G(\theta_2, s) + w_3\, G\,(\theta_3, s)$$

where

$w_1 + w_2 + w_3 = 1$ and each $G(\theta_i, s)$ is the expected gain from strategy s.

Equivalence of Two Approaches to Deriving Bayesian Strategies

We now show that the computations used in Chapter I to obtain Bayesian strategies are equivalent to the computations of the previous section as summarized in Table 5.3.

Computations in Table 5.3. In Table 5.3 we computed posterior probabilities on the basis of the data (a set Z) and solved the corresponding no-data problem for $B[P(\theta_i|Z)]$. We have from Bayes' formula that

$$P(\theta_i|Z) = p_i = \frac{P(\theta_i)\,P(Z|\theta_i)}{P(Z)} \quad \text{where}$$

$$P(Z) = P(\theta_1)\,P(Z|\theta_1) + P(\theta_2)\,P(Z|\theta_2) + P(\theta_3)\,P(Z|\theta_3).$$

Then for each z_k and a_j we obtain

$$G[P(\theta_i|Z),A] = \sum_{i=1}^{3} p_i\,u(\theta_i,A) = \frac{1}{P(Z)} \sum_{i=1}^{3} P(\theta_i)\,P(Z|\theta_i)\,u(\theta_i,A).$$

Maximizing $G[P(\theta_i|Z),A]$ over each element (action) of set A gave us $B[P(\theta_i|Z)]$ in Table 5.3 and the optimal strategy, that is, the strategy that tells us to take the action which maximizes

$$\sum_{i=1}^{3} P(\theta_i)\,P(Z|\theta_i)\,u(\theta_i,A) \text{ for any observation in } Z. \text{ This we called the}$$

Bayesian strategy.

Computations in Chapter I. In Chapter I we computed the average utility on the basis of the data (a set Z) for each state of nature-strategy combination and solved the resulting problem for the optimal strategy, using the prior weights (w_i). We called this optimal strategy a Bayesian strategy earlier in this chapter; that is, we defined the Bayesian strategy as the strategy s that maximized the expected average utility

$$G(s) = \sum_{i=1}^{3} w_i\,G(\theta_i,s).$$

Our $G(\theta_i, s)$ were obtained by multiplying the $P(z_k|\theta_i)$ by $u[\theta_i, s(z_k)]$, where z_k are observations in Z and $s(z_k)$ is the action taken in response to observation z_k for strategy s by summing over k. The summing over k gave the action probabilities of Chapter I. Thus

$$G(\theta_i,s) = \sum_{k} P(z_k|\theta_i)\,u[\theta_i,s(z_k)].$$

Now substituting into the original expression for $G(s)$ we obtain

$$
\begin{aligned}
G(s) = {} & w_1\,P(z_1|\theta_1)\,u[\theta_1,\,s(z_1)] + w_1\,P(z_2|\theta_1)\,u[\theta_1,\,s(z_2)] + w_1\,P(z_3|\theta_1)\,u[\theta_1,\,s(z_3)] \\
& + w_2\,P(z_1|\theta_2)\,u[\theta_2,\,s(z_1)] + w_2\,P(z_2|\theta_2)\,u[\theta_2,\,s(z_2)] + w_2\,P(z_3|\theta_2)\,u[\theta_2,\,s(z_3)] \\
& + w_3\,P(z_1|\theta_3)\,u[\theta_3,\,s(z_1)] + w_3\,P(z_2|\theta_3)\,u[\theta_3,\,s(z_2)] + w_3\,P(z_3|\theta_3)\,u[\theta_3,\,s(z_3)].
\end{aligned}
$$

Our objective is to select an action $s(z_k)$ for each k such that $G(s)$ is a maximum in Table 1.3. In other words, we want the Bayesian reaction to each observation z_k. To obtain the Bayesian action in response to z_1, we must find the action $s(z_1)$ that maximizes the expression

$$w_1\, P(z_1|\theta_1)\, u[\theta_1, s(z_1)] + w_2\, P(z_1|\theta_2)\, u[\theta_2, s(z_1)] + w_3\, P(z_1|\theta_3)\, u[\theta_3, s(z_1)]$$

composed of the 3 terms in $G(s)$ above, involving $s(z_1)$. To obtain the Bayesian actions in response to z_2 and z_3 we must find the actions $s(z_2)$ and $s(z_3)$ that maximize similar expressions of terms in $G(s)$ involving $s(z_2)$ and $s(z_3)$. Thus, in general, if an observation from Z is made, the Bayesian strategy is the one with the actions that maximize

$$\sum_{i=1}^{3} w_i\, P(Z|\theta_i)\, u(\theta_i, A).$$ But this is exactly

$$\sum_{i=1}^{3} P(\theta_i)\, P(Z|\theta_i)\, u(\theta_i, A),$$ the result that we obtained in the

previous subsection where $w_i = P(\theta_i)$. Therefore, the approaches of Chapter I and Table 5.3 are equivalent.

VALUE OF EXPERIMENT

One useful by-product of computing the optimal Bayesian strategy as shown in this chapter is that the value of employing the Z data can be readily determined. This point can best be demonstrated by rewriting the information in Table 5.3 in the format of Table 5.4. We first solve the prior problem (no-data problem) to obtain the expected utility as if no additional information is available. Table 5.4 shows that when the prior probabilities $P(\theta_i)$ are applied to the original utility table, action a_2 maximizes utility with a value of 39. We then solve the posterior problem (data problem) for the Bayes strategy which maximizes utility employing the Z data. Application of the posterior probabilities to the original utility table in Table 5.4 gives us the same information as shown earlier in Table 5.3: When z_1 is observed, action a_1 gives the highest expected utility of 42.68; when z_2 is observed, action a_3 gives the highest expected utility of 36.90; and when z_3 is observed, action a_3 gives the highest expected utility of 40.00. The z_k are observed with frequency $P(Z)$. Hence, the weighted average utility of the optimal strategy is:

$$42.68(0.52) + 36.90(0.29) + 40.00(0.19) = 40.49$$

We can now compare the expected utility from the data problem with that from the no-data problem to obtain the "value of using the Z infor-

TABLE 5.4

COMPUTATION OF THE "VALUE OF AN EXPERIMENT" AND THE "VALUE OF A PERFECT PREDICTOR"

States	Actions			Prior Probabilities	Posterior Probabilities		
	a_1	a_2	a_3	$P(\theta_i)$	$P(\theta_i\|z_1)$	$P(\theta_i\|z_2)$	$P(\theta_i\|z_3)$
θ_1	50	40	20	0.5	0.673	0.345	0.263
θ_2	30	50	30	0.3	0.288	0.310	0.316
θ_3	10	20	60	0.2	0.039	0.345	0.421
Expected Utility Using Prior Probabilities	36	*39*	31	—	—	—	—
Expected Utility Using Posterior Probabilities:				$P(Z)$			
$P(\theta_i\|z_1)$	*42.68*	42.10	24.44	0.52	"Value of the Experiment"		
$P(\theta_i\|z_2)$	30.00	36.20	*36.90*	0.29	= 40.49 − 39 = 1.49		
$P(\theta_i\|z_3)$	26.84	34.74	*40.00*	0.19			
Weighted Average Utility of the Optimal Bayes Strategy		40.49		—	"Value of a Perfect Predictor" = 52 − 39 = 13		
Expected Utility of a Perfect Predictor		52		—			

mation," commonly called the *value of the experiment*. In our use the value of the experiment is 40.49 − 39 = 1.49, meaning that by using Z information the administrator's expected utility can be increased by 1.49 utiles. If the gains table is expressed in dollars rather than utility, as is often the case in empirical work, the value of the experiment has a very direct meaning. It measures in dollar terms the expected money gain to be obtained by employing the Z data rather than relying on the prior probabilities alone. In the usual case when the Z information can be obtained only at some cost, the value of the experiment can be compared with the cost of obtaining the Z information to decide whether it will be profitable to obtain the data.

Another useful piece of information along these lines is the "expected value of a perfect predictor." Suppose that a perfect forecasting device were available. Then the $P(\theta_i|Z)$ matrix of Table 5.4 would contain values of one down the diagonal and zeros elsewhere. The true states of nature θ would be perfectly predicted by the Z values, hence $P(Z) = P(\theta)$. Under such a case when z_1 is observed, θ_1 is predicted with certainty and action a_1 is taken, since it maximizes utility for θ_1. Likewise, z_2 predicts θ_2 without error and a_2 is selected, and similarly for z_3, θ_3, and a_3. Therefore, the expected utility obtained, if a perfect predictor were available, is:

$$50(0.5) + 50(0.3) + 60(0.2) = 52.$$

The "value of a perfect predictor" is $52 - 39 = 13$, measuring the gain in utility possible from using a perfect predictor compared with using only the prior probabilities. Again, where the gain is measured in dollars, this value gives a measure of the potential value to be gained from predicting devices. In some cases, for example, the potential gain may be so small that there is little point in searching for additional information. In other cases, where potential gains are large, even a relatively inaccurate predicting device may increase the expected gain substantially.

To illustrate the procedure for finding the value of a perfect predictor where we have both the monetary outcomes of each action as well as a utility function, let us consider the "Wet or Dry" example again.

Suppose a specific decision maker is faced with the decision of what to do with 100 acres of grapes — a_1 = allocate all for raisins, a_2 = allocate all for wine crush, or a_3 = allocate half to each. Since Table 1.7 is on a per-acre basis, we can easily obtain the gains table for 100 acres, as shown in Table 5.5 (left-hand side). Let us suppose that the utility function as shown in Figure 5.J was derived for this decision maker from his preferences among risky prospects. Then we can convert each of the monetary values to utility values by reading from the graph the utility numbers associated with each monetary number. The utility values are shown in Table 5.5 (right-hand side).

If we had a perfect forecaster, then the true state of nature θ would be perfectly predicted. Then, if θ_1 were predicted, action a_1 would be taken, with monetary outcome \$6,020, or utility outcome 65; if θ_2 were predicted, action a_1 would be taken, with monetary outcome \$4,400, or utility outcome 60; and likewise for the other states of nature. The maximum monetary outcome and maximum utility outcome for each state of nature are outlined in Table 5.5. The maximum expected monetary value with a perfect predictor is \$4,104, and the maximum expected utility value with a perfect predictor is 51.67. Thus, the value of the perfect predictor is \$4,104 − \$3,222 = \$882 in terms of money, or $51.67 - 40.01 = 11.66$ in terms of utility.

The question that naturally arises at this point is, "Does the utility value bear any correspondence with the monetary value?" The answer is NO! This can be seen by looking at the graph in Figure 5.J for the utility

TABLE 5.5
MONETARY AND UTILITY GAINS FOR WET OR DRY PROBLEM

States of Nature	Monetary Gains			Utility Gains			
	a_1	a_2	a_3	a_1	a_2	a_3	$P(\theta)$
θ_1	$6,020	$1,850	$3,935	65	34	57	0.42
θ_2	4,400	1,850	3,125	60	34	50	0.14
θ_3	− 388	1,450	546	−10	28	11	0.32
θ_4	2,800	4,196	3,498	46	59	54	0.04
θ_5	1,620	4,196	2,908	30	59	47	0.07
θ_6	−2,320	3,357	518	40	52	10	0.01
Expected Value	3,222	2,005	2,614	36.04	35.01	40.01	
Max. with Perfect Predictor		$4,104				51.67	

value of $822: the gain from the perfect predictor over the expected gain from a_1 without the predictor is not equal to 11.66, the gain in utility from a perfect predictor. The reason for this is that the utility function is non-linear.[9]

The next question, then, is "What is the value, in terms of money, of the perfect predictor to the decision maker with a non-linear utility function?" After all, the decision maker with a non-linear utility function would have to pay for a perfect predictor in terms of money, since his utility is not transferrable. This question is answered by considering the amount of money (cost) that the decision maker would be willing to give up and remain as well off with the perfect predictor as he would have been with just his prior information.[10] That is, what cost must be subtracted from each monetary outcome (left-hand portion of Table 5.5) to obtain the same expected utility value as action a_3 provides? Since, with the perfect predictor, we are interested only in the maximum expected value, we need consider only those cells of Table 5.5 that are outlined. Thus, we are looking for a cost, c, which, when subtracted from these monetary gains and converted to utility, will provide a maximum expected utility of 40.01.

By trial and error we found a $c = $1,200$, which provides monetary gains that, when converted to utility, provides a maximum expected utility of 40.17, approximating the value of 40.01. The monetary and

[9] Any attempt to connect the difference between two utility numbers to a monetary value would be another illustration of committing Fallacy 3.

[10] This definition was suggested by D. R. Harvey, "A Note on the Value of Information in Decision Problems" (Term paper, University of New England, Armidale, N.S.W., Australia).

utility values are shown in Table 5.6. The utility values were read from the curve in Figure 5.J (page 129). (Since the utility values were read from a graph, the final result is only approximate.) Thus, we can say that the decision maker with such a utility function could not afford to pay more than $1,200 for a perfect predictor and remain as well off in terms of utility as he would have if he used only his prior information. In Chapter XI we shall consider other examples and look at the value of a specific predictor in comparison to a perfect predictor.

REGRESSION ANALYSIS AND ESTIMATION OF POSTERIOR DISTRIBUTIONS

Regression is a tool of analysis that is frequently used by economists and statisticians in a decision-making context. Normally in this context, there is a decision maker who must make a decision and the analyst who may be carrying out the regression analysis for the decision maker. In fact, this is the usual case in business where there is a manager who is the decision maker and a separate research department or staff persons who carry out the analyses. In the case of the agricultural extension service and the agricultural experiment station, there is a similar situation, except that the farm manager and the analyst may be physically separated by a greater extent than in business. In this type of situation the question arises: how does the decision maker incorporate into his decision making the results of the analyst, that is, how does the decision maker arrive at his posterior distribution over his states of nature?[11]

TABLE 5.6

MONETARY GAINS MINUS $1,200 COST OF PERFECT PREDICTOR AND CORRESPONDING UTILITY VALUES

States of Nature	Actions						
	Monetary Gains			Utility Gains			
	a_1	a_2	a_3	a_1	a_2	a_3	$P(\theta)$
θ_1	$4820			62.0			0.42
θ_2	3200			51.0			0.14
θ_3		$ 250			4.5		0.32
θ_4		2996			49.0		0.04
θ_5		2996			49.0		0.07
θ_6		2157			37.0		0.01
Maximum Expected Utility with Perfect Predictor							40.17

[11] We are indebted to Don Pierce of the Department of Statistics, Oregon State University, for help with this section.

FIGURE 5.J
UTILITY FUNCTION FOR DECISION MAKER IN WET-DRY PROBLEM

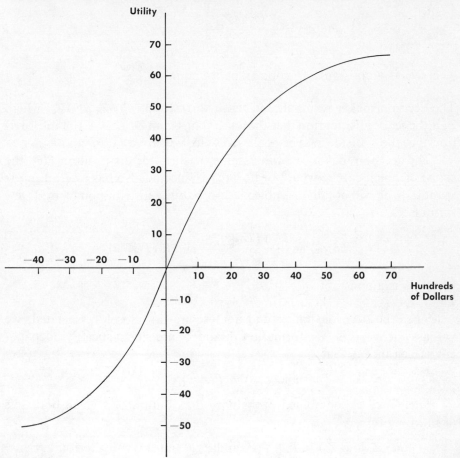

Viewing the separation between the decision maker and the analyst, one recognizes that each has an independent and different set of information upon which to base posterior distributions. The decision maker probably has his own personal experience with the problem and thus may have one particular set of information. Much of his information may be of a qualitative nature. The analyst with his own experiences, tools, and statistical data, has a different set of information, which may be of a more quantitative nature.

We shall state the problem in the following way: The analyst attempts to derive a probability distribution, call it $P(\theta|Z_1)$, where Z_1 is the information set available to the analyst. A reasonable assumption for the analyst to make is that $P'(\theta)$, the prior probability distribution, is a uniform distribution. Hence, Bayes' formula is

$$P(\theta|Z_1) = \frac{P'(\theta)\, P(Z_1|\theta)}{P(Z_1)} = K_1\, P(Z_1|\theta)$$

where K_1 is a constant of proportionality equal to $\dfrac{P'(\theta)}{P(Z_1)}$.

The decision maker wants the posterior distribution $P(\theta|Z_1 \text{ and } Z_2)$ where Z_1 is the set of information that the analyst has, and Z_2 is the set of information that the decision maker has. How do we derive $P(\theta|Z_1 \text{ and } Z_2)$?

The decision maker, we will assume, has a prior distribution $P(\theta)$, the shape of which can be whatever he likes. Since he also has a set of information Z_2, he will obtain his subjective probability distribution from Bayes' formula:

$$P(\theta|Z_2) = \frac{P(\theta)\, P(Z_2|\theta)}{P(Z_2)} = K_2\, P(\theta)\, P(Z_2|\theta)$$

where K_2 is a constant $= \dfrac{1}{P(Z_2)}$.

Since the decision maker and analyst are not closely associated, we will assume the sets of information Z_1 and Z_2 are stochastically independent, which means that

$$P(Z_1 \text{ and } Z_2|\theta) = P(Z_1|\theta)\, P(Z_2|\theta).$$

Therefore, the combined probability distribution of θ given both sets of information is[12]

$$P(\theta|Z_1 \text{ and } Z_2) \propto P(\theta)\, P(Z_1 \text{ and } Z_2|\theta) \text{ but, by substitution}$$
$$P(\theta|Z_1 \text{ and } Z_2) \propto P(\theta)\, P(Z_1|\theta)\, P(Z_2|\theta)$$

and finally by substitution

$$P(\theta|Z_1 \text{ and } Z_2) \propto P(\theta|Z_1)\, P(\theta|Z_2).$$

Application to Regression Analysis[13]

In this discussion the unknown parameter θ is assumed to be y_n, the true price of a commodity in period n. Let Z_1 be the set of data consisting

---

[12] The symbol $\propto$ means "proportional to."
[13] This section is based on D. V. Lindley, *Introduction to Probability and Statistics from a Bayesian Viewpoint, Part 2, Inference* (London: Cambridge University Press, 1965), pp. 203–213.

of previous prices of the commodity and related variables available to the
analyst, that is,

$$Z_1 = \{(y_1, X_1), (y_2, X_2), \ldots, (y_{n-1}, X_{n-1})\} = [y, X]$$

where the y_i are observed prices for $n - 1$ years, X_i are column vectors of
p independent variables associated with the respective prices, and y and
X are matrices.
Suppose that

$y = \beta X' + e$ where
$\beta = (\beta_1\ \beta_2\ \ldots\ \beta_p)$ and $\text{Var}\ (e) = \sigma^2 I$, where I is the identity matrix.

It is assumed, as in the usual regression case, that X is fixed and the set
y, i.e., $y_1, y_2 \ldots y_{n-1}$, is a set of independent normal random variables.
Further, it will be assumed that the analyst's prior distribution of

$$\beta_1, \beta_2, \ldots, \beta_p \text{ and } 1n\ \sigma^2$$

are uniformly and independently distributed. The uniform distribution of
β and $1n\ \sigma^2$ is to be interpreted in the sense that the analyst's prior knowledge of β and σ^2 is so diffuse that the prior density is sensibly constant over
the effective range of the likelihood function. The independence of β
and σ^2 is reasonable since typically knowledge of the variance of y will not
alter one's knowledge of the dependence of y on X, (i.e., of β).
It can be shown that the posterior distribution $P(y_n|Z_1, X_n)$, where y_n is
the true price in year n and the X_n contains the values of the independent
variables available for the forecast, i.e., $y_n = \beta X_n' + e_n$ is such that,

$$\frac{y_n - \hat{\beta} X_n'}{\sqrt{\left(X_n'(X'X)^{-1}X_n + \dfrac{1}{n} + 1\right)s^2}} = t.$$

This means that the expression has a t distribution with $n - 1 - p$ degrees of freedom. In this expression $\hat{\beta}$ is the estimate of β from the regression
analysis, s^2 is the error mean square, $(X'X)^{-1}$ is the inverse of the variance-
covariance matrix of the original X, and X_n is as defined previously. Since
y_n is the only random variable in the ratio above, the t value can be calculated. Using a table of the t-distribution (given in Appendix A),

$$P(y_n - \delta < y_n < y_n + \Delta|Z_1, X_n)$$

can be obtained, wherein δ and Δ are arbitrary. This set of probabilities
for intervals of varying length is the distribution that we called $P(\theta|Z_1)$ in
the previous section.

The decision maker's probability distribution $P(y_n|Z_2)$ will be taken to be of the form:

$$P(y_n|Z_2) = P_i \qquad \text{if } y_n \text{ is contained in the interval}$$
$$(y_n - \delta, \ y_n + \Delta) \text{ for the } i \text{ ranges of } y$$
$$= 0 \text{ otherwise.}$$

This is the distribution that we called $P(\theta|Z_2)$ above. Then it follows from the results of the previous section that the combined posterior distribution of y_n is

$$P(y_n|Z_1, X_n, Z_2) \propto P(y_n|Z_1, X_n) \, P(y_n|Z_2).$$

This can be evaluated by multiplying ordinates of the two distributions for the same intervals and rescaling to normalize the products. The procedure of getting a posterior distribution in a regression context will be illustrated by an example in Chapter VIII.

SUMMARY

This chapter concludes the presentation of the main body of decision theory under uncertainty. It was shown how the Bayes' solution provides an optimal strategy, that this strategy is a pure strategy, and that the solution is computationally easy to determine. It was shown how to derive the value of an experiment, whether the gains were stated in monetary or utility terms. The derivation of posterior probability distributions in the context of regression analysis was shown to illustrate the broad application of Bayes' formula and to lay the foundation for some of the interesting research applications to follow.

FURTHER READING

Chernoff, Herman, and Lincoln Moses. *Elementary Decision Theory*. New York: John Wiley & Sons, Inc., 1959, Chapter 6.

EXERCISES

1. Plot the weighted average of (2,2), (4,4), and (6,1) which give these three points the weights:
   a) $\frac{1}{2}, \frac{1}{2}, 0$
   b) .8, .1, .1
   c) .1, .8, .1
   d) $\frac{1}{3}, \frac{1}{3}, \frac{1}{3}$
2. Now represent each desired point of No. 1 as a weighted average of (6,1) and a point on the line connecting (2,2) and (4,4).

3. Express the point (4.4,2.4) as weighted average of the three points (6,1), (2,2) and (4,4).

4. Let S be a circle (circumference and interior). Delete one point P. Is the remaining set convex if P is on the circumference? If P is in the interior?

5. Which of the following sets are convex?
   a) $\{(x,y): \max(x,y) = 1\}$
   b) $\{(x,y): \max(x,y) \geq 1\}$
   c) $\{(x,y): \max(x,y) \leq 1\}$
   d) $\{(x,y): \max(x,y) < 1\}$

6. Using the following regret table and $f(Z|\theta)$ table, find the Bayesian action when a z_2 is observed. How much was that observation worth?

Actions

States of Nature	a_1	a_2	a_3
θ_1	0	1	2
θ_2	3	0	1
θ_3	4	3	0

Observations

States of Nature	z_1	z_2	z_3	z_4
θ_1	$\frac{1}{2}$	$\frac{1}{2}$	0	0
θ_2	0	$\frac{1}{2}$	$\frac{1}{2}$	0
θ_3	0	0	$\frac{1}{3}$	$\frac{2}{3}$

7. Mr. Decision Wrecker faces a choice among the following actions with the regrets as shown below for each possible state of nature.

	a_1	a_2	a_3
θ_1	5	6	0
θ_2	5	0	10
θ_3	6	3	0

He conducts an experiment, for which the $P(Z|\theta)$ is given below, and observes z_2.

	z_1	z_2	z_3
θ_1	0.7	0.3	0
θ_2	0.2	0.5	0.3
θ_3	0.1	0.3	0.6

   a) What action would you predict Mr. Decision Wrecker will take if he is a Bayesian type?
   b) How much was the observation worth to him?
   c) How much could he have paid for the experiment to be conducted?

8. The following numbered steps present most of the theorem which says that every admissible strategy is a Bayes strategy for some prior probabilities $1 - w$ and w. Each step contains a question.
   a) Let s_o be an admissible strategy represented by a point $\bar{U}$ on a diagram with $G(\theta_1,s)$ on the horizontal axis and $G(\theta_2,s)$ on the vertical axis.
   QUESTION: After locating s_o on your diagram, indicate a strategy s' that is not admissible.
   b) Then no point of S lies in the convex set T of points which lie above and to the right of $\bar{U}$.
   QUESTION: After locating S and T, indicate a circumstance that denies this condition.

c) Clearly, any line separating S and T must go through $\bar{U}$ and hence is a supporting line of S and T at $\bar{U}$.

QUESTION: After locating the supporting line, show one that is not a supporting line of T.

d) In the event that there is a supporting line of T at $\bar{U}$, the coefficients in the equation of that line satisfy certain conditions.

QUESTION: What are the conditions?

e) We can divide the coefficients by $a + b$ and obtain weights that satisfy certain conditions.

QUESTION: What are the conditions?

f) Thus, for any admissible strategy s_o represented by $\bar{U}$, there is a pair of weights so that $(1 - w) G_1 + w G_2 = c$ supports S at $\bar{U}$.

QUESTION: Furthermore, since T is above the line and S is below the line, what conditions are satisfied for all points of S and $\bar{U}$?

g) QUESTION: What conclusion follows from the last two conditions of f?

9. a) Draw a convex set representing the strategies of a decision-making problem under uncertainty. With $1 - w = \frac{1}{3}$ and $w = \frac{2}{3}$ for prior probabilities, show that the corresponding supporting line intersects the line $G_1 = G_2$ at the maximized value of $(1 - w) G_1 + w G_2$.

b) What is the relationship between a maximin and a Bayes solution to a problem of decision-making under uncertainty?

10. Suppose that a rancher can average \$100 per calf from calves sired by a bull which is homozygous dominant for a certain characteristic. He can average \$90 per calf if the bull turns out to be heterozygous dominant. Due to the genetics and breeding involved, one fifth of untested bulls for sale are homozygous dominant and four fifths are heterozygous, but these bulls cannot be visually distinguished. However, it is possible to "test" the sires by means of their offspring from certain costly crosses. The probability of a test calf showing the desired characteristic is 1.0, given that the sire is homozygous, and the probability is 0.5 if the sire is heterozygous. The cost of an untested sire is \$500, but the cost of a tested sire increases by \$100 for each tested offspring (where each tested offspring shows the desired characteristic). The question is, which of the following types of bulls would be the most profitable for the rancher to buy:

TYPE OF BULL	COST OF BULL
Untested	\$ 500
Tested, one out of one offspring with desired characteristic	600
Tested, 2 out of 2 with desired characteristic	700
Tested, 3 out of 3 with desired characteristic	800
Tested, 4 out of 4 with desired characteristic	900
Tested, 5 out of 5 with desired characteristic	1000
.	.
.	.
.	.
Tested, N out of N	$500 + \$100N$

11. Suppose there were a fertility test that could be given range bulls early in the spring. Suppose further that on the average, 40% of bulls for sale are infertile and 60% are

fertile. Of those that are fertile, 80% pass the test and of those that are infertile, only 40% pass the test.

a) What is the probability that a bull is infertile, given that he has passed the test?

b) If a fertile bull is worth $800 to the rancher and an infertile bull has zero value, what would the expected value be to the rancher of a bull that has passed the test?

12. Some men believe that some women's actions are predictable to the extent that a man can make a decision concerning which woman would make a good marriage partner. Suppose for the sake of this question that you are one of these men (and if married that such an opportunity would again present itself) and that you divide the states of nature into two categories: θ_1 = good marriage partner, or θ_2 = poor marriage partner. (Since most single men are naive about these matters, we can be assured that this is not a two-person game.) There are, for simplicity, only three actions that you need consider: a_1 is to play the field, a_2 is to restrict one's attention to blondes, and a_3 is to restrict one's attention to brunettes.

a) Make up your own loss table in terms of utility.

b) From casual observation assign prior probabilities and solve the no-data problem. State your criterion and show your calculations.

c) Now there are certain experiments that can be performed before the decision is made. One that is about as relevant as any is to ask the prospective partner to take an intelligence test. Six possible observations are: (1) blonde and above average, (2) blonde and average, (3) blonde and below average, (4) brunette and above average, (5) brunette and average, and (6) brunette and below average. Make up your own conditional probability densities.

d) Suppose you now observe a z_1. State a criterion of decision and determine what action it tells you to take. Show your calculations.

CHAPTER VI

Introduction to Empirical Applications

The purpose of the next chapters, VII through XI, is to show that the theoretical tools developed in earlier chapters can be widely used in practical decision settings. The examples are drawn from the broad area of agriculture and natural resource management. The wide range in types of decisions presented reflects our conviction that there are countless practical decision situations for which decision theory provides a meaningful framework for conceptualizing problems and organizing data for their solution. A rather thorough search of the decision theory literature reveals a sparseness of empirical applications in the areas of agriculture and natural resources. This is somewhat surprising in view of the tremendous uncertainties of weather, technology, disease, and prices that affect decisions in these fields.

The typical textbook treatment of decision making is (intentionally) cast in terms of "trivial" examples: whether to wear a raincoat when faced with weather uncertainty; whether to break eggs in a single bowl when faced with some probability of a rotten egg; whether to participate in parlor or gambling games with prizes and penalties; etc. A definite advantage in keeping the examples at a somewhat artificial level is that the reader is inclined to accept the problem posed for what it is, an illustrative example, and not question the simplifying assumptions involved. Experience with a large number of students suggests that the more "realistic" the examples, the more difficulty involved in focusing their attention on the theoretical aspects of the problem. Probably every teacher has had the discouraging experience of developing a carefully planned "realistic" example to illustrate a theoretical point, only to have a student interrupt with an irrelevant comment, such as pointing out that yields in his home county are greater than those used in the example.

Thus, the decision to illustrate the theoretical concepts with "nontrivial" empirical examples was made with some trepidation. Real problems have a way of becoming cluttered up with too many details. Readers may quarrel with data or assumptions rather than method. Despite these dangers, our preference for realistic examples was dictated by the experience that our own students have not really understood decision theory until they have tried to apply it themselves. We believe our presentation will take them one step further in this direction than the usual treatment. By trimming empirical description to bare essentials, we think we can give students a greater appreciation of decision theory by working through actual research illustrations.

The empirical material in each chapter is handled in ascending order of complexity, usually starting with problems involving a prior distribution only and working through cases of posterior distributions. In some of the more complex cases, the theory is adapted somewhat to handle the empirical problem adequately. We hope to show that, with some ingenuity, the theoretical concepts are relevant even for problems which initially do not appear to fit neatly into the usual decision theory mold.

A Preview of Empirical Applications

Chapters VII and VIII summarize three applications of decision theory in the field of agriculture. Chapter VII analyzes the problem of selecting an optimum stocking rate for cattle on California rangeland, where feed supplies are highly variable from year to year. From a subject-matter point of view, this application is suggestive of a wide range of problems dealing with population density related to an uncertain food supply, such as often faced in the fields of fish and game management. From an analytical point of view it is illustrative of many production planning decisions. The problem is posed successively as one with no prior distribution, then as one with a prior distribution, and finally as one incorporating predictions of feed supplies and development of a posterior distribution. The effect of alternative subjective prior distributions on decision strategies is illustrated. This particular problem is a relatively straightforward application involving discrete states of nature and a limited number of discrete acts. It thus provides the reader with the opportunity to grasp firmly the fundamentals of the approach before turning to somewhat more complex applications.

Chapter VIII contains two additional applications in agriculture. The first deals with the general problem of selecting the optimum proportions of crops in a cropping system when the net returns of the individual crops are subject to considerable variation due to price and weather uncertainty. This application is an illustration of the classical portfolio selection prob-

lem analyzed by Markowitz.[1] Only a prior distribution is used, but the
concept of a continuous rather than discrete distribution is introduced.
An expectation-variance (E-V) boundary of acts is derived using quadratic
programming and a choice among the acts based on alternative utility
functions.

The second application in Chapter VIII involves production planning
by turkey growers who must make a choice between various kinds of contract production and independent production. Turkey prices and death
rates are highly variable, but part of the grower risk can be transferred to
the contracting firm (turkey processor and/or feed company) by one of
several contractual arrangements. This application introduces the problem of incorporating price forecasts by regression analysis into the Bayesian framework. Continuous, nonnormal distributions are required
because turkey mortality rates clearly are not normally distributed. Time
is also introduced by way of a problem involving firm growth over a ten-
year period. The growth process for each strategy is simulated many times
with prices and mortality as stochastic variables, giving a probability distribution of terminal net worth for each strategy. The choice among
strategies is then made using decision theory principles.

Chapters IX through XI turn from applications in agriculture to those
in the natural resource fields of geology, forestry, and climatology. Chapter IX analyzes a problem typical of petroleum exploration and mining —
the question of whether or not to drill an oil well. The analytical framework is relatively straightforward in this problem, using both the prior
and posterior distributions. However, this application is noteworthy for
the serious attempt made to derive empirically the utility functions for a
sample of operators.

Chapter X introduces a typical problem in forest management. The
question posed is whether a vertically integrated firm in the pulp and paper
industry should supply its raw material by buying and developing its own
timberland or by purchasing raw material in the log market. In a typical
forest management problem of this type, extremely long time periods are
involved. Therefore, the concepts of discounting future costs and returns
to a common decision point are introduced. It is shown that the solution
to the problem is extremely sensitive both to the interest rate and to the
subjective prior probability distribution used.

Chapter XI presents a problem where climatological forecasts play a

[1] Harry M. Markowitz, *Portfolio Selection: Efficient Diversification of Investments*,
Cowles Foundation Monograph 16 (New York: John Wiley and Sons, 1959). Rudolf J.
Fruend, "The Introduction of Risk into a Programming Model," *Econometrica*, Vol. 24, No. 3
(July, 1956), pp. 253–263. Donald E. Farrar, *The Investment Decision Under Uncertainty*
(Englewood Cliffs, N.J.: Prentice Hall, 1962).

key role. Procedures are presented for evaluating a rainfall predicting device in a specific decision making setting. Although the setting involves selecting optimal fertilizer rates in an arid region of Australia, it illustrates how a climatologist could evaluate the value of a weather forecasting device.

Relationship of Analyst to Decision Maker

Before turning to the next chapter and the first of the empirical applications, it may be pointed out that the applications fall into two broad groups when viewed from the standpoint of the relationship between the analyst and the decision maker. The agricultural applications of Chapters VII and VIII and the problem in Chapter XI fall into one group. Here there is a sizable number of comparatively small individual producers who are the decision makers. The analyst or research economist is remote from his client and is trying to make general information available to many individuals in widely varying circumstances such that they can make better decisions under uncertainty.

The applications in Chapters IX and X fall into a second group where the firm making the decision is normally very large and hires its own research staff. Here the analyst is in close contact with a single decision maker or decision-making body and hence can narrow his efforts to the specific case at hand.

The distinction between these two general cases can be made more sharply by considering how research information might be summarized and presented in the decision framework of this book. The five components of this decision framework are actions, states, calculation of a monetary payoff table, conversion to utility values, and estimation of a probability distribution over the states (prior or posterior, or both). We believe that the analyst dealing with a remote client is generally in a position to present the first three components in his reports to decision makers. Since the last two components, utility functions and probability distributions, might differ widely among decision makers, it is generally impractical from the standpoint of time and cost to determine the utility function and subjective probabilities for each decision maker. Often, however, objective probabilities are presented by the analyst based on historical or other empirical evidence.

Results presented in the five-component decision framework can be interpreted by the remote decision maker in at least four ways:

1. The decision maker may accept the implicit linear utility function specified by the analyst as well as the empirical probabilities pre-

sented.   In this case, he can use the results directly; that is, he can adopt the criterion of maximizing expected monetary value and ascertain directly from the decision table an optimal action.

2. The decision maker may accept the linear utility function specified by the analyst but revise the probabilities presented.   In this case, he alters the probability distribution according to his own assessment and determines the action consistent with the revised subjective probabilities.

3. The decision maker may accept the probabilities presented by the analyst but believe that the utility function specified does not apply. In this case he should convert monetary payoffs to utility payoffs in accordance with his own assessments of utility, and determine the action consistent with his own preferences.

4. The decision maker may believe that neither the probabilities presented nor the utility function specified applies to his circumstances. Formally, he should revise or replace the probabilities and convert monetary payoffs to utility before determining the optimum action. However, in practice he more likely examines his probability distribution of the monetary consequences of each action and selects that action which intuitively makes him feel most comfortable or satisfied.   In effect, he is converting monetary values to utility values and introducing his own probabilities in this evaluation process, albeit in a somewhat informal way.[2]

In contrast, the analyst for a large firm might very well carry out the full five-step procedure by deriving both his client's specific utility function and his subjective probabilities for the decision in question.   Of course, even the problem of deriving empirical utility functions for farmers is not as impractical as once thought.[3]   However, the large numbers of farmers served by a typical agricultural research or extension economist would normally rule out a "complete" cataloging of utility functions.

One problem, however, is raised in the case of the large firm that is less important for the case of remote clientele.   Recall our assumption that the prior distribution of the decision maker is independent of the posterior dis-

---

[2] We have argued that such an informal procedure may lead to inconsistencies or unwitting violation of preferences underlying the utility function, and that only by formally deriving the utility function can one say that the decisions made conform to the preferences.   The formal procedure suggested for deriving a utility function is to ascertain preferences in an artificial situation and then to infer that the derived utility function can be applied to real situations. This inference has been criticized and the general applicability of the utility function has sometimes been questioned.   Dorfman, *op. cit.*, p. 144, expresses these doubts by reminding us that utility functions are derived empirically by a method which "replaces the problem of choosing among the actual alternatives with a number of artificial choice problems, each of which is simpler than the actual one (which is to the good) but also more artificial (which is to the bad)."

[3] For example, see the work by Officer and Halter, *op. cit.*, and the appendix to Chapter III.

tribution of the analyst. The prospect that this assumption will be met seems questionable in the case of an analyst and decision maker working closely together, having access to the same data and interacting together over a long period of time. This is a problem that needs more study.

EXERCISE

From here on you are on your own. We suggest you try your hand at a real world problem by attempting to apply decision theory tools to some original problem of your choice.

CHAPTER VII

Applications in Agriculture I

In this chapter we apply Bayesian decision theory to a stocking rate problem that is typical of many problems in agriculture. We present the problem in three stages of complexity; first assuming no prior distribution, then a prior distribution, and finally a posterior distribution. Throughout this chapter we assume that monetary values adequately reflect payoffs; that is, we assume a linear utility function for money.

THE STOCKING RATE PROBLEM

There are 30 million acres of foothill land in California suited primarily for livestock grazing. Rainfall in these areas is concentrated in the winter months with essentially no rainfall for at least six months in the summer and fall. Range land that is a lush green during the rainy season becomes parched and tinder-dry in late summer and fall. Thus, the feed supply is highly seasonal, with large amounts available during the winter and spring and little during the summer and fall. Some of the excess feed during the winter and spring can be reserved for summer or fall grazing although it loses a substantial portion of its feed value in the drying process. Year-around grazing operations are therefore feasible, although some supplemental feeding is required during late fall and early winter. The feed supply is not only variable seasonally, but between years, depending on rainfall, temperature, wind, and other factors. Historical studies show that feed supply in a "good" year can be double that in a "bad" year.

One fairly common type of livestock operation in this area is a beef cow herd (cow-calf operation). Brood cows graze year-around on the range land, and their calves are sold at weaning time (8 months of age) weighing around 500 pounds. This type of organization is rather inflexible in that cow numbers cannot be changed easily from year to year in response to weather conditions and feed supply. The rancher's dilemma is to decide on the size of herd to maintain: if the herd is too small, feed will be wasted in many years; if the herd is too large, the feed supply in many years will be inadequate, and expensive supplemental feeds must be purchased.

THE STOCKING PROBLEM UNDER COMPLETE IGNORANCE

We assume initially that the rancher has no idea of the probability distribution of range conditions (that is, no prior information), although this is probably quite unrealistic. As we have argued earlier, it is in fact extremely difficult to think of realistic problems where the decision maker does not have some information, however vague, about the probability of various states of nature.

Assume a rancher with 3,000 acres of range land of varying quality. In a "normal" year, the range produces sufficient feed to carry a 360-cow beef herd, with calves sold at an 8-month weight of 500 pounds. In a "very poor" year there is sufficient feed for only about 230 cows; in an "excellent" year the range can carry 460 cows. To analyze this problem in a decision framework, we define the three components common to all decision models — the states of nature, the actions, and the payoff for each state-action combination. This information is summarized in Table 7.1. We define six states of nature (range conditions) from θ_1 (very poor) to θ_6 (excellent). The six actions (herd sizes) range from a_1 (230 cows) to a_6 (460 cows). Thus, the six actions are selected to match the six states of nature, that is, action a_1 is the herd size which utilizes the feed produced in a very poor year (θ_1), a_2 the herd size that utilizes the feed produced in a poor year (θ_2), and so forth.

Each payoff entry in the body of Table 7.1 is the result of a budgeting computation indicating the net farm income that would accrue to the rancher for the specified action and state of nature. An example budget is shown in Table 7.2, indicating a net income of $5,800 for a 360-cow herd (a_4) with normal range conditions (θ_4). Payoff entries for the elements off the diagonal in Table 7.1 are obtained by adjusting net income either for (1) the additional cost of supplemental feeding (for entries above the diagonal), or (2) the small additional income from excess feed (hay) that can be sold (for entries below the diagonal).

In most problems of this type some minor questions arise concerning which costs to include in arriving at the payoff values. Would annual cash income be a more realistic measure of payoff than deducting depreciation (a deferrable cost) to arrive at net farm income? Should unpaid interest on investment (opportunity cost) be deducted in arriving at the payoffs? The general rule is that if a cost differs from cell to cell of the table, it must be considered as a cost in arriving at a complete comparison of payoffs. Thus, in Table 7.1 depreciation is included as a cost because it differs by actions, while unpaid interest is omitted because it is the same for all entries in the table.

TABLE 7.1
PAYOFF TABLE FOR A COW-CALF OPERATION UNDER UNCERTAINTY OF RANGE CONDITIONS

States of Nature: Range Conditions (θ_i)	Actions: Herd Size (a_i)						Criterion	
	a_1 230 Cows	a_2 280 Cows	a_3 320 Cows	a_4 360 Cows	a_5 415 Cows	a_6 460 Cows	Hurwicz $\alpha = .6$	Insufficient Reason
	Dollars							
θ_1 Very poor	−4,580	−6,290	−8,260	−10,040	−12,690	−14,930	0.6	1/6
θ_2 Poor	−3,330	− 870	−2,090	− 3,970	− 6,620	− 8,860	0	1/6
θ_3 Fair	−2,530	450	2,830	1,440	− 600	− 2,800	0	1/6
θ_4 Normal	−1,890	1,090	4,060	5,800	5,530	2,020	0	1/6
θ_5 Good	− 930	2,050	5,020	7,420	10,230	8,510	0	1/6
θ_6 Excellent	− 130	2,850	5,820	8,220	11,770	13,930	0.4	1/6
Hurwicz ($\alpha = .6$)	−2,800	−2,630	−2,630	− 2,740	− 2,910	− 3,390	—	—
Insufficient Reason $P(\theta) = 1/6$	−2,230	− 120	1,230	1,480	1,270	350	—	—

TABLE 7.2

COMPUTATION OF NET FARM INCOME FOR A 360-COW HERD (ACTION a_4) WITH NORMAL RANGE CONDITIONS (STATES θ_4)

Item	Subtotal	Total
	Dollars	
Gross Income (sale of calves, cull cows, and bulls)		53,000
Cash Variable Costs	24,200	
Cultural Costs (fertilizer, seed, gas, oil, etc.)	14,200	
Livestock Costs (veterinary, medicine, replacement bulls, purchased feed, etc.)	10,000	
Cash Fixed Costs (hired labor, taxes, insurance, paid interest, etc.)	15,700	
Depreciation	7,300	
Total Costs (excluding unpaid interest on investment)		47,200
Net Farm Income		5,800

We proceed now to evaluate the decision problem of Table 7.1 under the assumption of complete ignorance, that is, no prior probability distribution of range conditions is known. We apply successively the alternative criteria which have been proposed to handle this type of problem as discussed in Chapter IV.

Maximin Criteria

A rancher using the maximin criterion assumes that the worst consequence of each act will occur, then selects the action which offers the best of these unfavorable occurrences. In terms of Table 7.1, he in effect assumes that the very poor range conditions (θ_1) will occur, then selects a herd size of 230 cows (a_1) as the optimal action because the loss of $4,580 is less than for any other herd size. This criterion is clearly pessimistic or conservative in that the entire weight in the decision is given only to the worst possible outcomes. The dubious acceptability of this criterion is emphasized by observing that a rancher who stocked only 230 cows (a_1) would never sustain a profit regardless of the range condition which actually eventuates. A rancher using the maximin criterion would thus be forced out of business in the long run — exactly the consequence he is probably trying to avoid by being conservative! Intuitively it would appear that even a very conservative rancher should choose some other action such as a_2 which, although it has slightly worse consequences than a_1 if θ_1 should occur, has significantly better consequences for all other states of nature. Only if the rancher felt that nature were a conscious adversary, as in game theory, would action a_1 make much sense. Furthermore, such an attitude seems to imply that θ_1 is "more likely" to occur than other states, which appears inconsistent with our assumption of complete ignorance. This empirical decision problem should raise some doubts in the minds of those who feel that a conservative person should follow a maximin approach to decision making.

Maximax Criterion

Contrary to the maximin criterion, the maximax criterion places the entire emphasis in decision making on the best outcomes possible. In Table 7.1 the rancher using this criterion would stock 460 cows (a_6) since this action includes the possibility of the maximum profit of $13,930. This criterion hypothesizes a confirmed optimist who takes no account of the possibility of the less favorable consequences of his action. Note that if θ_1 should occur, the maximax action a_6 could result in a loss of $14,930. It is difficult to imagine a rancher who would ignore completely all the possibilities other than the most favorable in determining a stocking rate, again raising serious doubts about this as an acceptable criterion.

The Minimax Regret Criterion

The motivation for the minimax regret criterion is that a person feels dissatisfied when an opportunity has been missed. For example, suppose in Table 7.1 that action a_4 (360 cows) is selected and that θ_6 occurs. The rancher then makes a net income of $8,220, which is relatively favorable. On the other hand, if he had known that θ_6 would occur, he could have made $13,930 (by choosing a_6). His opportunity cost or income foregone of selecting a_4 was $13,930 − $8,220 or $5,710. In decision theory terms, the opportunity cost of $5,710 is known as regret. On the other hand, suppose a_4 were selected and θ_1 occurred. If θ_1 could have been anticipated, action a_1 would have been optimum, incurring a loss of $4,580 rather than $10,040; the regret involved in having selected a_4 when θ_1 occurs is then the difference between these two figures, or $5,460. In like fashion, the complete regret Table 7.3 is constructed corresponding to payoff Table 7.1. Computationally, to convert the gains to regrets, subtract from the largest gain for each state all the entries in the same row (state).

TABLE 7.3

**REGRET TABLE FOR THE COW-CALF OPERATION UNDER UN-
CERTAINTY OF RANGE CONDITIONS**

States of Na-ture: Range Conditions (θ_i)	Actions: Herd Size (aj)					
	a_1 230 Cows	a_2 280 Cows	a_3 320 Cows	a_4 360 Cows	a_5 415 Cows	a_6 460 Cows
	Dollars					
θ_1 Very poor	0	1,710	3,680	5,460	8,110	10,350
θ_2 Poor	2,460	0	1,220	3,100	5,750	7,990
θ_3 Fair	5,360	2,380	0	1,390	3,430	5,630
θ_4 Normal	7,690	4,710	1,740	0	270	3,780
θ_5 Good	11,160	8,180	5,210	2,810	0	1,720
θ_6 Excellent	14,060	11,080	8,110	5,710	2,160	0

The minimax regret criterion states that the rancher should act so as to minimize the maximum regret which could occur. In terms of Table 7.3 this means that action a_4 (stocking rate of 360 cows) is optimum since its maximum regret of $5,710 is less than the maximum regret for the other actions. While the maximin criterion directs attention to the worst outcomes, minimax regret directs attention to the largest opportunity losses. In both cases, the tone is pessimistic or conservative. However, the minimax regret is less so, since it takes into account the opportunities foregone in calculating regret. Both criteria, however, can be criticized as ignoring most of the information in the table in making the final choice.

Hurwicz Optimism-Pessimism Criterion

As discussed in Chapter IV, Hurwicz has proposed a compromise criterion that incorporates information on both the best and the worse consequences of each act. Specifically, indexes of relative pessimism (α) and optimism ($1 - \alpha$) are derived and used in assigning weights to the worst and best consequences of each action. The optimum decision is then the action with the maximum weighted average.

The value of α for the rancher could be estimated by confronting him with the following simple decision problem. The rancher is asked to select

	a_1	a_2
θ_1	0	x
θ_2	1	x

the value of x that would make him indifferent between action a_1 and a_2. The two extreme values of x would be 0 and 1. If the rancher should choose $x = 0$, the decision table would look as follows:

	a_1	a_2
θ_1	0	0
θ_2	1	0

Clearly no weight is being given to θ_2 if the rancher is indifferent between a_1 and a_2 — he is looking only at the worst that can happen. Thus, a value of $x = 0$ implies a maximin criterion. Conversely, if the rancher selects $x = 1$, the decision table would read as follows:

	a_1	a_2
θ_1	0	1
θ_2	1	1

Here no weight is given to θ_1 — the rancher is looking only at the best result for each action and hence is indifferent between a_1 and a_2; that is, he is following the maximax criterion.

Suppose the rancher picks some value for x between 0 and 1, such as $x = 0.4$. The table now reads:

	a_1	a_2
θ_1	0	0.4
θ_2	1	0.4

The implication now is that there is some set of weights α and $(1 - \alpha)$ for θ_1 and θ_2 that make the decision-maker indifferent between a_1 and a_2. That is,

$$\alpha 0 + (1 - \alpha)1 = (\alpha)\, 0.4 + (1 - \alpha)\, 0.4 \text{ or}$$
$$\alpha = 0.6 \text{ and } 1 - \alpha = 0.4.$$

(This assignment of values to α and $1 - \alpha$, given x, assumes that the decision-maker is indifferent between the two actions if they have the same expected value.) The α and $1 - \alpha$ indices so derived are then used in determining the $P(\theta)$ in *real* decision problems — a very special $P(\theta)$ in which the "worst" state of nature for each action is assigned a probability of α, the "best" state of nature a probability of $1 - \alpha$, and all other states a probability of zero. Viewed in this light, the maximin and maximax criteria are simply special cases of the Hurwicz criterion where the pessimism index (α) and optimism index ($1 - \alpha$), alternately, take values of 1.

To illustrate the Hurwicz criterion in the range stocking problem of Table 7.1, assume that an index $\alpha = 0.6$ has been derived as above for the rancher. The optimum action is now either a_2 or a_3 with a weighted average value of $-\$2,630$. To break the tie, the rancher would have to flip a coin. Intuitively, the Hurwicz criterion appears to be fairly reasonable in this case. However, the idea of ignoring all the information in the payoff table for intermediate states of nature θ_2 through θ_5 is somewhat disturbing. Certainly these values should carry some weight in arriving at a decision.

The Principle of Insufficient Reason: Equally Likely States

Since we are dealing with decision making under complete ignorance, a reasonable suggestion might be to assume that each state of nature is equally likely to occur. In terms of Table 7.1, this amounts to assuming that each of the six states of nature has a probability of one-sixth. The criterion of insufficient reason would then specify action a_4 (stocking 360 cows) as the optimum action since its expected value of $1,480 is the maximum of the six alternative actions.

This criterion has considerable appeal in the sense that all of the information in the payoff table is utilized in arriving at the optimum decision, whereas the criteria discussed above concentrate on particular values only. The difficulty with the principle of insufficient reason as a criterion is that it is sensitive to the way in which states are defined. The states of nature must be defined in such a way as to include all possible outcomes. But this can ordinarily be done in many different ways. Unfortunately, the optimum action may depend on these definitions even though the real problem is the same. Suppose, for example, that after developing the six states as specified in Table 7.1, the rancher has second thoughts. He decides that θ_6 ("excellent" range conditions) is too broad a definition to characterize accurately the more favorable conditions that could occur. Therefore, he replaces old θ_6 ("excellent" conditions) with a new θ_6 ("very good" conditions) and θ_7 ("ideal" conditions). He now assigns equal probabilities to the seven states of nature. The original states θ_1 through θ_5 now have probabilities of $\frac{1}{7}$ rather than $\frac{1}{6}$, and it is clear that the resulting decision could change.

Some may object that the new states θ_6 and θ_7 should be given probabilities of $\frac{1}{12}$ and $\frac{1}{12}$ since they simply split the old θ_6, which had a probability of $\frac{1}{6}$. But to do so would imply that we are not in a situation of complete ignorance about the likelihood of alternative states. That is, we would be saying that new θ_6 and θ_7 are each only half as likely as states θ_1 through θ_5. Thus, the principle of insufficient reason has the disquieting feature that arbitrary definitions of states may dictate different solutions to the same real problem.

Evaluation of Criteria

Our earlier examination in Chapter IV of the criteria employed in the range stocking decision problem of this chapter showed that there are serious objections to each. While the various criteria have elements which we have recognized in our own decision-making processes, it seems unlikely that we would be willing to turn our decision making under uncertainty over to a clerk who mechanically used any one of the criteria outlined.

We assert that there probably is no such thing as "complete ignorance" or "absolute uncertainty." Rather, most of us would or could be forced to attach probabilities to the various states of nature in real decision problems, even though these are highly subjective and based on fragmentary evidence. For example, in the range stocking problem, even a rancher with no previous experience in California is likely to have some information about various kinds of weather conditions and feed supplies that he could formulate into subjective probabilities. Alternatively, he might consult an experienced rancher to obtain more definite information, that is, to search for a suitable prior distribution. Another rancher with experience in California would have some personal basis for establishing his prior probabilities. Some ranchers may attempt to analyze published historical rainfall or weather data to supplement their personal experience. In other words, as Horowitz[1] has stated:

> In a sense, therefore, and even though there have been no explicit probability assessments, there is still the suggestion of some underlying subjective probability distribution(s) over the states of nature; for there is certainly a probability of distribution(s) over the states of nature against which the decision would be nonoptimal; the latter distribution must have been judged unlikely relative to the set of possible alternative distributions or a different decision would have been made. Thus it is indeed questionable whether or not we can justifiably treat any decision problem, particularly one that actually confronts us in the real world, as a problem under uncertainty.

[1] Ira Horowitz, *An Introduction to Quantitative Business Analysis* (New York: McGraw-Hill, 1965), p. 99.

Consistent with the above quotation, we have shown in Chapter IV that a particular action will be optimum for some probability distribution over the states of nature.   Thus, the fact that different people arrive at different decisions to the same problem can be partly explained by their different subjective judgments as to the probability distribution over the states of nature.

THE STOCKING PROBLEM WITH A PRIOR DISTRIBUTION

We pointed out above that it was highly unrealistic to assume that a rancher has no idea of the probability distribution of range conditions. Even without prior evidence, the rancher would probably search for some information on which to form a prior distribution.   One source of such information is the California Crop and Livestock Reporting Service, which has regularly reported an index of range conditions as of the first of the month from 1922 to date.   This report is widely circulated among ranchers; many have undoubtedly analyzed the historical record at least informally to gain some idea of the variability of range conditions from year to year.

These data are reported in Table 7.4, by month, January through June, from 1922 through 1965.   February through June is the period of year in which most of the plant growth occurs.   After June the plants dry out and remain essentially dormant until rains begin the following November or December.   Hence, the average range index over the February to June period is a good measure of the level of feed supply available for the entire year.   An average range condition of 78 was computed for the period February 1 to June 1 based on the 44 years of observations; this average was defined as a "normal" feed supply.   The index for this period, however, ranged from a low of 50 in 1937 to a high of 98 in 1927.   The distribution of range conditions was approximated by simply dividing the observations into class intervals and calculating directly the corresponding probabilities.   Thus, six class intervals are defined in Table 7.5, with a descriptive name given to each, as was done earlier in Table 7.1.   As the reader can verify from counting observations in Table 7.4, "very poor" range conditions (index <55) occurred in only 2 years out of 44, from which we estimate the probability of this state to be 0.045.   "Poor" range conditions (index 55 to 64) occurred in 5 years out of 44, or with a probability of 0.114.   The other probabilities in Table 7.5 are calculated in like manner.

Table 7.6 presents the same decision problem outlined in the previous

TABLE 7.4
INDEX OF MONTHLY RANGE CONDITIONS FOR THE
SACRAMENTO VALLEY, CALIFORNIA

Year	Jan.	Feb.	Mar.	Apr.	May	June	Average Range Condition, Feb. 1–June 1
1922	75	66	57	74	73	82	70
1923	96	99	94	65	98	98	91
1924	57	46	73	59	42	47	53
1925	84	71	94	105	108	95	95
1926	82	71	95	90	97	93	89
1927	95	95	96	102	100	96	98
1928	88	86	87	100	98	95	93
1929	80	80	74	76	66	63	72
1930	64	72	84	92	89	90	85
1931	55	62	77	76	50	52	63
1932	63	63	54	76	73	77	69
1933	55	55	50	63	68	63	60
1934	71	86	94	97	88	83	90
1935	94	90	96	96	102	99	97
1936	71	85	87	86	88	87	87
1937	45	23	32	58	70	68	50
1938	93	95	96	98	99	95	97
1939	74	67	53	58	54	56	58
1940	44	62	72	88	96	94	82
1941	86	84	88	92	92	97	91
1942	92	84	84	80	91	92	86
1943	81	75	81	90	90	84	84
1944	63	64	64	61	60	68	63
1945	91	86	84	87	81	79	83
1946	84	81	71	73	79	77	76
1947	71	56	72	84	86	79	75
1948	80	65	54	66	86	91	72
1949	65	44	47	74	68	67	60
1950	61	63	74	82	83	81	77
1951	92	88	89	84	79	85	85
1952	81	78	81	72	85	87	81
1953	76	81	67	70	73	82	75
1954	71	72	76	86	93	91	84
1955	73	69	66	61	70	78	69
1956	74	74	74	71	79	87	77
1957	66	60	73	81	85	88	77
1958	87	86	89	88	88	88	88
1959	63	74	79	70	72	68	73
1960	59	61	68	77	79	81	73
1961	81	80	81	83	80	83	81
1962	73	67	78	81	77	78	76
1963	90	68	85	87	90	92	84
1964	86	82	75	72	68	70	73
1965	84	82	81	85	91	88	85
1922–65 average							78

Source: Crop and Livestock Reporting Service, U.S. Department of Agriculture, Sacramento, California.

section, with six actions (herd sizes)[2] and six states (range conditions). There is now, however, the significant additional information represented by the long-run (prior) probabilities of each of the six states of nature $P(\theta)$. We are no longer in a situation of complete ignorance, but rather one of risk. By multiplying the payoff for each action by the corresponding probability and summing, we find the expected monetary value for each

TABLE 7.5
CALCULATION OF PRIOR PROBABILITIES OF RANGE CONDITIONS, SACRAMENTO VALLEY, CALIFORNIA

States of Nature: Average Range Conditions, February 1–June 1 (θ_i)			
Description	Range Index Interval	Number of Years Observed[a]	Prior Probabilities
θ_1 Very poor	Less than 55	2	0.045
θ_2 Poor	55 to 64	5	0.114
θ_3 Fair	65 to 74	8	0.182
θ_4 Normal	75 to 84	14	0.318
θ_5 Good	85 to 94	11	0.250
θ_6 Excellent	95 or over	4	0.091
TOTAL	—	44	1.000

[a] From Table 7.4.

action. For example, the expected monetary value of action a_6 is $1,850, calculated as follows:

$$(-14{,}930)(0.045) + (-8{,}860)(0.114) + (-2{,}800)(0.182)$$
$$+ (2{,}020)(0.318) + (8{,}510)(0.250) + (13{,}930)(0.091) = 1{,}850.$$

Action a_5 (stock 415 head) provides the maximum expected monetary value of $3,950. Under the assumptions outlined earlier, a linear utility function and subjective probabilities equal to the empirical probabilities of Table 7.5, we can say unequivocally that action a_5 (415 head) is the optimum stocking rate. In other words, it pays to stock the range at a rate corresponding to "good" conditions, knowing that conditions this favorable (or better) will probably occur about $\frac{1}{3}$ of the time. While action a_5 will

[2] In this particular case, each of the actions (say a_3) was defined as the maximum size of cow herd that can be maintained by optimally allocating the feed supply for the corresponding range condition (θ_3), assuming no supplemental feed is purchased for cattle on range. Thus, the actions were defined by solving six rather simple linear programming problems involving optimum allocation of feed supplies under given range conditions. The off-diagonal payoffs also represent linear programming solutions. They show how action a_j is adjusted to state θ_i with minimum loss (or maximum profit).

TABLE 7.6
PAYOFF TABLE FOR A COW-CALF OPERATION WITH PRIOR PROBABILITIES OF RANGE CONDITIONS

States of Nature: Range Conditions (θ_i)	Actions: Herd Size (a_j)						Prior Probabilities $P(\theta_i)$
	a_1 230 Cows	a_2 280 Cows	a_3 320 Cows	a_4 360 Cows	a_5 415 Cows	a_6 460 Cows	
	Dollars						
θ_1 Very poor	−4,580	−6,290	−8,260	−10,040	−12,690	−14,930	0.045
θ_2 Poor	−3,330	−870	−2,090	−3,970	−6,620	−8,860	0.114
θ_3 Fair	−2,530	450	2,830	1,440	−600	−2,800	0.182
θ_4 Normal	−1,890	1,090	4,060	5,800	5,530	2,020	0.318
θ_5 Good	−930	2,050	5,020	7,420	10,230	8,510	0.250
θ_6 Excellent	−130	2,850	5,820	8,220	11,770	13,930	0.091
Expected value	−1,890	820	2,980	3,800	3,950	1,850	1.000

involve buying supplemental feed in approximately $\frac{2}{3}$ of the years, the opportunities foregone by understocking are even more costly. It is significant to note that in the previous section, where we assumed complete ignorance, none of the criteria selected a_5 as optimal.

In some cases the problem is more complicated than suggested here. For example, the rancher might stock cows for below average range conditions and buy additional stocker animals to graze for a short period if above average feed supplies materialize.[3]

For the rancher who wishes to reevaluate the above problem using his own subjective probabilities, it is necessary to substitute these probabilities for the empirical probabilities, then recalculate the expected monetary values. For the rancher whose utility function is nonlinear, a different complexity arises. If we knew his utility function, we could simply evaluate the utility numbers corresponding to the various gains and losses, substitute the utility numbers for incomes in Table 7.6, and maximize expected utility rather than expected monetary value. However, if no utility function is available, we could make a rough check on whether the rancher's utility function is linear over the relevant range. We might suggest that he ask himself several questions, such as:

"Is my financial position such that I can take the long-run view of this problem, that is, that things 'will average out'?"

"Even if my financial position is such that I can afford to take the long-run view, does a bad year particularly worry me?"

"Is my financial position such that losses of the order which could occur in this decision problem would adversely affect my ability to stay in business?"

Affirmative answers to questions like these suggest that the rancher's underlying utility function is not linear over this range. A more rigorous check on the linearity of the utility function is the test proposed in Chapter III: Pick two dollar values that span the outcomes in the actual problem (for example, $-\$15,000$ and $\$15,000$ in our case). Find if the producer is indifferent between the average of these two values ($\$0$) for certain or a contract involving the two extremes values with probability 0.5 each. If the answer to this question is "no," we need to proceed by the methods of Chapter III to the derivation of the utility function.

One advantage of presenting decision problems in the framework similar to that of Table 7.6 is that it forces the decision maker to focus on the aspects of risk inherent in the problem. Most research studies make

---

[3] For readers interested in these more complex cases, see: G. W. Dean, A. J. Finch, and J. A. Petit, Jr., *Economic Strategies for Foothill Beef Cattle Ranchers*, California Agricultural Experiment Station Bulletin 824 (June, 1966).

recommendations based on single valued estimates, which do not allow the decision maker any flexibility to adjust to the risk in the situation.

THE STOCKING PROBLEM WITH A POSTERIOR DISTRIBUTION

We now turn to the case in which additional information is used in attempting to predict the state of nature (range condition) that will occur in a specific decision period.   In particular, we will be interested in showing how some observation, experiment, or other forecasting device will allow the decision maker to spy on the state of nature.   If the state of nature could be predicted prior to the decision with a high degree of accuracy, decisions could then be adjusted to the conditions expected and, over time, the value of gains increased.   Formally, as explained in Chapter V, we will estimate posterior probabilities $P(\theta_i|Z)$ where Z represents a set of predictors, z_k, and θ_i represents states of nature.   These posterior probabilities can then be used to derive the action that maximizes expected value, given the z_k observed prior to a particular decision.   An optimum action can thus be derived for any observed value of z_k.   This set of actions was called the Bayesian strategy; it is a complete set of rules that tells the decision maker how to act in response to any observed conditions z_k. The expected value of gains using the Bayesian strategy, that is, the data problem, can be compared with the expected value of gains using the optimal action from using the prior probabilities, that is, the no-data problem.   The increase in expected value from employing posterior rather than prior probabilities is a measure of the usefulness of the predicting device employed.   This gain we have called the value of the experiment in Chapter V.

To illustrate the concepts involved in problems employing posterior distributions, let us turn to a variation of the stocking rate problem on California range land.   Instead of a year-around cow-calf operation, we now consider another typical kind of operation of a more seasonal nature, where stocker cattle are purchased in early winter (during January) and sold in early summer (around July 1).   Thus, the cattle are on the range only during the green forage period of the year, and stocking rates can be varied easily from year to year depending on the outlook for range conditions.   The payoffs for six alternative stocking rates for this type of operation are shown in Table 7.7.   Using the same prior probability distribution of range conditions derived in the previous section (Table 7.5), the optimum stocking rate for the no-data problem is shown to be action a_4 (1,345 head).

By January, when the steers are purchased, the operator will have some

TABLE 7.7

PAYOFF TABLE FOR A STOCKER OPERATION WITH PRIOR PROBABILITIES OF RANGE CONDITIONS

States of Nature: Range Conditions (θ_i)	Actions: Stocking Rate (a_j)[a]						Probabilities $P(\theta_i)$
	a_1 841 Head	a_2 1,009 Head	a_3 1,177 Head	a_4 1,345 Head	a_5 1,513 Head	a_6 1,681 Head	
			Dollars				
θ_1 Very poor	−3,691	−5,585	−7,575	−9,411	−11,395	−13,307	0.045
θ_2 Poor	−3,007	237	−1,753	−3,589	−5,575	−7,485	0.114
θ_3 Fair	−2,407	969	4,147	2,311	327	−1,585	0.182
θ_4 Normal	−1,807	1,569	4,851	8,181	6,197	4,285	0.318
θ_5 Good	1,207	2,169	5,451	8,885	12,067	10,155	0.250
θ_6 Excellent	− 607	2,869	6,051	9,485	12,773	16,015	0.091
Expected value	−1,879	1,254	3,670	5,274	5,061	3,618	1.000

[a] Negative numbers represent negative net incomes (losses).

idea of whether range conditions during the spring are likely to be relatively favorable or unfavorable, that is, an opinion based on rainfall, temperature, and range conditions up to that date. The operator might use the observed range conditions in January as a predictor or indicator of the true range condition during the subsequent spring grazing period. Casual observation suggests that favorable spring grazing conditions tend to follow favorable conditions early in the season, and vice versa. This casual observation can be made more explicit and useful by judicious analysis of the data presented in Table 7.4. From these data, a table like Table 7.8 can be constructed that shows the conditional probabilities $P(Z|\theta)$, that is, the probabilities of observing a particular range condition in January given that the true spring season range condition is θ_i. With these conditional probabilities and his own subjective prior probabilities, we could compute the operator's posterior distribution over the states of nature using Bayes' formula.

The data from Table 7.4 are summarized on the left side of Table 7.8 and converted to the conditional probabilities, $P(Z|\theta)$, on the right side. To illustrate how these probabilities are calculated and interpreted, consider the second row of Table 7.8. We notice that three out of five years when the spring range conditions were poor, the January range condition was also poor; thus the probability of observing z_2 when θ_2 is the true state is $3/5 = 0.600$. Two years out of the five years when the spring range conditions were poor, the January condition was fair, which gives $P(z_3|\theta_2) = 0.400$. The other values in the table are obtained in the same manner. The conditional probabilities sum to 1.0 by rows.

The calculations required to obtain a posterior distribution of the spring range conditions using Bayes' formula are now shown. The conditional probabilities of Table 7.8 are reproduced in part A of Table 7.9 along with the ranch manager's prior probability distribution which, for the sake of convenience, we have taken to be the one derived in Table 7.5. Parts B and C of Table 7.9 are derived directly from the two distributions in part A. Part B shows the joint probabilities of the various combinations of θ and Z obtained by multiplying $P(Z|\theta) P(\theta)$. For example, part A of Table 7.9 shows that the probability of observing z_4 when the true range condition is θ_6 is $P(z_4|\theta_6) = 0.250$. The probability of θ_6 is $P(\theta_6) = 0.091$. Hence, the joint probability of observing z_4 and state θ_6 is

$$P(z_4|\theta_6) P(\theta_6) = (0.250)(0.091) = 0.023,$$

as shown in row θ_6, column z_4 of part B. The other cells of part B are derived similarly, by multiplying the conditional probabilities $P(Z|\theta)$ in each row of part A by the $P(\theta)$ for that row. Summing the probabilities in

TABLE 7.8

NUMBER OF YEARS OF OCCURRENCE OF VARIOUS COMBINATIONS OF RANGE CONDITIONS ON JANUARY 1 AND THE SUBSEQUENT SPRING PERIOD, AND CALCULATION OF CONDITIONAL PROBABILITIES

Spring Range Conditions (θ_i)	Observed Range Conditions, January 1							Conditional Probabilities, $P(Z\|\theta)$					
	z_1 Very Poor (<55)	z_2 Poor (55–64)	z_3 Fair (65–74)	z_4 Normal (75–84)	z_5 Good (85–94)	z_6 Excellent (>95)	Total	$P(z_1\|\theta)$	$P(z_2\|\theta)$	$P(z_3\|\theta)$	$P(z_4\|\theta)$	$P(z_5\|\theta)$	$P(z_6\|\theta)$
θ_1 Very poor (<55)	1	1					2	0.500	0.500				
θ_2 Poor (55–64)		3	2				5		0.600	0.400			
θ_3 Fair (65–74)		3	1	3	1		8		0.325	0.125	0.375	0.125	
θ_4 Normal (75–84)	1	1	5	5	2		14	0.071	0.071	0.357	0.357	0.143	
θ_5 Good (85–94)		1	2	2	5	1	11		0.091	0.182	0.182	0.454	0.091
θ_6 Excellent (>95)				1	2	1	4				0.250	0.500	0.250
TOTAL	2	9	10	11	10	2	44						

TABLE 7.9

DETERMINATION OF POSTERIOR PROBABILITIES OF SPRING RANGE CONDITIONS BASED ON OBSERVED RANGE CONDITIONS, JANUARY 1[a]

A. Conditional Probabilities, $P(Z|\theta)$

Spring Range Conditions (θ_i)	Observed Range Conditions, January 1 (z_k)						Sum	Prior Probability $P(\theta)$
	z_1 Very Poor	z_2 Poor	z_3 Fair	z_4 Normal	z_5 Good	z_6 Excellent		
θ_1 Very poor	0.500	0.500					1.000	0.045
θ_2 Poor		0.600	0.400				1.000	0.114
θ_3 Fair		0.375	0.125	0.375	0.125		1.000	0.182
θ_4 Normal	0.071	0.071	0.357	0.357	0.143		1.000	0.318
θ_5 Good		0.091	0.182	0.182	0.454	0.091	1.000	0.250
θ_6 Excellent				0.250	0.500	0.250	1.000	0.091

B. Joint Probabilities of θ and Z, $P(Z|\theta)\,P(\theta)$

Spring Range Conditions (θ_i)	Observed Range Conditions, January 1 (z_k)						Sum
	z_1 Very Poor	z_2 Poor	z_3 Fair	z_4 Normal	z_5 Good	z_6 Excellent	
θ_1 Very poor	0.022	0.022					
θ_2 Poor		0.068	0.046				
θ_3 Fair		0.068	0.023	0.068	0.023		
θ_4 Normal	0.023	0.023	0.114	0.114	0.045		
θ_5 Good		0.023	0.046	0.046	0.114	0.023	
θ_6 Excellent				0.023	0.046	0.023	
$P(Z)$	0.045	0.204	0.229	0.251	0.228	0.046	1.000

C. Posterior Probabilities, $P(\theta_i|Z)$

Spring Range Conditions (θ_i)	Observed Range Conditions, January 1 (z_k)					
	z_1 Very Poor	z_2 Poor	z_3 Fair	z_4 Normal	z_5 Good	z_6 Excellent
θ_1 Very poor	0.500	0.111				
θ_2 Poor		0.333	0.200			
θ_3 Fair		0.333	0.100	0.273	0.100	
θ_4 Normal	0.500	0.111	0.500	0.454	0.200	
θ_5 Good		0.111	0.200	0.182	0.500	0.500
θ_6 Excellent				0.091	0.200	0.500
Sum	1.000	1.000	1.000	1.000	1.000	1.000

[a] Original calculations rounded off to three places for presentation in table. Therefore, data presented in tables will not check exactly in the last decimal place.

each column of part B gives $P(Z)$, that is, the probability $P(Z)$ is given by $P(Z) = P(Z|\theta_1) P(\theta_1) + P(Z|\theta_2) P(\theta_2) + \cdots + P(Z|\theta_6) = \sum_{\theta=i}^{6} P(Z|\theta_i) P(\theta_i)$. The final section C of Table 7.9 shows the calculation of the posterior distribution $P(\theta|Z)$ from the components of Bayes' formula given in section B. That is, $P(\theta|Z) = P(\theta) P(Z|\theta) \div P(Z)$. Specifically, the joint probabilities $P(\theta) P(Z|\theta)$ in part B are divided by the marginal probability $P(Z)$ at the bottom of each column to provide the posterior distribution $P(\theta|Z)$ in part C. For example, $P(\theta_1) P(z_1|\theta_1) = 0.022$ in row 1, column 1, part B. $P(z_1) = 0.045$ at the bottom of column 1, part B. The posterior probability $P(\theta_1|z_1)$ in row 1, column 1, part C is then $P(\theta_1) P(z_1|\theta_1) \div P(z_1) = 0.022 \div 0.045 = 0.500$.

The posterior distributions given in part C of Table 7.9 could be obtained directly from the data in Table 7.8. If instead of dividing each element in a row by the row total, we divided each element in a column by the column total, we would obtain the posterior probabilities directly. For example, z_4 was observed in 11 years. Following a z_4, states θ_3, θ_4, θ_5, and θ_6 occurred 3, 5, 2, and 1 years, respectively. Hence, $P(\theta_3|z_4) = 3/11 = 0.273$, $P(\theta_4|z_4) = 5/11 = 0.454$, $P(\theta_5|z_4) = 2/11 = 0.182$, and $P(\theta_6|z_4) = 1/11 = 0.091$. These probabilities appear in the column headed z_4 in part C of Table 7.9. The other values in part C of Table 7.9 could be obtained similarly.

Although the direct method is a more convenient way of obtaining the posterior probabilities, it has the distinct disadvantage that it incorporates the prior distribution given by the same data. Thus, a ranch manager would have no way of modifying these posterior probabilities to conform to his own subjective prior probabilities if he believed that the prior distribution provided by the data did not describe his situation. The conditional probabilities $P(Z|\theta)$ can be used with any prior distribution whatever in Bayes' formula to obtain the posterior probabilities. It is for this reason that it would be more useful to decision makers to have experimental results summarized in the form of conditional probabilities $P(Z|\theta)$ than in the posterior probability form of $P(\theta|Z)$. This conclusion is made more vivid when one considers the situation in which the decision maker is physically removed from the experimenter or analyst, as is frequently the case in agriculture where the manager is far removed from his sources of information, such as the agricultural experiment station.

Obtaining the Bayesian Strategy

Table 7.10 summarizes the calculations involved in deriving the Bayesian strategy using the posterior probabilities derived in Table 7.9. The

TABLE 7.10
COMPUTATION OF BAYESIAN STRATEGY USING POSTERIOR PROBABILITIES: VALUE OF A PERFECT PREDICTOR; VALUE OF THE Z PREDICTOR

States of Nature: Range Conditions (θ_i)	a_1 841 Head	a_2 1,009 Head	a_3 1,177 Head	a_4 1,345 Head	a_5 1,513 Head	a_6 1,681 Head	$P(\theta\mid z_1)$	$P(\theta\mid z_2)$	$P(\theta\mid z_3)$	$P(\theta\mid z_4)$	$P(\theta\mid z_5)$	$P(\theta\mid z_6)$	$P(\theta)$
			Dollars						Posterior Probabilities, $P(\theta\mid Z)$				
θ_1 Very poor	−3,691	−5,585	−7,575	−9,411	−11,395	−13,307	0.500	0.111					0.045
θ_2 Poor	−3,007	237	−1,753	−3,589	−5,575	−7,485		0.333	0.200				0.114
θ_3 Fair	−2,407	969	4,147	2,311	327	−1,585		0.333	0.100	0.273	0.100		0.182
θ_4 Normal	−1,807	1,569	4,851	8,181	6,197	4,285	0.500	0.111	0.500	0.454	0.200		0.318
θ_5 Good	−1,207	2,169	5,451	8,885	12,067	10,155		0.111	0.200	0.182	0.500	0.500	0.250
θ_6 Excellent	−607	2,869	6,051	9,485	12,773	16,015				0.091	0.200	0.500	0.091

Expected net income from a perfect predictor = $(-3,691)(.045) + 237(.114) + \cdots + 16,015(.091) = \$7,691$

Expected Net Incomes Given Z Observation

Z Observation:	a_1	a_2	a_3	a_4	a_5	a_6	$P(Z)$
z_1	−2,749	−2,008	−1,362	*−615*	−2,599	−4,511	0.045
z_2	−2,549	197	*1,100*	424	−985	−2,895	0.204
z_3	−1,987	1,363	3,580	*5,381*	4,430	2,518	0.229
z_4	−1,752	1,633	4,877	*6,825*	6,261	4,818	0.251
z_5	−1,327	2,069	5,321	8,207	*9,860*	8,979	0.228
z_6	−907	2,519	5,751	9,185	12,420	*13,085*	0.046

Expected net income from Z predictor = $(-615)(.045) + (1,100)(.204) + \cdots + (13,085)(.046) = \$5,992$

Value of a perfect predictor = $\$7,691 - \$5,274^a = \$2,417$

Value of the Z predictor = $\$5,992 - \$5,274^a = \$718$

Bayesian strategy:

When z_1 observed, follow a_4
When z_2 observed, follow a_3
When z_3 observed, follow a_4
When z_4 observed, follow a_4
When z_5 observed, follow a_5
When z_6 observed, follow a_6

^{a} $5,274 represents the expected net income from the optimum action a_4 using only prior probabilities, as shown in Table 7.5.

upper left-hand portion of Table 7.10 repeats the payoff Table 7.7, while the upper right-hand portion gives the posterior probabilities. The first step is to derive the expected net income for each action, assuming a particular z_k observation. For example, suppose z_1 is observed. Given a z_1 observation (very poor range conditions in January), there is, according to the posterior probabilities $P(\theta|z_1)$, a 0.500 probability that θ_1 (very poor spring range conditions) will ensue and also a 0.500 probability that θ_4 (normal spring range conditions) will follow. Thus, we calculate the expected value of each of the actions when z_1 is observed. For action a_1, for example, this is $(-\$3,691)(0.500) + (-\$1,807)(0.500) = -\$2,749$. For action a_2 it is $(-\$5,585)(0.500) + (\$1,569)(0.500) = -\$2,008$. These values and those calculated for a_3 through a_6 are given in the first row of the lower section of Table 7.10. Thus, given a z_1 observation, action a_4 gives the greatest expected net income $(-\$615)$.

Given an observation of z_2 the probabilities $P(\theta|z_2)$ are applied to the original payoff table, resulting in expected values shown in the second row of the lower section of Table 7.10. Given an observation of z_2, action a_3 provides maximum expected net income (\$1,100). Optimum actions can be derived in a similar manner following each of the other observed values of z_k. It is seen that the Bayesian strategy is $(a_4, a_3, a_4, a_4, a_5, a_6)$. In other words, the optimum strategy is:

When *very poor* range conditions are observed in January, stock *1,345* head.
When *poor* range conditions are observed in January, stock *1,177* head.
When *fair* or *normal* range conditions are observed in January, stock *1,345* head.
When *good* range conditions are observed in January, stock *1,513* head.
When *excellent* range conditions are observed in January, stock *1,681* head.

While the strategy appears generally quite sensible, the careful reader will note the anomaly of "very poor" range conditions in January leading to a larger stocking rate than when "poor" range conditions are observed. This point is examined in more detail later in this chapter under the heading "Comments on the Adequacy of the Data."

The Bayesian Strategy with Different Prior Distributions.
Suppose the manager is willing to accept the conditional relationship $P(Z|\theta)$ between range conditions on January 1 and subsequent spring range conditions. However, suppose he believes that the past 44 years of observed range conditions have been generally more favorable than will be the case in the future. Hence, he forms his own subjective prior distribution $P'(\theta)$ independently from the range data observed in the past. Suppose he adopts a prior distribution as shown in the upper part of Table 7.11.

This distribution is considerably more pessimistic than the prior distribution $P(\theta)$ actually observed over the past 44 years (shown in the right-hand column of Table 7.9). Using the new prior distribution $P'(\theta)$ and the conditional distribution $P(Z|\theta)$ in Table 7.9, a different set of posterior probabilities $P'(\theta|Z)$ are calculated using Bayes' formula and presented in the upper part of Table 7.11. Applying these posterior probabilities to the payoffs (upper left-hand portion of Table 7.10), we arrive at the Bayes' strategy $(a_1, a_3, a_3, a_3, a_4, a_5)$. Not surprisingly this is a more conservative strategy than the previous strategy $(a_4, a_3, a_4, a_4, a_5, a_6)$.

Suppose another manager adopts an optimistic subjective prior distribution $P''(\theta)$ shown in the lower part of Table 7.11. Again, working through Bayes' formula to obtain the new set of posterior probabilities $P''(\theta|Z)$ shown in the lower part of Table 7.11 and applying them to the payoffs of Table 7.10, the Bayesian strategy $(a_4, a_4, a_4, a_4, a_5, a_6)$ is obtained. Because of the more optimistic prior distribution $P''(\theta)$, this strategy is somewhat less conservative than the original Bayesian strategy.

These examples demonstrate the way in which subjective prior probability can be incorporated with experimental conditional probabilities in decision making. The results demonstrate the sensitivity of the optimal strategy to the particular subjective prior distribution specified. Furthermore, the fact that operators employ different strategies in actual situations might be explained by their use of different subjective prior distributions, even though they are considering the same actions, states, and payoffs and employing the same source of information as summarized in the conditional probabilities $P(Z|\theta)$.

Comments on the Adequacy of the Data. The reader may raise a question concerning the relatively high stocking rate following a z_1 observation in the initial Bayesian strategy $(a_4, a_3, a_4, a_4, a_5, a_6)$. Examination of data in Table 7.8 indicates the source of this questionable result: There are only two z_1 observations over the 44 years, and one of these occurred in a year in which normal spring range conditions (θ_4) ensued. With only two observations, the probabilities $P(\theta|z_1)$ are likely to be misleading; likewise, $P(\theta|z_6)$ may also be misleading since z_6 occurred only twice in the 44 years. In the latter case, however, they occurred for θ_5 and θ_6, which is more intuitively reasonable. A manager confronted with the experimental probabilities $P(\theta|z_1)$ would likely revise the $P(\theta|z_1)$ distribution based on experience and intuition. For example, if he substituted subjective probabilities of $P(\theta_1|z_1) = 0.5$ and $P(\theta_2|z_1) = 0.5$ for those shown, the Bayesian strategy would be $(a_2, a_3, a_4, a_4, a_5, a_6)$.

The above adjustment in the $P(\theta|z_1)$ distribution indicates the im-

TABLE 7.11
POSTERIOR PROBABILITIES USING PESSIMISTIC PRIOR AND AN OPTIMISTIC PRIOR DISTRIBUTION

Posterior Probabilities with Pessimistic Prior

Spring Range Conditions (θ_i)	Pessimistic Prior Probability	Observed Range Conditions, January 1 (z_k)					
		z_1 Very Poor	z_2 Poor	z_3 Fair	z_4 Normal	z_5 Good	z_6 Excellent
θ_1	0.10	0.820	0.126				
θ_2	0.30	0.180	0.454	0.514			
θ_3	0.40		0.379	0.215	0.704	0.532	
θ_4	0.15		0.028	0.232	0.254	0.223	
θ_5	0.05		0.013	0.039	0.042	0.245	1.000
θ_6	0.00						
Sum	1.00	1.000	1.000	1.000	1.000	1.000	1.000

Posterior Probabilities with Optimistic Prior

Spring Range Conditions (θ_i)	Optimistic Prior Probability	Observed Range Conditions, January 1 (z_k)					
		z_1 Very Poor	z_2 Poor	z_3 Fair	z_4 Normal	z_5 Good	z_6 Excellent
θ_1	0.00						
θ_2	0.05	1.000	0.213	0.084			
θ_3	0.15		0.397	0.083	0.201	0.073	
θ_4	0.40		0.199	0.601	0.512	0.218	
θ_5	0.30		0.191	0.232	0.197	0.518	0.519
θ_6	0.10				0.090	0.191	0.481
Sum	1.00	1.000	1.000	1.000	1.000	1.000	1.000

portance of subjective knowledge even in the derivation of conditional probabilities $P(Z|\theta)$. Even after all the empirical evidence available is accumulated, there may be inadequacies in the data that will require revision of the empirical probabilities. These inadequacies may arise because of an insufficient number of observations or from errors and biases in reporting. For example, different people have been involved over the years in reporting and making estimates of indices and may not have been entirely consistent in their ratings. Also, in the case of $P(\theta|z_1)$ and $P(\theta|z_6)$, too few observations were available in some critical cells. Thus, an intelligent manager is not likely to use the probabilities mechanically. Instead, he will peruse them carefully and make any adjustments he feels necessary in order to bring them in line with his own subjective evaluation. He is not bound to accept the data uncritically, particularly when there are compelling reasons, such as those mentioned above, for suspecting that the data are inadequate.

The researcher or analyst whose job it is to make recommendations to decision makers based on inadequate data is faced with a somewhat different problem. He cannot simply substitute his own subjective probabilities into the problem where he thinks necessary and present this as objective information to his audience. There are procedures available to the analyst for handling analytical problems of this type, such as "smoothing" procedures that involve fitting continuous functions to the data. Such procedures will be used in later chapters.

Value of Experiment. What is it worth to consider additional information of the type used here in attempting to fit stocking rates to range conditions? One way of arriving at the potential worth of additional information is to suppose that we had a forecasting device for range conditions which was perfectly accurate, so that the true state of nature, θ, would always be known at decision time. In this case the $P(\theta_i|Z)$ values of Table 7.10 would be 1's down the diagonal and 0's elsewhere, that is, the true states would be perfectly predicted by the z_k values. Thus, when z_1 is observed θ_1 is predicted with certainty, and action a_1 is taken since it maximizes the payoff for that state. Likewise, z_2 predicts θ_2 without error and a_2 is selected, and similarly for the other observations and states. Therefore, the expected value obtained, if a perfect predictor were available, is \$7,691 as shown in Table 7.10. This value is compared with the expected value of the no-data problem, \$5,274, obtained earlier in Table 7.7. Therefore, the value of a perfect predictor is \$7,691 − \$5,274 = \$2,417. One way of interpreting this figure is to say that \$2,417 is the upper limit on the cost that should be expended in obtaining added information to predict the true state of nature.

It is also possible to calculate the value of the data actually used (January range conditions) as a predictor of the true spring range conditions. This value can be calculated using the solution to the data problem by weighting the expected net income of the actions making up the Bayesian strategy with the frequencies from the $P(Z)$ distribution. Hence, the weighted average return of the optimal strategy is \$5,992 (expected net income from Z predictor line in Table 7.10). Thus, the "value" of our simple Z predictor is \$5,992 − \$5,274 = \$718. Since this observation can be made at essentially no cost, it clearly should be used. However, the difference between the value of our predictor (\$718) and the value of a perfect predictor (\$2,417) suggests that it might be worthwhile to explore other and perhaps more sophisticated predicting devices.

SUMMARY

In this chapter we have examined a realistic, straightforward application of decision theory to the agricultural decision-making problem of range stocking rates for beef cattle under uncertainty. Initially, we made the unrealistic assumption that the decision must be made in a framework of complete ignorance (no prior distribution). We examined a number of possible decision criteria in this situation and found each to be seriously lacking when examined from a theoretical point of view. In fact, each of these criteria can be thought of as a special case of maximizing expected value in which the prior probability distribution is pre-specified in a very restricted way (for example, the maximax criterion implies a probability of 1.0 for the most favorable state of nature and zero for all others).

We therefore turned to examination of the range stocking problem in the more general framework of expected value maximization (of money or utility) to be used for the remainder of the empirical applications in this book. In these cases, the decision-maker forms objective or subjective probabilities rather than implicitly accepting a pre-specified "rule" regarding probabilities. In the range stocking problem a prior probability distribution of range conditions was developed from historical data, although it is recognized that individual ranchers might legitimately modify these probabilities either subjectively or on the basis of more detailed information or records regarding their own ranch conditions. On the basis of these probabilities the action that maximized expected monetary value (expected net income) was selected as the optimal decision.

We then examined a case in which the stocking rate decision could be realistically changed from year to year depending on a forecast of weather conditions. An elementary forecasting device of simply observing actual range conditions (Z) prior to the decision point was examined. Conditional probabilities, $P(Z|\theta)$, were derived from historical data and Bayes rule used to derive an optimal decision strategy for a given prior distribution. The expected monetary value (net income) from using the forecasting device (data problem) was compared with that from not using a forecasting device (no-data problem) to determine the value of the experiment or the value of the forecast. For the given problem the value of the forecast turned out to be about $720 per year. A "perfect" predictor would increase expected net income by about $2,400 per year. Therefore, a useful line of research would appear to be a search for predicting devices of greater accuracy.

It has been the authors' experience that the simple concepts of decision theory can be explained to and understood by ranchers. We have found that a simple decision framework often helps clarify issues that are often vague without such a systematic approach. A typical statement by ranchers is that their decisions are "just a wild gamble" or "pure guesswork." On closer examination, however, it is usually found that they are using some elements of a decision framework. We believe that decisions can be improved by making this framework more explicit.

In the next chapter we turn to somewhat more complex applications of decision theory in agriculture.

CHAPTER VIII

Applications in Agriculture II

In this chapter we present the results of two additional research studies in agriculture employing the decision-making principles of earlier chapters. These studies serve as concrete applications of some of the more sophisticated theoretical concepts developed in earlier chapters.

The first study concerns the selection of an optimum cropping system from among several individual crops differing in expected income and variance of income. This application illustrates several important concepts: the idea of a continuum of both actions and states, the E-V (expectation-variance) framework and quadratic programming, and use of both Von Neumann-Morgenstern and lexicographic utility functions.

The second study involves a series of decision problems concerning the form of financing (contracting versus independent production) that turkey growers should select. Growth strategies under uncertainty are also examined, using decision-making theory. New concepts include the use of regression analysis as the Bayesian "experiment" for deriving posterior probabilities, maximization of utility with nonnormal distributions of outcomes, simulation procedures, and adaptation of the Bayesian framework for finding improved growth strategies over time.

Selection of a Cropping System

The empirical problem is that of selecting a cropping system in an important irrigated farming area in the Sacramento Valley of California. The farms concerned are generally large-scale, mechanized operations with a high level of management. Recent surveys of the area[1] indicated that farms averaged about 1,100 acres of irrigated land with a gross income of about $200,000 per year. Hired labor cost alone averaged about $70,000 per year. This area has soil and climatic conditions well adapted to a wide range of crops. The major crops grown are alfalfa, sugar beets, tomatoes

---

[1] G. W. Dean and H. O. Carter, *Cost-Size Relationships for Cash Crop Farms in Yolo County, California*, Giannini Foundation Mimeo. No. 238, (Berkeley: University of California, Agricultural Experiment Station, December, 1960); John R. Wildermuth and H. O. Carter, "The Technological and Labor Induced Adjustment Process of Commercial Farms in the Sacramento Canning Tomato Area," *Proceedings* (Western Farm Economics Association, July, 1967).

for processing, and barley. Other grain crops, such as wheat, and specialized crops, such as safflower, utilize most of the remaining acreage. These
individual crops vary widely in the expectation and variance of net income.
The major variations in net income stem from variation in crop yields and
in product and factor prices. A wide range of possible crop combinations
is technologically and economically feasible. The major decision problem
involves selecting the crop combination that best achieves the goals of
management.

Derivation of an E-V Frontier

A useful theoretical framework for considering this problem initially
is the mean-variance (E-V) framework outlined earlier in Chapter IV.
This approach defines the efficiency frontier (boundary) as one providing
minimum variance (or standard deviation) of income for each level of
expected (mean) income. In decision-making terms, any action not on the
efficient boundary is dominated by some action(s) that lies on the efficient
boundary. That is, for any action off the efficient boundary there are
actions which give the same expected income with less variance, greater
expected income with the same variance, or greater expected income with
less variance. Thus, derivation of the efficient boundary simplifies the
final choice problem considerably by restricting the range of admissible
actions to those lying on the boundary itself. This simplification assumes,
of course, that the distribution of net incomes for any action can be accurately described by its first two moments, that is, the mean and variance.

Suppose the manager operates with a certain complement of fixed
resources of land and other capital investments such as machinery. The
fixed costs (rent, interest, depreciation, taxes, insurance) associated with
these resources are constant for all possible crop combinations and do not
affect the variance of the cropping system. The "net income" or gross
margin (I_i) for each individual crop is then defined as total revenue minus
the total variable cost attributable to that crop, $I_i = TR_i - TVC_i$. Assume that the per acre distribution of I_i is the same (has the same mean
and variance per acre) regardless of the number of acres grown. This
assumption appears reasonable on the basis of a study conducted in the
area showing that variable costs per acre tend to be constant over wide
ranges of output.[2] Suppose there are n crop alternatives. Let q_i represent

the proportion of the land area devoted to the ith crop ($\sum\limits_{i=1}^{n} q_i = 1$), σ_i^2

---

[2] Dean and Carter, *ibid.* However, there are significant economies of scale in the area for
farms of up to 700–800 acres due to declining fixed costs per acre of land farmed. Thus, as will
be shown later, the E-V boundary derived must be shifted to the left by the amount of the
fixed costs per acre.

the net income variance of the ith crop, and r_{ij} the correlation between net incomes of crop i and j.[3] The expected income from any cropping system is then the weighted average of the expected incomes from each crop included in the system. If a normal distribution of net income is assumed for each crop, the expected net income from the cropping system (I), expressed on a per acre basis, is specified by

$$\bar{I} = \sum_{i=1}^{n} q_i \, \bar{I}_i.$$

The net income variance per acre for the cropping system (σ_I^2) is given by

$$\sigma_I^2 = \sum_{i=1}^{n} q_i^2 \, \sigma_i^2 + 2 \sum_{\substack{i,\,j=1 \\ i>j}}^{n} q_i \, q_j \, r_{ij} \, \sigma_i \, \sigma_j$$

where interactions among crops are represented by the covariance terms $(r_{ij} \, \sigma_i \, \sigma_j)$.[4]

Table 8.1 provides the estimates of the means and standard deviations of the net income per acre of the major individual crops in the study area, as well as the correlation matrix of net incomes. The major sources of uncertainty, yields and prices, both are subject to some systematic tendencies. Yields have tended to rise over time due to technological changes; product and factor prices have generally risen or have followed long-term cyclical movements. These systematic components of the time series have been removed by the variate difference method,[5] so that the variances and covariances represent estimates from the random components only. The mean net incomes in Table 8.1 are averages of the most recent five years of the time series used. The argument is that, looking ahead, the recent average is the best estimate of the future expected value of the net income for each crop, while the best estimate of the future variance is the variance of the random component of the entire historical time series.

---

[3] In many farming areas the values of q_i are restricted (by tradition or biological reasons) to a limited number of values to permit only exact crop "rotations." For example, q_i values for crops $A, B,$ and C of $\frac{1}{2}, \frac{1}{4},$ and $\frac{1}{4}$ would imply a four-year sequence (rotation) of $A - A - B - C$ on any particular field. To maintain constant acreages of each crop annually, one half of the acreage of the farm would be devoted each year to A, and one-quarter each to B and C. Thus, it is possible to think of a hypothetical "typical" acre that contains $A, B,$ and C in the proportions $\frac{1}{2}, \frac{1}{4},$ and $\frac{1}{4}$. In California conditions growers do not generally think in terms of strict "rotations," but rather in terms of acceptable ranges of the q_i. The resulting land use is then called a cropping combination or a cropping system rather than a strict crop rotation.

[4] For more detail, see H. O. Carter and G. W. Dean, "Income, Price, and Yield Variability for Principal California Crops and Cropping Systems," *Hilgardia*, Vol. 30, No. 6 (October 1960), pp. 188–193.

[5] G. Tintner, *The Variate Difference Method* (Bloomington: Principia Press, 1940). Yield data are time series of county averages, whereas ideally the variances would be based on individual farm data. Our estimates probably tend to underestimate the income variability facing an individual farmer.

TABLE 8.1

CORRELATION MATRIX AND MEANS AND STANDARD DEVIATIONS OF INDIVIDUAL CROP INCOMES[a]

Crop	Alfalfa (A)	Sugar Beets (S_B)	Tomatoes Owned (T_O)	Tomatoes Leased Out (T_L)	Barley (B)	Wheat (W)	Safflower (S)
			Correlation Coefficients (r_{ij})				
A	1.00	−0.37	0.60	0.56	0.42	−0.36	0.26
S_B		1.00	−0.04	0.03	−0.05	0.28	0.10
T_O			1.00	0.93	0.16	−0.43	0.39
T_L				1.00	0.10	−0.43	0.45
B					1.00	0.60	−0.70
W						1.00	−0.31
S							1.00
			Dollars per Acre				
Mean Net Income ($\bar{I}_i$)	50	69	147	64	24	35	45
Standard Deviation of Income (σ)	16	12	29	6	4	3	10

[a] Estimates from Carter and Dean, *ibid.*

Given the estimates of Table 8.1, the variance (or standard deviation) and mean from any crop combination desired can be computed directly from the equations presented above. In practice, not all crop combinations are feasible due to certain institutional or agronomic restrictions. For example, typically, tomatoes and sugar beets each are restricted to a maximum of 25 percent of the land because of marketing contracts, processor allotments, and disease (nematode) problems. Within these restrictions, the mean and standard deviation of net income per acre for all feasible crop combinations could be derived using the above equations. Selected crop combinations are plotted in Figure 8.A and read as follows:

FIGURE 8.A
$E - \sqrt{v}$ BOUNDARY FOR THE CROP COMBINATION PROBLEM

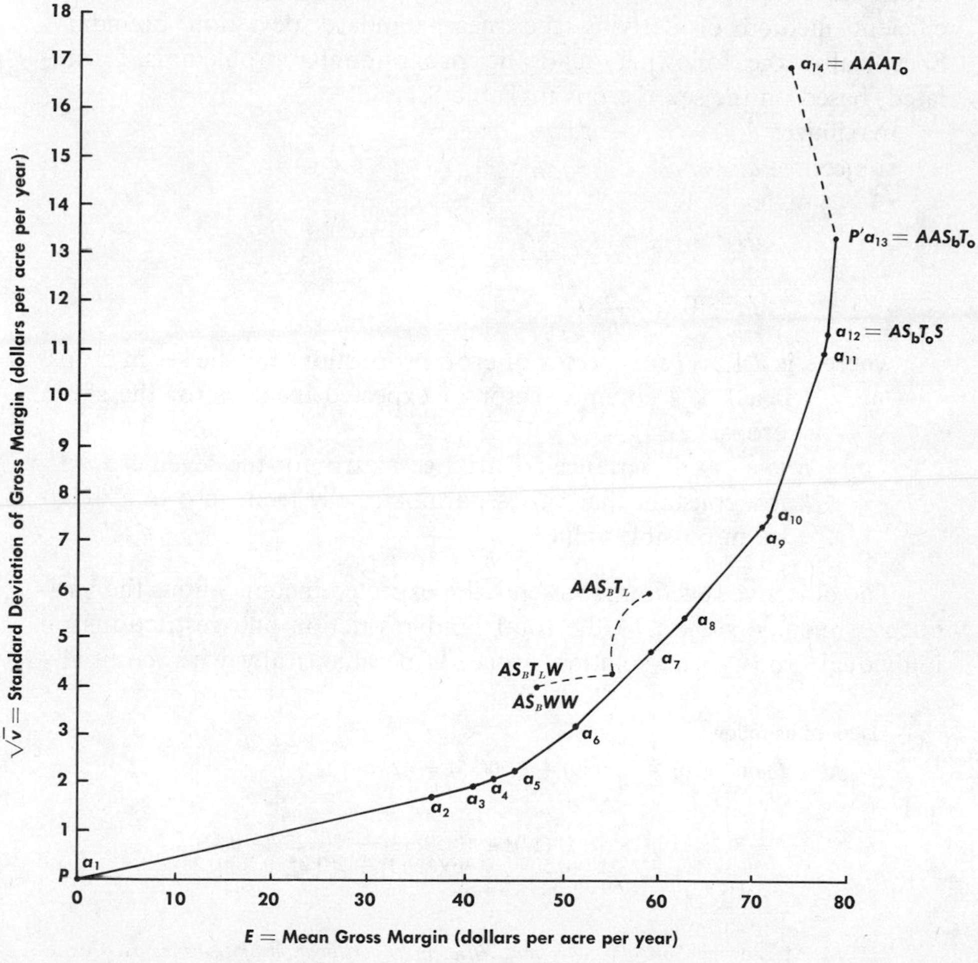

Rotation A-S_B-W-W specifies a crop combination in which $\frac{1}{4}$ of the land is planted to alfalfa, $\frac{1}{4}$ to sugar beets, and $\frac{1}{2}$ to wheat. The mean income of this rotation is \$47.25 per acre with a standard deviation of \$4.07 per acre.[6] Rotation A-S_B-T_L-W specifies a crop combination of $\frac{1}{4}$ alfalfa, $\frac{1}{4}$ sugar beets, $\frac{1}{4}$ tomatoes leased out, and $\frac{1}{4}$ wheat. The dashed line connecting these two points shows the mean and standard deviation of net income as tomatoes leased out (T_L) replace wheat (W) in the rotation. Intermediate points are calculated as a basis for drawing the connecting dashed line. All other points on the lines shown in Figure 8.A are interpreted similarly.

Computation of a sufficiently large number of points to approximate the E-V boundary by this "brute force" direct calculation method would be a formidable task. Fortunately, quadratic programming[7] provides a more efficient method of deriving the mean-standard deviation boundary. Specifically, the following quadratic programming problem is formulated, based on the seven crops in Table 8.1:

maximize: $F(q) = q'I - q'Bq$

subject to: $q_1 + q_2 + \cdots + q_7 \leq 1$

$\qquad\qquad q_2 \leq \frac{1}{4}$

$\qquad\qquad q_3 + q_4 \leq \frac{1}{4}$

$\qquad\qquad q'I = k$

$\qquad\qquad q_i \geq 0$

where q is a 1×7 row vector of crop proportions for the seven crops.

$\quad$ I is a 1×7 column vector of expected incomes for the seven crops.

$\quad$ B is a 7×7 variance-covariance matrix for the seven crops.

$\quad$ k is a constant that varies parametrically from zero to a maximum possible value.

The objective function represents the expected income minus the variance of income subject to the total land restriction and restrictions on individual crops. The solution proceeds parametrically with k initially

---

[6] Derived as follows:

$$I = 0.25(50) + 0.25(69) + 0.50(35) = 47.25$$

and

$$\sigma_I^2 = (0.25)^2(16)^2 + (0.25)^2(12)^2 + (0.50)^2(3)^2 + 2(0.25)^2(-0.37)$$
$$(16)(12) + 2(0.25)(0.50)(-0.36)(16)(3) + 2(0.25)(0.50)(0.28)$$
$$(12)(3) = 16.59$$

$$\sigma_I = 4.07$$

[7] H. M. Markowitz, *Portfolio Selection, Efficient Diversification of Investments*, Cowles Foundation Monograph 16 (New York: John Wiley and Sons, Inc., 1959); and P. Wolfe, "The Simplex Method for Quadratic Programming," *Econometrica*, Vol. 27 (July, 1959), pp. 382–398.

equal to zero. Thus, the parametric solution shows the maximum difference between expected income and variance for each level of expected income $q'I$. This is equivalent to finding the minimum variance for each level of expected income, which is, by definition, the E-V boundary.[8] The step-by-step parametric solution is shown in Table 8.2 and the E-V points plotted out as line PP' in Figure 8.A. Each action a_i on PP' refers to a crop combination specified by the proportions in Table 8.2. All points above PP' are dominated by some points on the line; all points below the line are impossible to attain.

Solutions of the Problem Using a Quadratic Utility Function

Suppose now that we wish to use the E-V frontier developed above to find the optimum cropping system on a 1,000-acre farm in the area. The first step is to convert the per-acre E-V frontier of gross margins in Figure 8.A and Table 8.2 to the E-V frontier of net farm income for a 1,000-acre farm. This involves two steps: (1) the expectation (E) and standard deviation ($\sqrt{v}$) of Table 8.2 are multiplied by 1,000; (2) the total annual fixed costs of $60,000 (interest or rent on land and depreciation, interest, taxes, and insurance on machinery) are subtracted.[9] These computations and the resulting expectation and standard deviation of net income for 13 actions for a 1,000-acre farm are given in Table 8.3, columns (1) through (5). Only actions 8 through 13 show a positive expected net income when all resources are priced at market (opportunity cost) prices.

We could present these results to the farmer and let him make a choice, hoping that his choice would be consistent with his underlying utility function. Suppose, however, that we derive his utility function by the methods discussed in Chapter III, either because we wish to give him a definite cropping system recommendation that is consistent with his utility function or because we wish to predict his actions in this or other risky situations. Suppose the utility function is quadratic, of the form $u = M - 0.02M^2$, where u = utility and M = monetary value (in $1,000). Recall from Chapter IV that, knowing the expectation and variance of the monetary outcomes M of any action (a_i), the expected utility of the action a_i is given by:

$$u(a_i) = u[E(M)] + \tfrac{1}{2}\,\sigma_M^2\,\frac{d^2u[E(M)]}{dM^2}$$

[8] The solution was obtained in less than three minutes on an IBM 7044 computer using a quadratic programming routine developed by Professor Leon Wegge, Department of Economics, University of California, Davis.

[9] Note that when the assumption of a linear utility function is dropped, the conclusion of conventional economic theory that fixed costs do not affect decisions is no longer correct.

TABLE 8.2

PARAMETRIC SOLUTION TO THE QUADRATIC PROGRAMMING PROBLEM

Solution Step	Expected Gross Margin[a] ($/Acre)	Standard Deviation ($/Acre)	Value of q_i for Activites in the Solution							Σq_i[b]
			Alfalfa	Sugar Beets	Tomatoes Owned	Tomatoes Leased Out	Barley	Wheat	Safflower	
1	0	0	—	—	—	—	—	—	—	—
2	36.89	1.73	0.01	—	—	0.25	—	0.57	0.02	0.84
3	41.10	1.95	0.01	—	—	0.25	—	0.66	0.03	0.94
4	42.92	2.05	0.03	—	—	0.25	—	0.69	0.04	1.00
5	44.77	2.22	0.02	0.05	—	0.25	—	0.63	0.03	1.00
6	51.62	3.26	—	0.13	0.06	0.19	—	0.60	—	1.00
7	59.68	4.81	—	0.20	0.12	0.13	—	0.54	—	1.00
8	62.95	5.47	—	0.25	0.15	0.10	—	0.50	—	1.00
9	71.50	7.43	—	0.25	0.25	—	—	0.50	—	1.00
10	71.60	7.47	—	0.25	0.25	—	—	0.49	0.01	1.00
11	77.44	11.05	0.19	0.25	0.25	—	—	—	0.31	1.00
12	77.75	11.32	0.25	0.25	0.25	—	—	—	0.25	1.00
13	79.00	13.25	0.50	0.25	0.25	—	—	—	—	1.00

[a] Represents total revenue minus total variable costs per acre only.
[b] Due to rounding Σq_i in this table not always exactly equal to 1.0 from steps 4–13.

TABLE 8.3
MEAN AND STANDARD DEVIATION OF INCOMES FOR 13 ACTIONS ON A 1,000-ACRE FARM

Action	Expected Gross Margin[a]	Total Fixed Costs[b]	Expected Net Income	Standard Deviation of Net Income[a]	Expected Utility[c]
(1)	(2)	(3)	(4)	(5)	(6)
			Dollars		
1	0	60,000	−60,000	0	−132.00
2	36,890	60,000	−23,110	1,730	−33.85
3	41,100	60,000	−18,900	1,950	−26.12
4	42,920	60,000	−17,080	2,050	−22.99
5	44,770	60,000	−15,230	2,220	−19.97
6	51,620	60,000	−8,380	3,260	−9.99
7	59,680	60,000	−320	4,810	−0.78
8	62,950	60,000	2,950	5,470	2.29
9	71,500	60,000	11,500	7,430	7.75
10	71,600	60,000	11,600	7,470	7.79
11	77,440	60,000	17,440	11,050	8.92
12	77,750	60,000	17,750	11,320	8.89
13	79,000	60,000	19,000	13,250	8.27

[a] Data from Table 8.3 times 1,000.
[b] Includes land interest or rent and machinery depreciation, interest, taxes, and insurance.
[c] Based on the quadratic utility function, $u = M - 0.02M^2$, where u = utility and M = monetary value (in $1,000).

In this case $u[E(M)] = M - 0.02M^2$ and

$$\frac{d^2u[E(M)]}{dM^2} = -0.04.$$

To illustrate the calculations, the expected utility of action a_8 of Table 8.3 is:

$$u(a_8) = [2.950 - .02(2.950)^2] + \tfrac{1}{2}(5.470)^2(-0.04) = 2.29.$$

The results of similar calculations for the other actions are shown in column (6), Table 8.3. Action a_{11}, a cropping system of 19% alfalfa, 25% sugar beets, 25% tomatoes (owned), and 31% safflower (see Table 8.2), is shown to provide the greatest expected utility, with a utility value of 8.92 (see Table 8.3). Action a_{11} appears to be a satisfactorily precise solution. In some cases, however, it may be desirable to obtain a more mathematically precise point of maximum utility. Such a point could be found by first approximating the E-V boundary with an appropriate function, $V = f(E)$, then maximizing the utility function $u(a_i) = f(E,V)$ subject to the E-V frontier $V = f(E)$. For example, if the frontier is approximated by a quadratic function $V = a + bE + cE^2$ where a, b, and c are appropriate constants, the function to be maximized is:

$$\text{Max } u(a_i) = (E - .02\ E^2) + \tfrac{1}{2} V(-0.04) + \lambda(V - a - bE - cE^2)$$

where λ is a Lagrangian multiplier. Setting the partial derivatives of the function with respect to E, V and λ equal to zero and solving simultaneously would give the E-V point that maximizes expected utility.

It is clear from Table 8.3 and Figure 8.A that a person with a linear utility function should select action a_{13} where expected income is maximized. For the quadratic utility showing decreasing marginal utility as hypothesized above, however, the optimum action is a_{11}: in this case the marginal utility associated with an increase of expected income by \$310 in moving from a_{11} to a_{12} is more than offset by the marginal disutility of an increase in the standard deviation of income of \$270. Of course, should we have found a person with increasing marginal utility in this range, we might have an optimum at some point like a_{14} (rotation $AAAT_0$) on the "back side" of the efficiency frontier.

Solution of the Problem Using a Lexicographic Utility Function

A possible alternative to the continuous utility function used in the last section is a form of lexicographic utility. To illustrate its application, we resolve the cropping problem using the following lexicographic utility function:

$$z = (z_1, z_2)$$

where

$z_1 = $ a risk aversion goal. The satisfactory level of z_1 is designated as $z_1{}^*$, stating that income in any year must be $\geq \$0$, with probability ≥ 0.90

and

$z_2 = $ a profit maximization goal, defined as maximum expected income.

In this case the decision maker feels that a negative income would be a serious threat to firm survival. He is willing to run a risk of 10 percent of this eventuality. Given this side restriction, he attempts to maximize profits. We now apply this utility function to the cropping problem. Figure 8.B shows the income at the lower 10 percent point of the probability distribution of income for each action. Clearly, actions a_9, a_{10}, a_{11},

FIGURE 8.B

$E - \sqrt{V}$ FRONTIER AND LOWER 5 AND 10 PERCENT POINTS ON THE
NET INCOME PROBABILITY DISTRIBUTION OF A 1,000-ACRE FARM

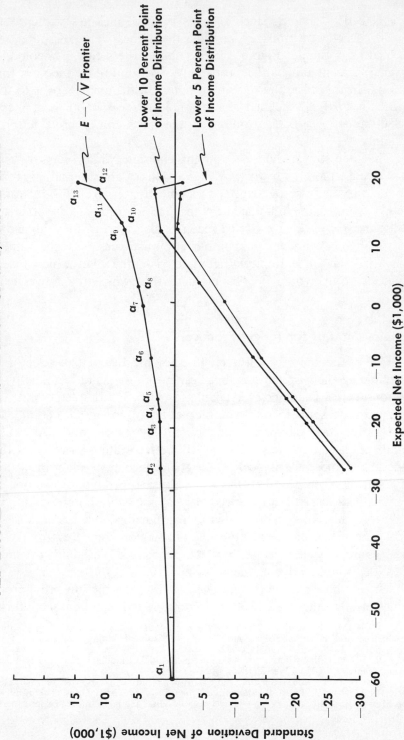

and a_{12} satisfy goal z_1, since all have positive incomes with probability ≥ 0.90. Of these actions, a_{12} provides the highest value of z_2 and hence is selected as optimal.   Figure 8.B also shows the series of incomes at the lower 5 percent tail of the probability distribution of incomes for each action.   In this case, the maximum point on the curve moves to the left. Hence, a goal z_1^* defined, for example, as: probability of income $\geq$ $-\$800$ must be ≥ 0.95, would show the more conservative action a_{11} as optimal.

The interesting conclusion from this example, which seems to be in substantial agreement with work by McFarquhar[10] and Merrill[11], is that even though variance rises as expected income rises in crop production along the E-V frontier, the high income plans tend to dominate the others.   That is, the plans with high expected incomes also tend to have higher "minimum" incomes under unfavorable circumstances.   Hence, unless the individual has an extreme aversion to risk, the plan which maximizes expected utility would be very close to that which maximizes expected income.

Decision Models for Turkey Producers[12]

One of the key decisions facing turkey producers is to select the form of financing their operations that best meets their goals annually and in the long run.   The choices available range from completely independent production to some form of contractual arrangement with commercial or cooperative feed companies and/or turkey processors.   Although the details of these contracts vary, we will concentrate on two types that are widespread and quite typical: (1) a guaranteed price plan and (2) a base payment plan, plus bonuses based on physical production factors.

The *independent* turkey producer is one who purchases all inputs, makes all decisions, arranges his own financing, and assumes all of the risk.   The risk in independent turkey production emanates from two principal sources, variability in product prices and variability in mortality rates (death losses) during the growing period.

Under the *guaranteed price contract* the contracting firm (processor) agrees prior to the starting of the feeding period to purchase all turkeys at

[10] A. M. M. McFarquhar, "Rational Decision Making and Risk in Farm Planning—An Application of Quadratic Programming in British Arable Farming," *Journal of Agricultural Economics*, Vol. 14, No. 4 (1961), p. 552.

[11] W. C. Merrill, "Alternative Programming Models Involving Uncertainty," *Journal of Farm Economics*, Vol. 47, No. 3 (1965), p. 574.

[12] This section is adapted from a more complete study by Vernon R. Eidman, Harold O. Carter, and Gerald W. Dean, *Decision Models for California Turkey Growers* Giannini Foundation Monograph No. 21 (Berkeley: University of California, Agricultural Experiment Station, July, 1968).

market weight for a specified price per pound.   The grower agrees to furnish all of the financing for the operation and must sell the turkeys to the
buyer at market time or pay a substantial fine for failure to perform the
contract.   Under this agreement, the grower has shifted the price risk to
the contracting firm and incurs income variability due only to variability
in mortality rates.

The *base payment plus bonuses contract* is a considerably more complex
arrangement that reduces income variability still further.   Under this contract the grower furnishes only the fixed resources (land, buildings, and
equipment), labor, and machinery.   The contracting firm furnishes the
remainder of the variable inputs (including feed), maintains ownership of
the flock, and makes the major production and marketing decisions.
When the flock has been marketed, the grower receives a base payment for
all live birds sold, plus a bonus for *liveability*, defined as the ratio of birds
sold to birds started.   A second bonus is paid for efficiency of *feed conversion*, defined as pounds of feed fed per pound of turkey sold.

Our analysis of this decision problem is limited to a choice among these
three alternatives.   To simplify, the results are presented only for an
operation of a given size, two broods of 10,000 birds each.   This size of
operation is typical of the smaller California producers faced with the independent versus contract decision.

The No-Data Problem

As pointed out above, the two major sources of income variability in
turkey production are prices and mortality.   We first must estimate the
probability distributions of mortality, price, and income for each of the
three alternatives.   In this first section we assume that no additional information is gathered in attempting to forecast either mortality or prices for
the particular decision period.   Hence, this decision is made on the basis
of prior probabilities.   Later, however, a turkey price forecasting model is
devised, and it is shown how the decision is modified using posterior
probabilities.

Mortality Distribution.   The mortality distribution was estimated
from observations obtained from a sample of growers' records and data of
the California Extension Service.   Mortality rates in the sample ranged
from 4.5 to 25.8 percent. The modal class interval was 7.0 to 7.9 percent,
and the distribution appeared to have a significant positive skew, that is,
skewed toward larger mortality rates.   While a number of theoretical

distributions permit positive skewness, the lognormal distribution[13] realistically describes a variable such as mortality that must be greater than zero and positively skewed.   The mean ($\bar{m}$) and standard deviation ($\hat{\sigma}$) of the logarithmic transformation of mortality, estimated by the maximum likelihood method, are given below:

$$\bar{m}_{log} = 0.98890$$
$$\hat{\sigma}_{log} = 0.19329.$$

A chi-square test of goodness of fit utilizing the actual and theoretical frequencies of the mortality distribution indicated that the hypothesis that the sample is drawn from a lognormally distributed parent population cannot be rejected at the 5 percent level.   Consequently, the parameters estimated were used in subsequent calculations of income variability.

Price Distributions.   Turkey prices declined sharply from 1950 to 1957, but since have fluctuated around an average level of 22 cents per pound.[14]   The grower's subjective distribution of prices would undoubtedly take this downtrend into account; that is, he is likely to feel that the high prices of the early 1950's will not occur again in the near future.   To approximate the grower's subjective prior distribution of prices (that is, for the no-data problem), we have first estimated a quadratic regression equation in time, $P = f(T,T^2)$, that is, attempting to take account of the historical downtrend in price.   The price forecast and the standard error of the price forecast from this equation, where T is set at the value for the forecast year ($T = 16$), are the parameters of the distribution of forecasted price.   The results for this equation are presented in the upper portion of Table 8.4.

Income Distributions.   An independent grower is one who furnishes all inputs, makes all decisions, and assumes all risk of the enterprise. The return for an independent grower of the size assumed is given by the equation below, where S is the number of poults started in thousands, m represents the proportion of mortality, and P is the price per pound of turkeys.[15]

---

[13] J. Aitchison, and J. A. C. Brown, *The Lognormal Distribution* (Cambridge, England: Cambridge University Press, 1957), 176 pages.
[14] Price represents a weighted average of tom and hen prices sold in the months from August through December.
[15] The equation is an average for turkeys and hens assuming they are marketed at the same price P.   Turkeys are marketed at 24 weeks at 26.4 lbs. and hens at 19 weeks at 14.4 lbs.   Thus 20,400 is the sale weight of 1,000 birds at an average of 20.4 lbs.   The second term ($-20,765m$) is a correction for mortality, including birds dead on arrival at the processing plant.   The term ($3,575 - 1,975m$) S is the variable cost function and 6,418 is fixed cost.   More details are available in the reference cited earlier: Eidman *et al.*, *ibid.*

$$R_1 = S[P(20,400 - 20,765m)] - S(3,575 - 1,975m) - 6,418$$

This equation represents gross returns (price per pound times number of pounds produced) minus the variable cost of production (but excluding the operator's and family's labor), minus fixed costs (depreciation, taxes, insurance, and maintenance). Hence, R_1 represents returns to fixed capital, the operator's and family's labor, and management.

The guaranteed price contract specifies that the grower must furnish all of the financing for the operation and sell the turkeys to the contractor at market time for a specified price per pound. The return equation for this contract is identical to that given above for an independent grower if the guaranteed price is substituted for P.

Returns for the base payment plus bonuses contract are summarized by the equation below, where the base payment per bird marketed is 27 cents for hens and 32 cents for toms.

$$R_2 = S[0.27(500 - 470m) + 0.32(500 - 530m) + 0.01X$$
$$(1,000 - 1,000m) + b(1,000 - 1,000m)] - 6,418 - 16S$$

The bonus for liveability is included by setting $X = 11 - m$ when $0 \leq m \leq 11$ and $X = 0$ when $m > 11$. The feed conversion bonus per bird is b, where the feed conversion is computed as

$$b = (66,500 - 48,689m) \div (20,400 - 20,765m)$$

The problem now is to estimate the variance of net returns under each of the three production alternatives. The equation given above for the independent grower can be expressed as returns to the fixed factors, family labor, and management per 1,000 poults started by subtracting the fixed costs ($6,418) and dividing the remainder by S. The resulting expression can be represented by the equation below:

$$\text{Returns per 1,000 poults } (R_1) = P(a - bm) + fm + k$$

where the letters a, b, f, and k represent four numerical coefficients. The expected value and variance of this expression are shown below:

$$\text{Expected returns per 1,000 poults } (\bar{R}_1) = \bar{P}(a - b\bar{m}) + f\bar{m} + k$$
$$\text{Variance of returns per 1,000 poults} = E(R_1 - \bar{R}_1)^2$$

where $\bar{P}$, $\bar{m}$, and $\bar{R}_1$ are mean values of the respective distributions. Substituting into the variance equation the two preceding equations and assuming that the covariance of price and mortality is zero,[16] the resulting expression[17] is:

---

[16] This implies that price and mortality are independent, which is reasonable for the individual grower, although it would not be for the industry in aggregate.

[17] For details of the derivation, see Appendix C, Eidman, Carter, and Dean, *ibid.*

Variance of returns per 1,000 poults $= a^2\sigma_p^2 + f^2\sigma_m^2 + b^2[\sigma_p^2(\sigma_m^2 + \bar{m}^2) + \bar{P}^2\sigma_m^2] - 2\,ab(\sigma_p^2\bar{m}) - 2bf\,(\bar{P}\sigma_m^2)$

Substituting in this expression the relevant values of the coefficients, based on an expected price of 22 cents per pound, and a variance of price based on the variance of the forecast from the no-data problem of Table 8.4, the standard deviation of net returns per 1,000 poults is $512[18] or $10,240 for the 20,000 flock size considered in this problem.

Prices in the above equations, however, are normally distributed while mortality is lognormally distributed. To find the form of the resulting distribution of returns, a Monte Carlo simulation technique was used to generate 1,000 sets of estimates of prices and mortality, based on the appropriate variance and covariance terms among prices and mortality, where prices follow a normal distribution and mortality rates follow an independent lognormal distribution of mortality. The resulting net returns distribution was not significantly different from the normal distribution with the same mean and variance when tested with the chi-square goodness-of-fit test at the 5 percent level of significance.

While the above procedure established that the distribution of net returns is approximately normal for independent production, this is not the case for the two types of contract production. The distribution of net returns for the guaranteed price contract is lognormal since the returns equation is a linear function of mortality. The distribution of net returns from the base payment plus bonuses contract is discontinuous because of the discontinuous nature of the liveability bonus provision. However, these discontinuities prove to be of minor importance and the net returns distributions for this contract is again approximately lognormal. The distribution of net returns for the two contract alternatives were derived by a simulation procedure resulting from successive substitution of values of M in the two net returns equations for contract production.

The first three moments (mean, variance, and skewness) of the three actions (independent, guaranteed price contract, and bases plus bonuses contract) are summarized in Table 8.5. As expected, the contract alternatives have lower mean income than independent production but also much lower variances. While returns from independent production are normally distributed and therefore have no skewness, both contracts have a negative skewness of net returns due to positive skewness of mortality rates.

---

[18] This figure is only approximated by the expression above. For the exact expression using separate price forecasting equations for hen and tom turkeys, see V. R. Eidman, G. W. Dean, and H. O. Carter, "An Application of Statistical Decision Theory to Commercial Turkey Production," *Journal of Farm Economics*, Vol. 49, No. 4 (November, 1967), p. 860.

TABLE 8.4

REGRESSION EQUATIONS FOR FORECASTING TURKEY PRICES

	Estimates of Regression Coefficients and t-Values						
Equation	Constant Term	Time (T)	Time^2 (T^2)	Hens on Farms (H)	Cold Storage Inventories (I)	R^2	Standard Error of the Forecast for $T = 16$
No-data Problem	0.3472 (13.39)	−0.0161 (−2.16)	0.0004 (0.94)			0.71	0.0390
Data Problem	0.5154 (8.62)	−0.0217 (−3.67)	0.0007 (2.00)	−0.0996 (−1.91)	−0.0386 (−2.88)	0.87	0.0275[a]

[a] Computed with H and I at $\bar{H}$ and $\bar{I}$.

TABLE 8.5

THE FIRST THREE MOMENTS OF THE DISTRIBUTIONS OF NET RETURNS FOR INDEPENDENT AND CONTRACT PRODUCTION OF TURKEYS: 20,000-POULT OPERATION

Action	Mean	Standard Deviation	Variance	Skewness
a_1 = Independent	$5,740	$10,240	$104,857,600	$ 0
a_2 = Guaranteed Price Contract	2,060	2,165	4,688,020	− 12,302,112,000
a_3 = Base Plus Bonuses Contract	1,890	1,100	1,210,000	− 601,828,000

Solution of the Problem Using Cubic Utility Functions

It is clear that a choice among the three actions in Table 8.5 can be made only with reference to a specific utility function. Assume the cubic utility function $u = M - .05M^2 + .001M^3$ plotted out in Figure 8.C. This function shows sharply increasing marginal disutility of losses, dimin-

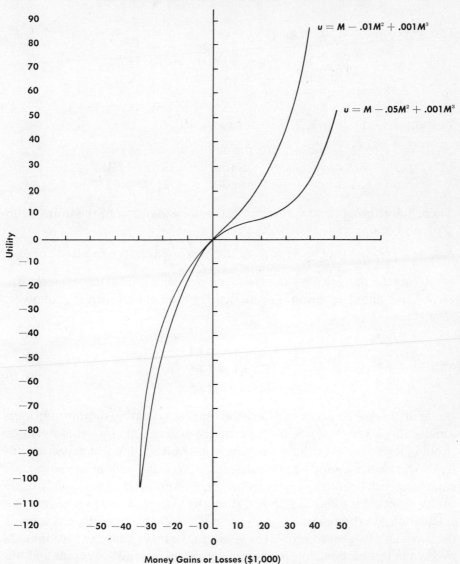

FIGURE 8.C
ALTERNATIVE CUBIC UTILITY FUNCTIONS

$u = M - .01M^2 + .001M^3$

$u = M - .05M^2 + .001M^3$

Utility

Money Gains or Losses ($1,000)

ishing marginal utility for gains up to \$16,667 (the inflection point where $u'' = 0$) and increasing marginal utility for larger gains. Using the Taylor expansion of the utility function as developed in Chapter IV, the expected utility $Eu(a_i)$ of action a_i with money outcomes M is:

$$Eu(a_i) = u[E(M)] + u'[E(M)]E[M - EM] + u''[E(M)]\frac{E[M - EM]^2}{2 \cdot 1}$$
$$+ u'''[E(M)]\frac{E[M - EM]^3}{3 \cdot 2 \cdot 1} + \cdots$$

From the utility function given above:

$$u' = 1 - .10M + .003M^2$$
$$u'' = -.10 + .006M$$
$$u''' = .006$$

For any action $a_i(i = 1, 2, 3$ in our case), let

$$\overline{M}_i = \text{mean value for action } a_i = E(M)$$
$$\sigma_i^2 = \text{variance for action } a_i = E(M - EM)^2$$
$$S_i = \text{skewness for action } a_i = E(M - EM)^3$$

Then, substituting these values in the Taylor expansion of the utility function, we obtain:

$$Eu(a_i) = (\overline{M}_i - .05\overline{M}_i^2 + .001\overline{M}_i^3) + \tfrac{1}{2}\sigma_i^2(-.10 + .006\overline{M}_i) + \tfrac{1}{6}S_i(.006)$$

Using the numerical values for mean, variance, and skewness from Table 8.5, the above equation is evaluated for each action with the following results:

$$Eu(a_1) = 0.84$$
$$Eu(a_2) = 1.66$$
$$Eu(a_3) = 1.65$$

With this particular utility function, reflecting sharply diminishing marginal utility over the critical range of the utility function, this operator should pick action a_2 (although action a_3 has almost identical expected utility). This choice should be made despite the fact that actions a_2 and a_3 have smaller expected monetary gain than independent production. Only if the utility function is cubic (as above) does the skewness term enter into the calculation of expected utility; otherwise $u''' = 0$ and the skewness term of the Taylor series goes to zero. However, in the numerical calculations carried out in this particular case, the variance term is quite important and the skewness term relatively unimportant.

To illustrate the importance of the utility function, we consider the same problem with the second cubic utility function $u = M - .01M^2 + .001M^3$ shown in Figure 8.C. An individual with this utility function also has an increasing marginal disutility for losses, although less drastic than for the first individual shown. Also, the second individual shows increasing marginal utility for gains beyond \$3,333 (the inflection point). Thus, it is to be expected that this individual will tend to select higher risk actions. The numerical computations, analogous to those carried out for the first individual, bear out this hypothesis. The expected utilities of the actions are:

$$Eu(a_1) = 13.15$$
$$Eu(a_2) = 2.00$$
$$Eu(a_3) = 1.85.$$

We see, in fact, that with the new utility function, the ordering of actions is completely reversed.

The Posterior Problem: Use of a Price Forecast

Suppose now that the grower tries to obtain some additional information in attempting to forecast prices. If he could forecast prices perfectly, he could select the form of production each year (independent or contract) to maximize profits. When price is high, independent production would be more profitable; when price is low, contract production would give greater profits. Although no price forecasting device is perfect, the extent to which it is accurate will improve decisions.

Suppose that an analyst remote from the decision maker has developed a price forecasting model. We now examine how this information might be incorporated into the grower's decisions. The analyst has identified two variables that influence potential industry supply. These variables are (1) the number of breeder hens on farms, January 1, and (2) cold storage inventories of turkey on hand in January. This information is available at the first of the year prior to the time when growers must sign contracts. The analyst also includes time as a variable to remove trend unrelated to annual quantity variations. The analyst develops a formal price forecasting model including these variables as indicated below:

$$P = f(T, T^2, H, I, U)$$

where P = price forecast for the August to December marketing period, T = time, H = ratio of number of breeder hens on farms at the start of the year relative to the previous year, I = ratio of cold storage inventories at the start of the year relative to those of the previous year, and U = unexplained residual. The statistical result for a linear equation in these variables is presented in the lower part of Table 8.4. The R^2 value is increased from 0.71 to 0.87 in moving from the naive time trend prediction equation of the decision maker (no-data problem) to the more sophisticated forecasting equation (data problem) of the analyst. The standard error of the forecast from this model is reduced to 2.75 cents per pound compared with 3.90 cents per pound for the decision maker's predicting equation.

The procedure for combining the additional information of the analyst's price forecast with the decision maker's prior subjective distribution of prices is now presented. Suppose the decision maker has made a price forecast for period $T = 16$, the first year beyond the fifteen-year period that generated the data to which the price forecasting equations were fit. The price forecast of the decision maker alone is 19.20 cents per pound. Suppose that the observed values of H and I on January 1 are 82.90 percent and 41.45 percent, respectively; the price forecast of the analyst is then 25 cents per pound. The resulting distributions of prices follow the t-distribution and can be approximated by discrete intervals as shown in the first two columns of Table 8.6. The two distributions are combined in the last column of Table 8.6 by multiplying together the probabilities corresponding to the same intervals of the two independent distributions and normalizing. The mean and standard deviation of the new combined normalized distribution are 22.96 cents and 2.57 cents, computed directly from their definitions.[19] The mean and variance of this new combined price distribution are incorporated into the equations presented earlier for computing the mean and variance of the distribution of net returns for independent producers given a price forecast of 25 cents per pound. The mean and standard deviation of net income for the 20,000 poult operation so derived are $16,770 and $7,388, respectively, as shown in the sixth row of Table 8.7. The mean and standard deviations of net incomes given other levels of price forecasts also are summarized in Table 8.7.

----

[19] The two independent distributions are t-distributed. Using the normal approximation to the t-distribution, the mean and variance (M_2 and σ_2^2) of the combined distribution can also be approximated from the means and variances (M_0, σ_0^2 and M_1, σ_1^2) of the two independent distributions as follows:

$$M_2 = \frac{M_1 \left(\frac{1}{\sigma_1^2}\right) + M_0 \left(\frac{1}{\sigma_0^2}\right)}{\frac{1}{\sigma_1^2} + \frac{1}{\sigma_0^2}}$$

$$\sigma_2^2 = \frac{\sigma_0^2 \sigma_1^2}{\sigma_0^2 + \sigma_1^2}$$

For example, see: John Forester, *Statistical Selection of Business Strategies* (Homewood, Ill.: Richard D. Irwin, 1968), Chapter 13.

TABLE 8.6

DERIVATION OF COMBINED DISTRIBUTION FROM DECISION MAKER'S PRIOR DISTRIBUTION AND ANALYST'S POSTERIOR DISTRIBUTION FOR A PRICE FORECAST OF 25 CENTS PER POUND

Price Intervals	Prior Distribution of Decision Maker[a]	Posterior Distribution of Analyst for Price Forecast of 25 Cents per Pound[b]	Combined Distribution	Normalized Combined Distribution[c]
$ per Pound		Probability		
< 0.04	0.0025	0	0	0
0.04 — 0.06	0.0025	0	0	0
0.06 — 0.08	0.0045	0	0	0
0.08 — 0.10	0.0096	0	0	0
0.10 — 0.12	0.0273	0	0	0
0.12 — 0.14	0.0588	0	0	0
0.14 — 0.16	0.1096	0.0042[d]	0.00046032[d]	0.0058[d]
0.16 — 0.18	0.1666	0.0106	0.00176596	0.0222
0.18 — 0.20	0.1970	0.0353	0.00695410	0.0874
0.20 — 0.22	0.1760	0.1013	0.01782880	0.2240
0.22 — 0.24	0.1213	0.2111	0.02560643	0.3216
0.24 — 0.26	0.0674	0.2750	0.01853500	0.2329
0.26 — 0.28	0.0322	0.2111	0.00679742	0.0854
0.28 — 0.30	0.0139	0.1013	0.00140807	0.0177
0.30 — 0.32	0.0058	0.0353	0.00020474	0.0026
0.32 — 0.34	0.0025	0.0106	0.00002650	0.0003
> 0.34	0.0025	0.0042	0.00001050	0.0001
Summation	1.0000	1.0000	0.07959784	1.0000

[a] $\bar{P}_{dm} = 0.1920$, $\sigma_{dm} = 0.0390$, following the t-distribution.
[b] $\bar{P}_a = 0.2500$, $\sigma_a = 0.0275$, following the t-distribution.
[c] $\bar{P}_{combined} = 0.2296$, $\sigma_{combined} = 0.0257$.
[d] Represents entire area < 0.16.

TABLE 8.7

PARAMETERS OF NET INCOME DISTRIBUTION AND EXPECTED
UTILITY FOR INDEPENDENT PRODUCTION GIVEN
ALTERNATIVE PRICE FORECASTS

Price Forecast: $ per Pound	Parameters of Net Income Distributions			Expected Utility[a]
	Mean	Standard Deviation	Variance	
0.15	− $19,980	$6,726	45,239,076	− 52.89
0.17	− 12,630	6,810	46,376,100	− 26.70
0.19	− 5,280	6,920	47,886,400	− 9.97
0.21	2,070	7,054	49,758,916	− .31
0.23	9,420	7,208	51,955,264	3.54
0.25	16,770	7,388	54,582,544	7.44
0.27	24,120	7,586	57,547,396	10.21
0.29	31,470	7,800	60,840,000	15.55

[a] Based on the utility function $u = M - .05M^2 + .001M^3$, where M is measured in thousands.

Each of the mean-variance situations in Table 8.7 can be converted to expected utility as shown in the last column, using the same utility function for the first operator assumed earlier. Recall that the expected utility of the best contract alternatives was 1.66. Thus, Table 8.7 indicates that when the price forecast is for about 22 cents per pound or less, expected utility is maximized by selecting contract production. However, for price forecasts above 22 cents per pound, independent production maximizes expected utility. Thus, the Bayesian strategy is:

When $\hat{P} \leq 0.22$, produce under a guaranteed price contract (action a_2):
When $\hat{P} > 0.22$, produce as an independent (action a_1).

Solution of the Data and No-Data Problem Assuming a Lexicographic Utility Function

To further illustrate the usefulness of the price forecasting device, we present the results of Table 8.7 in more extended tabular form as shown in Table 8.8. As an alternative utility function to those used in the previous section, assume the following lexicographic utility function:

$$u = f(z_1, z_2)$$

where

z_1^* = a satisfactory level of the firm survival goal specified as probability (income $\geq -\$10,000$) ≥ 0.95, and
z_2 = a profit maximizing goal defined as maximum expected income.

TABLE 8.8

GAINS (NET RETURNS) FOR ALTERNATIVE TURKEY PRODUCTION ARRANGEMENTS (BASED ON TWO BROODS OF 10,000 EACH)[a]

Probability of Obtaining a Smaller Return	Independent Production	Guaranteed Price Contract	Base Plus Bonuses Contract	Independent Production Given Alternative Price Forecasts							
				$\hat{P} = .15$	$\hat{P} = .17$	$\hat{P} = .19$	$\hat{P} = .21$	$\hat{P} = .23$	$\hat{P} = .25$	$\hat{P} = .27$	$\hat{P} = .29$
	(1)	(2)	(3)	(4)	(5)	(6)	(7)	(8)	(9)	(10)	(11)
0.01	−18,060	−5,590	−1,060	−35,630	−28,480	−21,380	−14,340	−7,350	−420	6,470	13,320
0.05	−11,090	−2,390	280	−31,050	−23,830	−16,660	−9,540	−2,440	4,620	11,640	18,640
0.10	−7,370	−1,050	530	−28,600	−21,360	−14,150	−6,970	180	7,300	14,400	21,470
0.20	−2,870	300	790	−25,640	−18,360	−11,110	−3,870	3,350	10,550	17,730	24,900
0.50	5,740	2,260	2,010	−19,980	−12,630	−5,280	2,070	9,420	16,770	24,120	31,470
0.80	14,360	3,610	2,830	−14,320	−6,900	540	8,010	15,490	22,990	30,500	38,040
0.90	18,860	4,130	3,170	−11,360	−3,900	3,590	11,110	18,660	26,240	33,840	41,470
0.95	22,580	4,500	3,400	−8,920	−1,430	6,100	13,670	21,280	28,920	36,600	44,300
0.99	29,550	5,040	3,750	−4,330	3,210	10,820	18,480	26,190	33,960	41,770	49,620
Expected return	5,740	2,060	1,890	−19,980	−12,630	−5,280	2,070	9,420	16,770	24,120	31,470

[a]Returns to fixed capital investment, family labor, management, and risk.

Using this utility function, reconsider the no-data problem summarized by the first three columns of Table 8.8. The optimal action would be the guaranteed price contract—independent production has a higher expected value but does not meet the first goal $z_1{}^*$ since it shows losses of $11,090 at the lower 5 percent probability level.

Let us turn now to the data problem where our price-forecasting equation provides an estimate of expected price each year. Columns 4 through 11 of Table 8.8 illustrate the distributions of net returns from independent production for eight alternative price forecasts ranging from 15 cents to 29 cents per pound. The net income at any ordinate of the normal distribution of net returns can be found as the mean ± the appropriate number of standard deviations. For example, given a price forecast of 21 cents per pound (column 7, Table 8.8), the net return at the lower 1 percent tail of the distribution is equal to the mean minus 2.3267 standard deviations, that is, $2,070 − 2.3267($7,054) = −$14,340.

Table 8.8 shows that the optimal Bayes strategy for the data problem, if a criterion of unrestricted maximization of monetary values is assumed, is for the producer to remain independent if the price forecast is higher than about 21 cents per pound and to use contract A if the price forecast is lower. The "value" of the prediction equations was tested by use of the actual price pattern (with trend removed) generated over the 1950–1964 period. The guaranteed price contract would have been more profitable in 5 of the 15 years and independent production more profitable in the other 10 years. The price-prediction equation would have correctly predicted the optimum form of production in 12 of the 15 years. The value of our price predictor would have averaged $600 annually over this period. The value of a perfect predictor would have been $2,700 per year.

Optimal Decision Strategies over Time

A more rigorous test of the alternative decision strategies outlined in the previous sections was conducted by simulating the capital accumulation of the firm over a period of time. Four alternative strategies were specified. The first three are of the no-data type, employing a single action over a period of time: (1) select independent production each year, (2) select base plus bonus contract production each year, (3) select guaranteed price contract production each year. The other strategy is the data strategy, where the action taken each year depends on the prices predicted by the price-predicting equations: Specifically, given the price prediction each year, select that action (independent or contract) which gives the greatest expected value. As before, this strategy involves selecting independent production if the price forecast is higher than 21 cents per pound and the guaranteed price contract when the price forecast is lower.

Comparisons among the four alternative strategies are made from the results of a series of simulations of firm growth over a period of time under each of the strategies. Thirty individual runs of 10 years each were simulated for each strategy. Three hundred paired values of actual price, predicted price, and mortality rate were generated from the appropriate distributions for use in the simulation procedure. The following procedure was used to obtain the values for a given year: The simulated "actual" price was computed as the weighted mean price (21.72 cents) over the 1957–1964 period plus a random normal deviate times the standard deviation of prices over this period (2.43 cents). Given this "actual" price for the year, the simulated "predicted" price was estimated as the "actual" price plus a second random normal deviate times the standard error of the forecast of the price-prediction model. The simulated mortality rate (in logs) was computed as the mean (in logs) plus a third random normal deviate times the standard error of mortality (in logs). The antilog of this result provided the observation of the mortality rate. Thus, to provide the 300 paired observations, 900 random normal deviates were used. For each paired value (the data for one year) the predicted and actual prices were related as they would be if the price-prediction equation were used. The mortality rate was independent of both prices. The same set of observations on these three variables was used to investigate changes in the firm's financial position for each of the four strategies. Therefore, differences observed in the results are not due to selection of alternate sets of random variables but are comparable in the sense that the values of prices and mortality were the same for each strategy.

Since financial growth is a goal of most managers, growth in net worth over the simulated 10-year period is selected as the basis for comparing the alternative strategies. The starting net worth of the firm was assumed to be $30,000. It was also assumed that if the net worth of the firm dropped below $15,000 at any time during the simulation, the operator would sell out and reinvest his capital at 6 percent interest elsewhere.

The frequency of ending net worth for each strategy is presented in Table 8.9. On the average over the 30 simulated 10-year periods, the two contracts did not maintain the original net worth (that is, mean ending net worth dropped to $26,600 and $27,170, respectively). Continuous independent production produced substantial growth averaging $71,710 at the end of the 10-year period. The data strategy, however, had an even higher mean income, a higher minimum, and a smaller range. Thus, the data strategy appears to clearly dominate the other actions.

TABLE 8.9
FREQUENCY OF ENDING NET WORTH RESULTING FROM 30 SIMU-
LATION RUNS FOR EACH OF FOUR ALTERNATIVE GROWER
STRATEGIES, PARAMETERS OF THE INCOME DISTRIBUTION,
AND EXPECTED UTILITY

	Frequency of Ending Net Worth			
	No-Data Strategies			
Range in Net Worth	Independent Production	Base Plus Bonuses Contract	Guaranteed Price Contract	Data Strategy
Thousands of Dollars	Number of Years			
−5 to 5	1	0	0	0
5 to 15	2	3	0	0
15 to 25	0	10	8	0
25 to 35	3	11	22	0
35 to 45	1	6	0	1
45 to 55	0	0	0	1
55 to 65	6	0	0	4
65 to 75	5	0	0	5
75 to 85	2	0	0	5
85 to 95	1	0	0	4
95 to 105	2	0	0	2
105 to 115	3	0	0	3
115 to 125	1	0	0	2
125 to 135	2	0	0	2
135 to 145	1	0	0	1
145 to 155	0	0	0	0
155 to 165	0	0	0	0
165 to 175	0	0	0	0
175 to 185	0	0	0	0
	Dollars			
Lower limit of income	1,340	9,520	19,060	44,170
Upper limit of income	142,470	42,210	34,070	136,130
Range of income	141,130	32,690	15,010	91,960
Mean income	71,710	27,170	26,600	87,200
Expected utility[a]	66	32	33	79

[a] Based on utility function: $u - 1.32N - .0044N^2$, where N = net worth at the end of 10 years.

To complete this illustration we might also calculate expected utility for this problem, even though examination of Table 8.9 suggests that the data strategy is dominating. In this case, assume that our utility function is:

$$u = 1.32N - 0.0044N^2$$

where

$$N = \text{net worth at the end of ten years.}$$

Such a utility function would have to be derived with respect to future net worth. Specifically, the questions would have to be framed in terms of options between a "certain" net worth ten years hence and a reference contract involving a higher and a lower net worth, with given probabilities, ten years hence. Using the specific utility function assumed, the ordering of strategies is the data strategy, independent production, the guaranteed price contract, and the base plus bonuses contract, with expected utilities of 79, 66, 33, and 62, respectively.

SUMMARY

Agricultural economists have traditionally devoted a substantial proportion of their research effort to increasing efficiency in agriculture by providing recommendations to individual firms regarding profitable uses of their resources. Almost without exception, these recommendations have been based on point estimates of expected profitability for each of several alternative decisions. Given the prevalence of uncertainty in agriculture, recommendations that also include information about the risk associated with the alternatives would allow decision-makers a more rational basis for choice. This chapter presented two studies on agricultural production in which the risk of alternative actions is examined by way of the E-V (expectation-variance of income) approach.

The first study dealt with selection of an optimum cropping system. Typically this type of problem has been solved using linear programming, assuming certainty in all components of the problem (that is, net returns vector, input-output matrix, and constraint vector). In our study the important sources of risk affect only the net returns vector; this is often reasonable since variations in prices, yields, and costs generally enter the objective function only. Thus, quadratic programming was used to derive the E-V boundary showing the set of cropping systems that provide minimum variance for given expected incomes. Given the E-V boundary, the optimum cropping system was derived assuming, successively: (1) that the decision maker examines the E-V data and makes his choice directly; (2) that the decision is made on the basis of a particular quadratic utility function; and (3) that the decision is made using a particular form of lexicographic utility. Because of the nature of the E-V boundary, most plausible utility functions provide recommendations close to the action that maximizes expected income.

The second study derives *E-V* relationships for the three major alternatives facing California turkey growers — independent production and two types of contract production.   In this case, the study shows the possibility of using a price forecasting model as an "experiment" to convert the problem from the no-data to the data category.   A procedure is demonstrated for combining the additional information of the analyst's price forecast with the decision-maker's prior subjective distribution of prices. The result is a Bayesian strategy which says that if the analyst's price forecast exceeds a certain level, the decision-maker should choose independent production; if the price is lower than this level, contract production should be selected.   The Bayesian decision strategy was tested against other alternative decision rules by simulating firm growth over ten-year intervals using each of the rules.   The Bayesian strategy was dominating in the sense that it provided a higher mean income and a lower risk.

CHAPTER IX

Applications in Geology

This chapter expands the area of empirical applications of decision making under uncertainty from agriculture to the field of petroleum exploration. The drilling decisions by oil and gas operators represent decision making under an extreme environment of risk and uncertainty. Grayson[1] has written a fascinating book that first describes how investment decisions are made by oil and gas operators and then prescribes decision theory techniques as a possible way of helping them to make more rational decisions. This chapter attempts to summarize only some of the principal elements of the drilling problem in a decision theory framework as presented by Grayson. Readers interested in more descriptive detail should consult Grayson's book.

This application centers around a singular uncertainty decision — the decision by oil and gas operators to drill, or not to drill, a well. In practice, a sequence of decisions is directed toward the final payoff question: Should I invest in this well? If so, how much should I risk and how much of the risk should I share with others? At an earlier stage the operator also faces the question: Should I purchase added information about this project before making the final drilling decision? This sequence of decisions can usefully be divided into the no-data problem using only prior probabilities of the states of nature, and the data problem where additional information such as seismographic readings is used to develop posterior probabilities of the states of nature. In the latter case it is necessary to decide if the additional information gained from the seismographic reading will be worth the costs and, if so, to develop a complete strategy for drilling or not drilling following each possible type of seismographic reading.

The No-Data Drilling Problem

While most business decisions are characterized by some degree of uncertainty, few involve as much uncertainty as drilling an oil well. A well

---

[1] C. Jackson Grayson, Jr., *Decisions under Uncertainty; Drilling Decisions by Oil and Gas Operators* (Boston: Harvard Business School, Plimpton Press, 1960). Professor Grayson and the Harvard Business School have kindly given us permission to quote and summarize material from this study.

may cost from $5,000 to $2,000,000, depending on the depth and difficulties encountered during drilling.   For this cost, the payoff may be
$10,000, $50,000,000, or — a hole in the ground.   The firms making the
drilling decision may be relatively small independent operators where the
major decision making is lodged in a single individual, or they may be one
of the giant oil companies (called majors by Grayson) where decision
making is highly institutionalized.   Because our interest is primarily in
applications of individual decision making, we limit the discussion to
independent operators.

Perhaps the best way to capture the essence of the drilling decision is
to set up an example payoff table, then to discuss the components of that
table in some detail.   Table 9.1 is such a payoff table for a fairly repre-
sentative type of oil drilling problem.

The actions in Table 9.1 are more complex than the "drill," "don't
drill" choice implied earlier.   Action a_1 is the don't drill decision.   But
the drill decision can take many forms.   Action a_2 represents drilling with
100 percent interest; that is, the operator incurs all costs and earns 100 percent of all returns.   However, because of risk, capital limitations, or other
personal or financial considerations, the operator may seek to drill the well
under some other arrangement.   Action a_3 represents a 50–50 partnership
where costs and returns are split with some other operator or major company.   Action a_4 is quite conservative: This action (farm-out, keep $\frac{1}{8}$
override) grants the right to drill the property to another operator in return for $\frac{1}{8}$ of the oil revenues if the well is a producer.   It is impossible to
lose in this deal except in the opportunity-cost sense of income foregone if
the well is a big producer.   Action a_5 represents still another arrangement
for farming-out the drilling to another operator.   In this case, if the well
hits, our operator receives 50 percent of the oil revenues but only after the
driller recovers his entire investment in the well.

This quick sketch of five typical actions does no more that scratch the
surface of possible deals that might be worked out.   Grayson (Chapter 8
particularly) considers many other variations and suggests the complexities
that can arise in putting together a drilling deal.   However, for our purposes, the above sketch of actions should suffice.

We now turn to the definitions of the states of nature.   These are
defined in Table 9.1 as five discrete events ranging from "dry hole" to "1
million barrels."   Of course, anything is possible.   The well might find 100
million barrels.   Also, logically, the state of nature is a continuous variable.
However, oil drillers tend to think in discrete terms such as "this looks
like a 100,000-barrel well."   In general, the operator can make some statement of the range of possibilities that are in his realm of contemplation.

TABLE 9.1
PAYOFF TABLE FOR AN OIL DRILLING DECISION PROBLEM MONETARY VALUES

Actions

States of Nature		Don't Drill a_1	Drill With 100 Percent Interest a_2	Drill With 50 Percent Partner a_3	Farm-out, Keep $\frac{1}{8}$ Override a_4	Farm-out, Come Back in for 50 Percent Interest After Payout a_5	$P(\theta)$
Dry hole	θ_1	$0	$-50,000	$-25,000	$0	$0	.60
50,000 bbls.	θ_2	0	-20,000	-10,000	6,250	0	.10
100,000 bbls.	θ_3	0	30,000	15,000	12,500	15,000	.15
500,000 bbls.	θ_4	0	430,000	215,000	62,500	215,000	.10
1,000,000 bbls.	θ_5	0	930,000	465,000	125,000	465,000	.05
EMV		$0	$62,000	$31,000	$15,000	$47,000	

If he later protests that the list is incomplete, it can be expanded to include other states.

The next step is to calculate the payoff for each action-state combination. It is relatively easy to assign monetary consequences to all actions under state θ_1 (the first row of Table 9.1); the firm loses whatever it invests. (It is assumed that a dry well costs $50,000, and a producing well $70,000.) If the well is a producer (states θ_2 through θ_6), we must place a monetary value on the oil reserves represented by the well. If the firm plans to convert the oil immediately into dollars through sale of the well, then the monetary gain from the prospective sale could easily be assigned. If, for example, the firm immediately planned to sell the reserves for $1 a barrel, then 100,000 barrels would be worth $100,000. After paying $70,000 for the completed well, the net monetary payoff would be $30,000.

Most firms, however, plan to produce the oil themselves and convert it into dollars over a 10-to-20-year period. In this case, the stream of cash earnings over time must be projected and discounted back to a present value equivalent. For example, if cash earnings per year were $85,000 for the first two years and then declined steadily until the well went out of production after the tenth year, the present value (PV) equivalent of the income stream discounted at rate r might be:

$$PV = \frac{\$85,000}{1 + r} + \frac{\$85,000}{(1 + r)^2} + \frac{\$60,000}{(1 + r)^3} + \cdots + \frac{\$5,000}{(1 + r)^{10}}.$$

The relevant discount rate is the rate at which the decision maker thinks he could invest the dollars if he had them today. Often, with capital limitations, this rate is well above the cost of borrowed capital — 6 percent to 8 percent — often used by persons making discount calculations.

To keep the calculations of Table 9.1 as simple as possible, we assume a present value assignment of $1 a barrel (after all operating expenses, including income taxes, are deducted). On this basis, the remaining payoffs in Table 9.1 can be readily calculated. For example, in the cell represented by action a_3, state θ_3, the payoff computation is:

50 percent of 100,000 barrels at $1 per barrel   = $50,000
50 percent of $70,000 in drilling and completion costs = $35,000
payoff on 50 percent partnership = $15,000

The next step in the decision problem is to assign probabilities to the states of nature. In oil drilling it is unlikely that the decision maker (or his geologist) knows nothing about the likelihood of the occurrence of the states of nature (complete uncertainty). He has some information — vague, incomplete, and imperfect though it may be. Some operators simply make a subjective evaluation that certain states are more or less probable than others. In some cases, these are expressed as numerical probabilities. To apply decision-making principles it is essential that subjective probabilities be assigned. This may be done by introspection based on data or other miscellaneous information available to the decision maker. In some cases it may be necessary or helpful in assigning subjective or personal probabilities to use the idea of a standard bet or reference contract outlined earlier in Chapter II. The probabilities assigned to the θ_i in Table 9.1 are listed in the right-hand column.

Choice Criterion and Utility Functions

Using the criterion of expected monetary value (*EMV*) the optimal action in Table 9.1 is a_2 — drill with 100 percent interest. It might be noted that both actions a_1 and a_3 are dominated by action a_5; that is, action a_5 has a payoff equal to or greater than a_1 or a_3 irrespective of the state of nature θ_i. Closer examination of the payoff table also raises the question of whether it is reasonable to assume a linear utility function over the range of outcomes − \$50,000 to \$930,000. This, of course, is the assumption implied by the criterion of maximum expected monetary value.

Grayson[2] derived utility functions for a number of individual oil drillers using a variation of the von Neumann and Morgenstern method discussed at length in Chapter III. Figure 9.A shows a comparison of the utility functions derived for four individuals involved in actual oil drilling decisions. It may be interesting to compare the utility functions of Bill Beard, owner, and Fred Hartman, his geologist. The geologist, Fred Hartman, has less preference for small increments in dollar gains (his curve is lower at smaller dollar values) than that for Bill Beard. But when larger amounts of dollar increments are involved, he attaches much greater utility to these increments (the curve rises steeply) than does Mr. Beard. On the negative side of the curve, Hartman does not consider increasing losses much more seriously than small losses (the curve is almost flat) until he passes \$150,000 where the curve falls off sharply. This could be a reflection of his own attitude toward risk, or partly due to the fact that, as a geologist, he feels less direct involvement in losses. Bill Beard has a utility function exhibiting diminishing marginal utility over the entire range of outcomes. However, there is sharp curvature about the origin with the remaining parts of the function nearly linear. This function could be approximated by a quadratic algebraic form.

The utility function of Charles Scott, landman, shows constant (but

[2] Grayson, *op. cit.*, Chapter 10.

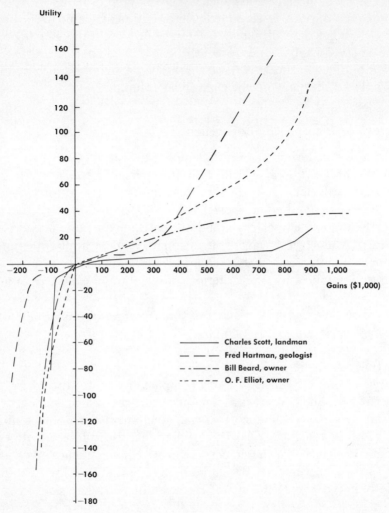

low) marginal utility for gains up to about $800,000, then sharply increasing marginal utility. Utility for losses drops sharply below a $100,000 loss. The curve for O. F. Elliott, owner, is somewhat similar in that it is nearly linear (but with a high marginal utility) up to about $800,000, with sharply increasing marginal utility for higher monetary values. His disutility for losses drops off more rapidly and steadily, however.

Grayson found that probabilities created the greatest difficulty in deriving the utility functions of these individuals. Some operators do not normally use numerical probabilities in their decisions, and they found it strange to try to reach a decision on the basis of probabilities. One operator could not respond at all to the utility experiment, saying that his mind could not conceive of probability relationships. After some explanation, however, other operators could proceed.

Judging by some responses, several operators evidently had difficulty in thinking of probabilities as being objective. When they were offered a prospect with certainty, most responded that this was ridiculous — "There is no such thing as certainty in drilling wells." If they introduced a sub-

FIGURE 9.B
HYPOTHETICAL UTILITY FUNCTION FOR AN OIL DRILLER

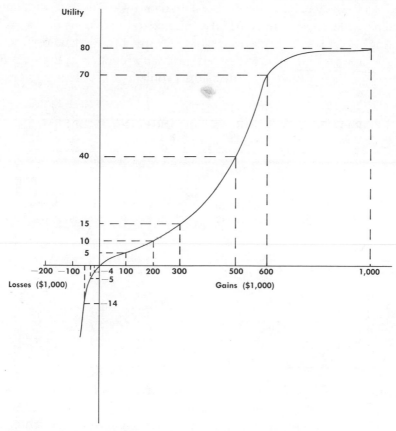

jective "correction" into the probabilities at this level (that is, where $P = 1$), then it is possible that they may have introduced unknown subjective adjustments elsewhere. If the individual subjectively adjusts the objective odds in answering the reference contract questions, his responses will include an unknown mixture of subjective probabilities and utilities, and the curve will not be a true utility-of-money curve. As mentioned in Chapter III, one way of reducing the possibility of introducing subjective probabilities into the responses would be to hold the probabilities constant — say at 50–50 — and vary the payoffs to find indifference points. Another possibility would be to spend additional time in explaining the meaning and use of objective probabilities.

Intransitivities, or inconsistencies, were also sometimes encountered in the responses. In the case of serious inconsistencies, these data were plotted and presented to the decision maker. Confronted with an inconsistency, the decision maker had a chance to "police his decisions" by indicating which response more nearly conformed to his true preferences.

Now suppose that we have derived the utility function in Figure 9.B for the operator facing the earlier decision problem of Table 9.1. Reading

TABLE 9.2
PAYOFF TABLE FOR AN OIL DRILLING PROBLEM
UTILITY VALUES

States of Nature		Actions			
		Drill with 100 Percent a_2	Farm-out, Keep $\frac{1}{8}$ Override a_4	Farm-out, Come Back in for 50 Percent After Payout a_5	$P(\theta_i)$
Dry hole	θ_1	−14	0	0	.60
50,000 bbls.	θ_2	− 4	.4	0	.10
100,000 bbls.	θ_3	2	.8	1	.15
500,000 bbls.	θ_4	30	3.5	11	.10
1,000,000 bbls.	θ_5	80	6	34	.05
EUV		− 1.5	1.89	2.95	—

from the utility function the utility values corresponding to the monetary consequences in Table 9.1, we form Table 9.2 in terms of utility (only nondominated actions a_2, a_4, and a_5 are included). Using the criterion of maximizing expected utility value (EUV), action a_5 is seen to be optimal. Action a_2, which was optimal using the criterion of EMV, becomes the least desirable action using the criterion of EUV.

On the whole, the operators' responses to using utility functions and *EUV* in helping to make decisions were favorable. However, most had some reservations about its practicality, mainly based on criticisms that the procedures were complex and time consuming. However, Grayson concludes (p. 319):

> The decision procedure is already complex and, while these procedures are strange at first and require some effort to master, they can be learned. And when this is done, decisions can be made easier, faster, and more consistently. But even if such procedures are not adopted in total now, the mere discussion of them may help operators (1) to realize the problems that they are now handling implicitly in their minds, and (2) to think about them in a more formal manner. Indeed, I believe that this may be the highest payoff for application of decision theories in the early stages.

The Data Drilling Problem

The data drilling problem is one of deciding whether to purchase additional information before making a final decision. In petroleum exploration and production, this situation occurs at many points — decisions as to whether to purchase magnetometer, gravitimeter, or seismic information; decisions as to whether to obtain information by a drill stem test, coring, drilling deeper, or setting pipe. At each decision point the operator has two possible choices: (1) despite the uncertainty, go ahead and make a final decision with present information; (2) in hopes of reducing the uncertainty, obtain more information and then make a final decision. What complicates the choice is that (a) the information usually is not free, and (b) the purchased information is not a perfect predictor of outcomes.

To illustrate a typical problem of the above sort, Grayson[3] analyzes the decision of whether or not to purchase seismic information, or in an oilman's terms, "Should we shoot the prospect?" To keep the problem simple, consider only two actions — drill and don't drill — and three possible states — dry hole, 200,000 barrels, and 500,000 barrels. Payoffs for each action-state combination are shown in the upper left-hand portion of Table 9.4 In this form, we have a no data problem. If the operator attaches subjective probabilities to the three states of nature as shown, $P(\theta_i)$, action a_2 (drill) has the higher expected monetary value (*EMV*) of $34,000. For this entire exercise we assume a linear utility function and therefore use *EMV* as our decision criterion.

We now pose the question: Is it worthwhile to search for additional information? As an outside limit to what could be paid for more informa-

[3] Grayson, *op. cit.*, Chapter 11.

tion we can readily calculate the value of a perfect predictor as illustrated in previous chapters.   In this case it is $35,000 calculated as follows:

$$.7(\$0) + .2(\$130,000) + .1(\$430,000) - \$34,000 = \$35,000.$$

It is clear that there are sizable potential gains from a good predictor.   Let us try to evaluate the gains from one of the possible predictors — seismic information.   Suppose it costs $10,000 to obtain seismic information — "shoot the prospect."   Is this imperfect predictor worth the cost?

Suppose an examination of statistics for 100 past seismic shots in the particular geological area under consideration reveals the data in Table 9.3.

TABLE 9.3
SEISMIC AND WELL DATA FOR THE XYZ AREA

Seismic Interpretation	Dry Hole	200,000 Barrels	500,000 Barrels	Total
Good and structure-closed	9	15	6	30
Structure-not closed	15	3	2	20
No structure	13	1	1	15
Fair and structure-closed	3	6	1	10
Structure-not closed	9	1	0	10
No structure	12	3	0	15
Total	61	29	10	100

Letting the six possible seismic interpretations in Table 9.3 represent possible values of the predictor $(z_1, z_2, \ldots, z_6)$, and noting that the three outcomes (dry, 200,000 barrels, and 500,000 barrels) correspond to our original three states of nature $(\theta_1, \theta_2, \theta_3)$, it is easy to convert the above data into conditional probabilities $P(\theta|Z)$ as shown in the right-hand portion of Table 9.4.   The probabilities of each of the seismic readings, $P(z_i)$, are also readily calculated as shown in the bottom row of the right-hand portion of Table 9.4.

With this information, Grayson diagrams the decision problem as a decision tree, as shown in Figure 9.C.   Think of the diagram as a road map. The decision maker starts at (a) and can proceed down one of two roads. Suppose he decides on the "don't buy seismic" route.   At point (b) he again has an option.   If he chooses the "no drill" path, his income is $0. If he chooses the "drill" path, one of three outcomes (−$50,000, $130,000, $430,000) ensue with probabilities .7, .2, and .1, giving an expected monetary value of $34,000.   Thus, if he initially chooses the "don't buy seismic" path at (a), his optimal action gives an *EMV* of $34,000.   This result corresponds to the no-data problem already solved in the upper left portion of Table 9.4.

TABLE 9.4
The Data Drilling Problem

Actions

States of Nature		Don't Drill a_1	Drill a_2	$P(\theta_i)$
Dry hole	θ_1	$0	$-50,000	.7
200,000 bbls.	θ_2	0	130,000	.2
500,000 bbls.	θ_3	0	430,000	.1
EMV No Data		$0	$ 34,000	

$P(\theta|Z)$

	Good and Structure			Fair and Structure		
	Closed	Not Closed	No Structure	Closed	Not Closed	No Structure
	z_1	z_2	z_3	z_4	z_5	z_6
	.30	.75	.86	.30	.90	.80
	.50	.15	.07	.60	.10	.20
	.20	.10	.07	.10	0	0
$P(Z)$	.30	.20	.15	.10	.10	.15

$EMV|Z$	a_1	a_2	$P(Z)$
$EMV|z_1$	$0	$ 136,000	.30
$EMV|z_2$	0	25,000	.20
$EMV|z_3$	0	-4,000	.15
$EMV|z_4$	0	106,000	.10
$EMV|z_5$	0	-32,000	.10
$EMV|z_6$	0	-14,000	.15
EMV Data	$0	$56,400	

Value of the seismograph information $z_i =$
$$\$56,400 - \$34,000 = \$22,400$$

210

FIGURE 9.C

DECISION TREE FOR THE DATA DRILLING PROBLEM

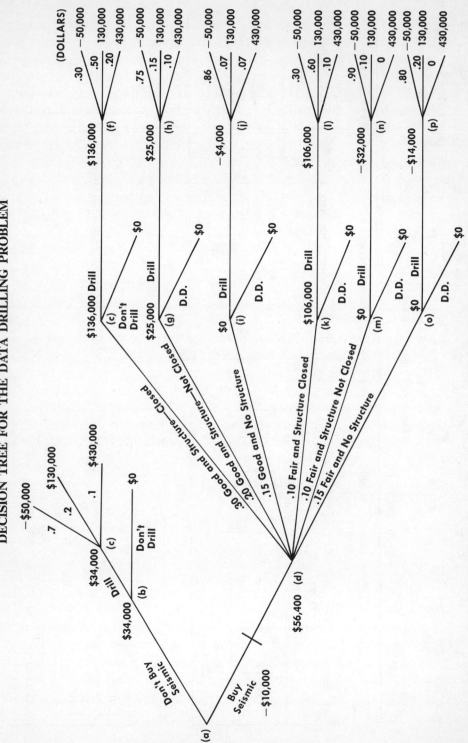

Suppose the operator at (a) in Figure 9.3 chooses the other path, buy seismic. This move will cost $10,000 as shown. Then nature makes her move shown as one of the six alternative branches of the road at point (d). These moves occur with the probabilities $P(Z)$ already calculated in Table 9.4. Suppose that nature selects the upper branch at (d)—"good and structure-closed." At point (e) the operator must select between the two branches labeled "drill" and "don't drill." Again, if he selects "don't drill" his income is $0. (Of course, to arrive at this point has cost him the $10,000 recorded along the road from (a) to (d), but this cost is the same for all outcomes beyond (d) and is accounted for later.) If at point (e) he selects the "drill" path, there are again three outcomes (dry hole, 200,000 barrels and 500,000 barrels, with dollar payoffs of $-\$50,000$, $130,000, and $430,000). The probabilities of these three outcomes are now the conditional probabilities, $P(\theta|z_1)$—.30, .50, and .20—shown in the first column of the upper right-hand portion of Table 9.4. In our terminology, these represent the posterior probabilities of state θ, given the type of seismic reading z_1. The *EMV* of following the "drill" path at point (e) is now easily calculated as $136,000, and the "drill" action would be chosen following a seismic reading of z_1—good and structure-closed.

It now remains only to evaluate the "drill," "don't drill" options following each of the other seismic readings z_2 through z_6, represented in Figure 9.C by the decision points (g), (i), (k), (m), and (o). In each case, the "don't drill" decision has a value of $0, while the "drill" decision has an *EMV* based on the posterior probabilities, given the particular seismic reading obtained. Evaluating this *EMV* of the "drill," "don't drill" decision at each point, we can devise the following decision strategy:

(1) Drill, if seismic interpretation is
    Good and structure-closed
or, Good and structure-not closed
or, Fair and structure-closed
(2) Don't dill if seismic interpretation is
    Good and no structure
or, Fair and structure-not closed
or, Fair and no structure

We can now calculate the *EMV* of buying the seismic information. The cost was $10,000. The expected return is the *EMV* of the best decision following each seismic reading multiplied by the probability of obtaining that reading. This value is $56,400 calculated as follows:

.30($136,000) + .20($25,000) + .15($0) + .10($106,000) + .10($0) +.15($0) = $56,400.

Thus, the expected value of the seismic information is clearly worth the $10,000 cost. The *EMV* of the "buy seismic" branch is then $56,400 −$10,000, or $46,400 compared with $34,000 for the "don't buy seismic" branch.

The diagrammatic decision tree of Figure 9.C makes quite clear the nature of the information decision. However, a more efficient way of obtaining the solution is shown in Table 9.4 where the lower portion shows the *EMV* of each action (a_1 and a_2), given the predictor z_i. These values are calculated simply by applying the relevant posterior distribution $P(\theta|z_i)$ to the original payoff table. The optimal decision for each value of z_i is then chosen, giving the same decision strategy as the decision tree:

If z_1, z_2, or z_4 are observed, take action a_2;
If z_3, z_5, or z_6 are observed, take action a_1.

The *EMV* of this strategy is $56,400 calculated as before by applying the *P(Z)* to the *EMV* of the optimal actions.

The "value of the seismographic information z_i" is now the difference between the *EMV* of the data problem minus the *EMV* of the no-data problem ($56,400 − $34,000) = $22,400. Thus, the operator could afford to pay up to $22,400 for the seismic information. If it costs only $10,000 as assumed here, the decision is clearly to buy the information.

This example has been carried out entirely in terms of monetary value rather than utility. If the utility function were nonlinear over the range −$50,000 to $430,000, it would be necessary to substitute utility for monetary values in the no-data table to find the action that maximized *EUV*. In the data problem we would first subtract the $10,000 seismic cost from each entry in the payoff table and then proceed as above. Finally, we would compare the *EUV*'s of the data and no-data problems to find if the additional information was worth the cost when considered in utility terms.

SUMMARY

This chapter has illustrated the possibilities of employing decision-theoretic concepts to improve decision making in still another field — petroleum exploration. The no-data problem involved a choice between "not drilling" and several "drilling" alternatives where the operator formed his subjective probability distribution of the possible outcomes based on his personal experience, miscellaneous data, and "hunches" concerning the particular drilling location. The data problem involved deciding whether to purchase seismic information in the specific location before making a final decision.

The decision criterion was considered first to be expected monetary value. A second decision criterion of maximizing expected utility was also used, based on utility functions derived for several individuals involved in oil drilling decisions. All of the utility functions showed fairly sharply declining utility for losses, but there were substantial variations among individuals in the shape of the utility function with respect to gains. Interestingly, three of the four individuals interviewed revealed an increasing marginal utility of money for large gains. Perhaps individuals with this type of utility function are attracted to a field like oil drilling where there are small probabilities of extremely large gains. It would be interesting to compare these utility functions with those for individuals involved in economic activities of a more conservative, "safe" nature. A hypothesis for testing might be that the shape of an individual's utility function determines his choice of occupation — that is, whether he selects a high risk, moderate risk, or low risk occupation.

CHAPTER X

Applications in Forest Management

This chapter is concerned with the application of the decision-making framework to an important problem in forest management.[1] Vertically integrated firms in the southern pulp and paper industry face the problem of how much of their raw material to supply from their own timberlands and how much to purchase from other producers. The magnitude of the problem can be seen if one considers a typical firm that uses 500,000 cords of raw material per year at an average cost of $18 per cord—an annual acquisition cost of $9 million. Another interesting aspect of the problem is that, if the firm decides to buy land and plant trees to grow its own supply, it will be between 20 and 30 years before the raw material is available. Because of the long planning horizon in forestry problems—and the resulting high degree of uncertainty of prices, productivity, and markets — application of our decision-making framework to forest management problems appears potentially fruitful.

Raw Material Acquisition Problem

The problem to be discussed is for a hypothetical firm that can supply its raw material needs internally, externally, or by an internal-external combination.[2] The question is: What degree of internal supply is optimal for the firm? Internal supply is determined by the level of land ownership along with the intensity of silvicultural practices chosen. The firm's objective is to minimize the present worth of the stream of raw materials costs over its planning horizon. For convenience, the set of actions will be defined as the following discrete acts:

---

[1] This chapter is adapted primarily from: Emmett F. Thompson, "Consideration of Uncertainty in Forest Management Decision-Making" (Ph.D. thesis, Oregon State University, 1966).

[2] Other forestry problems that can be considered within the decision-making framework developed in this book are discussed in: Emmett F. Thompson, "The Theory of Decision under Uncertainty and Possible Applications in Forest Management," *Forest Science*, Vol. 14, no. 2 (1968) pp 156–163.

$$a_1 = 0 \text{ percent} \qquad a_4 = 60 \text{ percent}$$
$$a_2 = 20 \text{ percent} \qquad a_5 = 80 \text{ percent}$$
$$a_3 = 40 \text{ percent} \qquad a_6 = 100 \text{ percent}$$

where the percentages reflect the percentage of raw material supplied internally at some future point in time.

The definition of the states of nature is based upon the assumption that the firm will continue to use the given quantity of raw material regardless of the cost of the raw material. While there is some level of raw material cost for which the firm would reduce its raw material consumption, we will accept historical cost trends as being within the realm of feasible raw material costs. Therefore, the states can be defined in terms of relative, rather than absolute, costs.

Thus, the states of nature are defined as the annual percentage change in the cost of external wood minus the annual percentage change in the cost of internal wood over the firm's planning period.

Six discrete states of nature are defined:

$\theta_1 = -3$ percent difference (annual percentage change in cost of external wood minus annual percentage change in cost of internal wood)

$\theta_2 = -2$ percent difference

$\theta_3 = -1$ percent difference

$\theta_4 = $ No difference

$\theta_5 = 1$ percent difference

$\theta_6 = 2$ percent difference

The definitions of the states of nature and the probabilities of each (to be shown later) were determined by using the data in Table 10.1, which show the average cost of external wood and an index of the production cost of internal wood for the period 1938 to 1963. By examining ten-year periods starting with 1938, one obtains 16 observations that show changes in the relative costs of external relative to internal wood.[3] These changes

---

[3] Let c_{Et} = cost of external wood in year t, c_{It} = production cost index of internal wood in year t, r_{Et} = annual percentage change over a ten-year period in the cost of external wood, starting from year t, and r_{It} = same as r_{Et} except for internal wood. Then:

$$c_{It}(1 + r_{It})^{10} = c_{I\ t+10}$$

and

$$r_{It} = \left[\frac{c_{I\ t+10}}{c_{It}}\right]^{1/10} - 1 \text{ or } (1 + r_{It})^{10} = \frac{c_{I\ t+10}}{c_{It}}$$

Likewise

$$r_{Et} = \left[\frac{c_{E\ t+10}}{c_{Et}}\right]^{1/10} - 1 \text{ or } (1 + r_{Et})^{10} = \frac{c_{E\ t+10}}{c_{Et}}$$

The state of nature variable θ is defined as:

$$\theta = r_{Et} - r_{It}$$

TABLE 10.1
AVERAGE EXTERNAL WOOD COST AND INDEX
OF INTERNAL WOOD PRODUCTION COST,
1938–1963

Year	Cost of External Wood[a]	Index of Internal Wood Production Cost[b] 1957–1959 = 100
1938	3.85	22
1939	4.40	22
1940	4.60	22
1941	5.00	27
1942	6.65	36
1943	8.00	47
1944	8.70	56
1945	9.15	63
1946	10.75	68
1947	11.70	73
1948	12.30	76
1949	11.80	74
1950	12.55	74
1951	14.70	82
1952	14.70	87
1953	14.70	88
1954	14.75	87
1955	15.05	89
1956	16.45	93
1957	16.35	96
1958	16.10	99
1959	16.60	105
1960	17.20	107
1961	16.85	110
1962	17.35	112
1963	17.40	116

[a] E. F. Thompson, *loc. cit.* Reference is made to Herbert A. Knight, "Pulpwood Prices in the Southeast, 1963," (Asheville, North Carolina: U.S. Forest Service, Southeastern Forest Experiment Station Research Note SE-28); and Herbert A. Knight and Agnes C. Nichols, "Southern Pulpwood Production" (Asheville, North Carolina; U.S. Forest Service, Southeastern Forest Experiment Station Resource Bulletin SE-3, 1963).

[b] For details see Thompson, *loc. cit.*, where it is shown that the USDA farm wage rate index reflected the annual changes in the cost of producing internal wood for the period considered.

range from a −3 percent difference to a +2 percent difference and are grouped into the six states of nature shown above.

The outcomes for each state-action combination are defined as the present value of the cost of a cord of wood. The resulting decision table is shown in Table 10.2. The after-tax costs per cord of wood delivered to the

TABLE 10.2

PRESENT VALUE OF RAW MATERIAL COSTS FOR HYPOTHETICAL FIRM USING 500,000 CORDS OF RAW MATERIAL PER YEAR, 20-YEAR PLANNING HORIZON AND 5 PERCENT INTEREST RATE BY STATE OF NATURE AND ACTION

State of Nature	Action						$P(\theta)$
	a_1	a_2	a_3	a_4	a_5	a_6	
	Million Dollars						
θ_1 (-3% difference)	88.3	85.1	85.2	87.4	92.2	99.4	0.05
θ_2 (-2% difference)	95.2	90.3	88.8	89.4	92.9	99.1	0.15
θ_3 (-1% difference)	103.0	96.3	93.1	92.0	93.9	98.5	0.30
θ_4 (No difference)	112.2	103.2	97.8	94.8	94.7	97.5	0.25
θ_5 (1% difference)	122.7	111.3	103.4	98.0	95.6	96.6	0.20
θ_6 (2% difference)	134.8	120.0	109.3	101.2	96.2	94.7	0.05
Expected monetary value	—	100.8	96.1	93.8	94.3	97.8	—

firm by source of supply and state of nature are shown in Table 10.3. The differences in costs among actions shown in Table 10.3 reflect the differences in hauling costs and silvicultural practices, that is, as the percentage of internal supply increases from 0 to 100 percent, the firm should use more intensive silvicultural practices to produce higher volumes on land near the mill to help offset the higher hauling costs associated with wood produced from land farther from the mill.

TABLE 10.3

AFTER-TAX COST PER CORD FOR WOOD DELIVERED TO MILL SITE BY SOURCE OF SUPPLY AND STATE OF NATURE

Source of Supply	State of Nature	Action					
		a_1	a_2	a_3	a_4	a_5	a_6
		Dollars					
External	All States	18.00	17.40	16.80	16.05	15.15	0
Internal	θ_1	0	13.50	14.35	14.95	15.50	15.95
	θ_2	0	13.45	14.30	14.90	15.45	15.90
	θ_3	0	13.35	14.20	14.80	15.35	15.80
	θ_4	0	13.20	14.05	14.65	15.20	15.65
	θ_5	0	13.05	13.90	14.50	15.05	15.50
	θ_6	0	12.70	13.55	14.20	14.75	15.20

The differences in costs between states of nature shown in Table 10.3 reflect the change in the relative value of external wood to internal use. For example, assuming θ_3 were the state of nature, there would be a relative decrease of 1 percent per year in external wood cost.

For our hypothetical firm using 500,000 cords of raw material per year, a 20-year planning horizon, and a 5 percent discount rate, the present values of each state-action combination are summarized in Table 10.2. As an example, we will consider the calculation of the outcome of state θ_1 and action a_4 (60 percent internal and 40 percent external supply).

Sixty Percent Internal Supply

Three hundred thousand cords per year at \$14.95 (θ_1, a_4, Table 10.3) per cord is \$4,485,000 per year. Present value at 5 percent interest of \$4,485,000 per year for 20 years is \$55.9 million.

Forty Percent External Supply

Average cost over the first decade of the planning period is $[16.05 + 16.05(1.03)^{-10}] \div 2 = \$14$ per cord (\$16.05 from "All States," a_4, Table 10.3). The total cost of 200,000 cords per year at \$14 per cord is \$2,800,000 per year. Present value, at 5 percent for 10 years, is \$21.6 million.

Average cost over the second decade of the 20-year planning period is $[16.05(1.03)^{-10} + 16.05(1.03)^{-20}] \div 2 = \$10.41$ per cord. The total cost of 200,000 cords per year at \$10.41 per cord is \$2,082,000 per year. Present value, at 5 percent for 10 years beginning in 10 years, is \$9.9 million.

Total Present Value of Internal and External Wood

Total present value from above $= 55.9 + 21.6 + 9.9 = \$87.4$ million.

It should be observed in Table 10.2 that regardless of the true state of nature, actions a_2, a_3, and a_4 are preferred to action a_1, that is, a_1 is dominated and the decision maker need not consider it further in his choice of action. At least one of the remaining admissible acts is preferred, given some state of nature. We also know from Chapter IV that there is some prior probability distribution on the states of nature for which the preferred action for a given state is optimal. The decision maker's task is to identify the probability distribution upon which he will base his decision.

In the present example there are some historical data available (Table 10.1) from which a decision maker could approximate a prior distribution.

The six states of nature occurred (after smoothing the data) with the frequencies shown along the right-hand side of Table 10.2. The smallest expected monetary value (cost) occurs when a_4 is chosen, that is, the firm would adopt a policy of supplying 60 percent of its raw material from internal supply. If a decision maker did not accept these prior probabilities as his own, he could subjectively assign others. As a guide to such an assignment he could calculate the minimum probabilities that could be assigned to any state and still leave the preferred action for that state as the optimal one. Following the procedure in Chapter IV, we calculated these minimum probabilities as shown in Table 10.4.

TABLE 10.4
MINIMUM PROBABILITIES THAT LEAVE THE PREFERRED ACTION OPTIMAL FOR THE RAW MATERIAL ACQUISITION PROBLEM

State of Nature	Minimum Probability	Preferred Action
θ_1	.99074	a_2
θ_2	.93103	a_3
θ_3	.72464	a_4
θ_4	.97959	a_5
θ_5	.66667	a_5
θ_6	.82759	a_6

The minimum cost of raw material acquisition for each state of nature was outlined in Table 10.2. The preferred actions were a_2, a_3, a_4, a_5, a_5, and a_6 for the six states, respectively. The minimum probabilities in Table 10.4 associated with each state, are those which leave the preferred action optimal against a probability equal to or greater than those shown. There are three states θ_1, θ_2, and θ_4 that have probabilities greater than 0.9. This means that the decision maker's subjective probability of any one of these three states would have to be greater than 0.9 before he would choose the preferred actions a_2, a_3, and a_5. However, a probability of two-thirds or greater on θ_5 would make a_5 optimal. Note that a probability as high as .72 on θ_3 would make a_4 the optimal action, that is, the same action as our historical frequency distribution made optimal. However, in that case the probability assigned to θ_3 was .30. This procedure only gives some guides to the decision maker as to the magnitudes of probabilities that would make a difference in his decision. In getting at more precise estimates of the decision maker's subjective probabilities, we would suggest the procedures of Chapter II.

Modification in Underlying Assumptions

One factor that is well known to be critical in forest-management planning is the discount rate. When the discount rate is considered in the context of decision making under uncertainty, it provides some new and interesting insights. The rate of discount that was used in Table 10.2 was 5 percent. However, the 1964 U.S. Census reported that a rate of approximately 8 percent would be closer to the industry's true opportunity cost of capital.[4] The present value of the raw material costs were recalculated for our hypothetical decision maker, assuming an 8 percent discount rate and are shown in Table 10.5.

TABLE 10.5

PRESENT VALUE OF RAW MATERIAL COSTS FOR HYPOTHETICAL FIRM USING 500,000 CORDS OF RAW MATERIAL PER YEAR, 20-YEAR PLANNING HORIZON, AND 8 PERCENT DISCOUNT RATE BY STATE OF NATURE AND ACTION

State of Nature	Action						$P(\theta)$
	a_1	a_2	a_3	a_4	a_5	a_6	
	Million Dollars						
θ_1	70.9	76.3	84.6	94.5	106.6	120.8	0.05
θ_2	75.9	80.2	87.2	95.9	107.2	120.3	0.15
θ_3	81.6	84.6	90.2	97.7	107.7	119.8	0.30
θ_4	88.4	89.6	93.8	99.8	108.4	119.3	0.25
θ_5	96.0	95.4	97.8	102.2	109.1	118.6	0.20
θ_6	104.8	102.0	102.3	104.7	109.8	117.6	0.05
Expected Monetary Value	85.95	87.81	92.50	99.05	108.13	119.45	

The results are drastically different than those of Table 10.2 where a 5 percent discount rate was used. Firstly, action a_1 is no longer dominated, but instead dominates actions a_5 and a_6. Secondly, using the prior probability distribution that was used in Table 10.2, action a_1 is now optimal, that is, the firm should supply none of its raw material internally.

It is of interest to note that many firms within the southern pulp and paper industry own a considerable amount of forest land. The justification for corporation ownership of forest land is expressed by one forester in the following quotation:[5]

[4] See Thompson, *op. cit.*, p. 82.
[5] John Fedkiw, "Capital Budgeting for Acquisition and Development of Timberlands," *Financial Management of Large Forest Ownerships*, School of Forestry Bulletin No. 66 (New Haven: Yale University, 1960), p. 5.

The main justification for investment in forest enterprises among integrated wood processing firms has been the strategic value of company control over the source of supply of its basic raw material. The term strategic is used because the major benefits are largely risk-reducing in character; real enough but difficult to quantify, accruing more or less to all other parts of the business, and extending more or less indefinitely into the future. The forest enterprise is expected to sustain a certain flow of wood to company plants, protect the firm against risks with respect to price, quantity and delivery schedule associated with outside supply sources, and supply long-term security for the firm's share of the product market and its profit position.

The peculiar quality of internal raw material as expressed in the above quotation is commonly referred to within the industry as "the insurance value of company wood." The strategic aspect of internal raw material would indicate that a discount rate lower than 8 percent should be used. Some foresters suggest using 5 percent. The difference in the expected values of the two resulting actions should provide some indication of the magnitude of this insurance value. Using the same prior frequency distribution that was used to calculate the expected monetary values in Table 10.2 to obtain the expected values in Table 10.5, we see that the insurance value of company wood is $7.85 million. That is, it is the difference between the expected value ($93.8) million when a_4 (Table 10.2) is the optimal action and the expected value when a_1 (Table 10.5) is the optimal action. It is apparent that this specific dollar value pertains only to this particular prior distribution and choice of discount rates. Other prior distributions and/or discount rates would show different "insurance values." Rather than using the firm's cost of capital and an arbitrary discount rate (5 percent in the example), a more meaningful comparison would result from using the firm's cost of capital and the forestry enterprise's internal rate of return.

SUMMARY

Almost all forest management decisions having any degree of significance over time contain inherent uncertainty. Present theoretical concepts of forest-management decision making take inadequate recognition of uncertainty. If forest managers are going to make decisions in which uncertainty is an integral factor — and they must make such decisions often — the theory underlying their decision-making processes should be capable of recognizing and systematically considering uncertainty. We believe that significant contributions to the solution of forest-management problems will come through development and adoption of decision-making models capable of systematically coping with uncertainty.

Although the example developed in this chapter is in reference to a hypothetical firm, we make no apologies for its lack of immediate application, for the underlying implications to similar forest management problems are more important. The example, in the context of the decision-making model of this book, has shown that when the components are quantified, the model will produce a decision which is optimal given the level of available information and the decision maker's knowledge of the situation. When the model is quantified consistent with the decision maker's knowledge, it will provide an explicit basis for corporate forest policy. As additional information becomes available, the model can be updated and the decisions modified. As this new information becomes available, changes in policy can be based on explicit data produced by a logical and systematic process.

It should be emphasized that defining the decision-making problem is a critical aspect of decision making. Unless the problem is defined in a manner that is compatible with a decision-making model, the model by itself cannot solve the problem.

CHAPTER XI

Applications in Climatology

One of the areas in which decision theory appears to be potentially very useful is climatology. The importance of weather on the economics of various private businesses and public enterprises has led to at least two broad lines of inquiry. One is to develop improved means for forecasting weather conditions (rainfall, freezes, heat waves, hurricanes, etc.) so that these enterprises can better adjust to the expected conditions. A second line of attack is to develop methods of weather modification (cloud seeding, fog dispersal methods, etc.) designed to change weather conditions in some desired way.

Decision problems involving weather forecasting are usually of the following nature: Can a private firm or public agency increase its expected profit or utility by employing some type of weather forecasting device? If the weather forecast is publicly available, does the forecast increase expected profit and utility? If the forecast is made privately and is available only at some cost to the user, does the expected gain from better decisions outweigh the cost? From society's point of view is the new benefit from weather forecasting greater than the cost of developing these forecasts?

The second area of application — weather modification — raises some additional difficult questions. Suppose, as is usual, that a private firm (such as a farming corporation) or public agency (for example, a municipal airport) decides to use weather modification equipment. From a private point of view, the question of whether or not to use weather modification and the particular techniques best adapted depends only on a comparison of expected benefits and expected costs expressed in terms of utility. But there is considerable debate over possible external effects. For example, does cloud seeding in one geographic area steal moisture from other areas? Can those who lose be identified? If so, will compensation actually be paid? Thus, this general area of application could quickly involve one in difficult questions of externalities and welfare effects.

The application presented in this chapter is of the first type — use of a weather predictor to improve decisions of private firms. Specifically, a rainfall predictor will be evaluated with respect to applications of fertilizer by wheat farmers in Australia. Because rainfall is the dominant variable

223

in the response of wheat production to nitrogen fertilizer, the rainfall predictor may have value in formulating strategies for wheat fertilization.[1]

Rainfall Predictor

One approach to forecasting annual rainfall is to examine historical data for serial correlation in the form of patterns or cycles. Predictions of annual rainfall one year ahead can be made on the basis of a smoothed trend of past rainfall data. In this chapter we illustrate the derivation of the value of such a rainfall predictor in a specific decision-making situation. Details of how the predictions are made are not of interest here, only how to carry out the evaluation.

One of the steps in the evaluation is the derivation of the $P(\theta|Z)$ distribution for the rainfall predictor.[2] It was derived by pooling data from 90 locations. Annual rainfall data for each location were classified into deciles (10 percentage points), thus converting rainfall for each location to a relative basis and allowing interregional pooling of the data. The predictions for each location, for the same year as the observed rainfall, were classified according to the type of prediction and the rainfall in the previous years. For example, prediction $1D$ indicates that a downward prediction (D) is forecast when rainfall in the previous year was in the first decile (1). The results are shown as a two-way table of frequencies in Table 11.1.

The posterior distribution of annual rainfall for each prediction, $P(\theta|Z)$, was estimated by converting the frequency distribution of Table 11.1 to a series of relative frequency distributions conditional upon the type of prediction. Because this estimate was based on a relatively small number of observations, several adjustments for finiteness were made.[3] The posterior probabilities of annual rainfall for the predictions are shown in Table 11.2.

To obtain the posterior distribution of annual rainfall for a single location, it is necessary to establish the correspondence between deciles (relative measure) and rainfall in inches (absolute measure) at that location. As an example location, Byerlee selected Ororoo, South Australia.[4] The mean annual rainfall at this location is 13.29 inches with a standard deviation of 4.01 inches, and the mean growing season rainfall (May to October) is 8.28 inches with a standard deviation of 2.79 inches.

---

[1] Material for this application comes from D. R. Byerlee, "A Decision Theoretic Approach to the Economic Analysis of Information" (M.S. thesis, University of New England, Armidale, N.S.W., August, 1968).

[2] θ represents actual annual rainfall and Z represents the predictions of annual rainfall.

[3] For details, see D. R. Byerlee, *loc. cit.*

[4] Byerlee, *op. cit.*, p. 65.

TABLE 11.1
FREQUENCIES OF OBSERVED RAINFALL AND PREDICTED TREND

Observed Rainfall θ Deciles	Type of Prediction[a] Z														
	1D	2D	3D	5D	8D	9D	10D	1U	2U	3U	5U	8U	9U	10U	Total
	Frequencies														
1	5	3	8	35	5	4	2	3	3	5	4				77
2	4	1	4	19	1	4	6	2	4	2	6				53
3			1	21	2	10	3	9	1	4	11		1		63
4–7		2	3	50	17	12	13	35	15	17	62	3	1		230
8				6		5	1		5	2	19	2	1		41
9				1	2	1			3	2	17	3	1		30
10				1		1			2	2	7	1		1	15
	9	6	16	133	27	37	25	49	33	37	126	9	4	1	509

[a] The predictions are named according to the predicted trend and the rainfall in the previous year, for example, 1D indicates that a downward prediction (D) is predicted when rainfall in the previous year was in the first decile (1).

TABLE 11.2
POSTERIOR PROBABILITIES $P(\theta|Z)$ OF ANNUAL RAINFALL, GIVEN THE PREDICTIONS

Rainfall θ	Type of Predictions Z													
	1D	2D	3D	5D	8D	9D	10D	1U	2U	3U	5U	8U	9U	10U
Deciles														
1	.55	.31	.36	.17	.17	.09	.03	.05	.06	.09	.02			
2	.36	.24	.33	.17	.06	.12	.11	.03	.09	.08	.03			
3	.09	.10	.11	.15	.06	.21	.04	.14	.09	.06	.07	.05	.10	
4–7		.25	.15	.38	.48	.34	.60	.60	.34	.48	.38	.15	.25	
8		.10	.05	.07	.06	.09	.14	.04	.21	.06	.15	.11	.10	.09
9				.03	.08	.09	.03	.11	.12	.06	.17	.33	.24	.36
10				.02	.09	.06	.05	.03	.09	.17	.17	.36	.31	.55
Total	1.00	1.00	1.00	1.00	1.00	1.00	1.00	1.00	1.00	1.00	1.00	1.00	1.00	1.00

The relative frequencies of rainfall for a period of 95 years were accumulated to smooth the data, providing a cumulative prior probability distribution over inches, as shown in Figure 11.A. The decile ranges are then marked off along the rainfall (in inches) scale. Using these decile ranges, the posterior probabilities of annual rainfall from Table 11.2 were cumulated and plotted to give the cumulative posterior distribution for each prediction. The cumulative posterior distribution for prediction 5D is plotted in Figure 11.A. Let us consider Point A in Figure 11.A, which is the eighth decile. In Table 11.2 we see that the cumulative posterior probability for decile 8 is .94 for 5D. The upper limit of the eighth decile from the prior distribution is approximately 17 inches. Thus, Point A

FIGURE 11.A
OBTAINING CUMULATIVE POSTERIOR DISTRIBUTION OF ANNUAL RAINFALL GIVEN THE PREDICTION, 5D

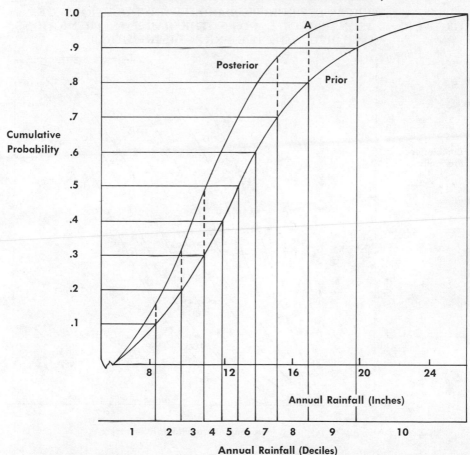

represents the cumulative posterior probability of rainfall being less than or equal to 17 inches.

To use the rainfall predictions in the context of the specific decision problem to follow, it was necessary to convert the annual rainfall distributions of Figure 11.A to growing season distributions. This was done by obtaining the probability, $P(G|A)$, of growing season rainfall (G), conditional upon the annual rainfall (A) for the data at the location under consideration.[5] Then these conditional probabilities were multiplied by the prior distribution $P(A)$ and summed over A to give $P(G)$. This is the prior cumulative distribution and the reference line used to obtain the cumulative posterior probability distributions of growing season rainfall, given the rainfall predictions as shown in Figure 11.B.

Each cumulative distribution in Figure 11.B was divided into two seg-

FIGURE 11.B

CUMULATIVE POSTERIOR PROBABILITY DISTRIBUTIONS OF GROWING SEASON RAINFALL GIVEN THE RAINFALL PREDICTIONS, COMPARED WITH THE PRIOR DISTRIBUTION

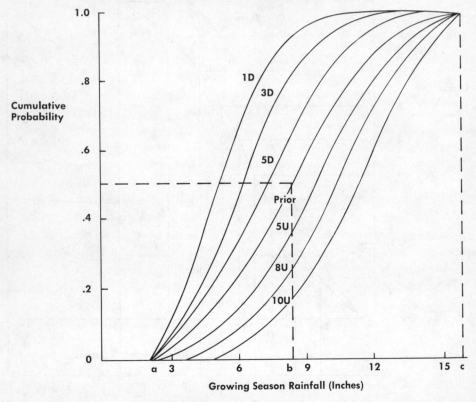

[5] The $P(G|A)$ distribution is not shown.

ments about $P(G) = 0.5$, and a cubic equation fitted to each segment. This was done so that the subsequent analysis could be done with continuous probability functions. Thus, having an algebraic expression for the cumulative distribution, the probability density function could be obtained by differentiation. If $P^1(G)$ is the polynomial expression for the cumulative distribution for the segment $a \leq G \leq b$, and $P^2(G)$ the expression for $b \leq G \leq c$, then the probability density function is given by:

$$\frac{dP^1(G)}{dG} = p^1(G) \text{ for } a \leq G \leq b \text{ and}$$

$$\frac{dP^2(G)}{dG} = p^2(G) \text{ for } b \leq G \leq c.$$

The segments a to b and b to c are shown in Figure 11.B for the prior cumulative distribution. This procedure was followed to obtain a set of probability density functions $p_k(G)$ $[k = 1, \ldots, 6]$ corresponding to the set of rainfall predictions z_k $[k = 1, \ldots, 6]$.[6]

Economic Evaluation of Predictors

Rainfall predictors have a wide variety of uses, and no doubt would be of different values depending upon the specific situations in which the predictors are used. Our main purpose here is to illustrate how to derive the value of a specific predictor and the value of a perfect predictor. One is interested in the value of a perfect predictor in comparison with a specific predictor to see whether it is worthwhile to attempt to improve upon the specific predictor. As mentioned in the introduction to this chapter, the rainfall predictor will be evaluated with respect to the application of nitrogen fertilizer to wheat in Australia, although it could also be used for many other purposes. It is suggested that variable climatic influences may explain why little nitrogen fertilizer has been used in the past. Because of the extreme climatic effect, the rainfall predictor may have value in formulating strategies for applying nitrogen to wheat in the future.

The analysis here proceeds in three stages: (1) the estimation of a production function in which the key variables are nitrogen and rainfall, (2) the computation of a Bayesian strategy for nitrogen application based upon the rainfall predictor, and (3) the evaluation of the predictor in relation to a perfect predictor.

[6] The number of predictions was reduced to 6 instead of the original 20 because many of the posterior distributions were almost identical to the prior distribution, and were judged to contain negligible amounts of additional information. See Byerlee, *op. cit.*, p. 67.

Estimation of the Production Function

The production function, in general, can be written as

$$y = f(x_1, x_2, \ldots, x_i, \ldots, x_n)$$

where y denotes output, and x_i is the ith input. For our purposes, it is well to partition the inputs into two subsets, the inputs under control of the decision maker, and those not under control of the decision maker at the time of making the decision. The uncontrolled variables are those like climatic conditions, levels of soil moisture, etc. Each of these subsets can be further partitioned into two more subsets. In the case of the controlled inputs, the inputs are classified as fixed and variable. In the case of the uncontrolled inputs, the inputs can be further classified into those for which reliable sample information is available and those for which either no information is available or a predictor is required to provide information. Thus, the production function can be written as:

$$y = f(x_j, x_k, x_l, x_m) \quad (j = 1, 2, \ldots, V)$$
$$(k = V + 1, V + 2, \ldots, F)$$
$$(l = F + 1, F + 2, \ldots, S)$$
$$(m = S + 1, S + 2, \ldots, P)$$

where x_j = variable inputs under control of decision maker,

x_k = fixed inputs under control of decision maker,

x_l = inputs not under control of the decision maker during the time period of the decisions, but sample information is available,

x_m = inputs not under control of the decision maker, but predictors are available.

In the nitrogen application problem we have, in general terms, the following production function:

$$y = f(N, S_m, S_n, G, F)$$

where y = response in wheat yield (bushels per acre),

N = pounds of nitrogen applied per acre (controlled input),

S_m = coefficient of soil texture (soil moisture percentage at 15 atmospheres) (uncontrolled input for which sample information is available),

S_n = parts per million (p.p.m.) of initial soil nitrate (uncontrolled input for which sample information is available),

G = inches of growing season rainfall (uncontrolled input for which the rainfall predictor can be used),

F = inputs under control of decision maker, but fixed for this time period.

The data used for fitting the production function were obtained from nitrogen fertilizer trials from 16 widely scattered areas of South Australia, where average annual rainfall varied from 11.5 inches to 19.9 inches.[7] The trials were conducted at each location for a period varying from one to six years. In all, 52 location-year combinations are represented in the data. In each trial, yield was measured at nitrogen applications of 0, 11.5, 23, and 46 pounds per acre. Soil analyses were conducted at planting time and rainfall recorded over the period from May to October. The function that was selected after fitting various algebraic forms[8] was:

$$y = 0.05274N - 0.00156N^2 + 0.01755NG - 0.00498NS_m$$
$$- 0.00119NGS_n.$$

Computation of Bayesian Strategies

We will assume in this chapter that the decision maker has a linear utility function and hence is interested in maximizing expected monetary value. In our case of nitrogen fertilizer application, he will maximize expected profit, $E(\pi)$,

where $E(\pi) = E(R_y\, y - r_N N)$ and
R_y = net price of wheat = $1.10/bushel,
r_N = price of nitrogen fertilizer = 12.5 cents per pound of N.

To maximize expected profit, we set the following derivative equal to zero:

$$\frac{\partial E(\pi)}{\partial N} = E\left(R_y \frac{\partial y}{\partial N} - r_N\right) = 0, \text{ or}$$

$$E\left(\frac{\partial y}{\partial N}\right) = \frac{r_N}{R_y}.$$

To obtain the solution of this last equation, we need the expectation on the left-hand side. This is given by the sum (integral) of the product of the probability density functions times the derivative functions. The probability density functions are those estimated above, $p^1(G)$ and $p^2(G)$, corresponding to the cumulative distributions shown in Figure 11.B. Since we want a Bayesian strategy, we will have a solution to the above equation for each prediction, k, and hence we will use a separate probability density

[7] Reported in J. S. Russell, "Nitrogen Fertilizer and Wheat in a Semi-Arid Environment, 1, Effect on Yield," *Australian Journal of Experimental Agriculture and Animal Husbandry*, Vol. 7, pp. 453–461.

[8] For greater detail, see Byerlee, *op. cit.*, p. 63.

function for each k. The Bayesian strategy is then given by the solution of the following equation for each k:

$$E\left(\frac{\partial y}{\partial N}\right) = \int_a^b \left(\frac{\partial y}{\partial N}\right) p_k^1(G)dG + \int_b^c \left(\frac{\partial y}{\partial N}\right) p_k^2(G)dG = \frac{r_N}{R_y}.$$

The Bayesian strategies for six rainfall predictions, four levels of soil texture, and five levels of soil nitrate are given in Table 11.3.

TABLE 11.3

**BAYESIAN STRATEGIES FOR SIX RAINFALL PREDICTIONS
IN COMPARISON WITH THE NO-DATA OPTIMAL ACTION
AT VARIOUS LEVELS OF SOIL TEXTURE
AND SOIL NITRATE**

Soil Texture Coefficients	Soil Nitrate	No-Data Actions	Bayesian Strategies					
			Type of Prediction					
			1D	3D	5D	5U	8U	10U
Percent			Pounds N per Acre					
3	1	18.1	4.0	8.4	13.3	25.7	31.7	36.2
3	2	15.0	2.0	6.1	10.5	22.0	27.6	31.8
3	3	11.9	0.0	3.7	7.8	18.4	23.5	27.4
3	5	6.7	0.0	0.0	2.3	11.1	13.4	18.6
3	7	0.0	0.0	0.0	0.0	3.9	7.2	9.8
6	1	13.3	0.0	3.7	8.5	20.9	26.9	31.4
6	2	10.2	0.0	1.3	5.7	17.2	22.8	27.0
6	3	7.1	0.0	0.0	3.0	13.6	18.7	22.6
6	5	1.0	0.0	0.0	0.0	6.3	10.6	13.8
6	7	0.0	0.0	0.0	0.0	0.0	2.4	5.0
9	1	8.5	0.0	0.0	3.7	16.1	22.1	26.7
9	2	5.4	0.0	0.0	0.9	12.5	18.0	22.3
9	3	2.3	0.0	0.0	0.0	8.8	13.9	17.9
9	5	0.0	0.0	0.0	0.0	1.5	5.8	9.0
9	7	0.0	0.0	0.0	0.0	0.0	0.0	0.2
12	1	3.7	0.0	0.0	0.0	11.3	17.3	21.9
12	2	6.6	0.0	0.0	0.0	7.7	13.2	17.5
12	3	0.0	0.0	0.0	0.0	4.0	9.2	13.1
12	5	0.0	0.0	0.0	0.0	0.0	1.0	4.3
12	7	0.0	0.0	0.0	0.0	0.0	0.0	0.0
Probability of occurrence of predictions[a]			.011	.036	.254	.254	.036	.011

[a] Since some of the predictions were judged to contain little or no information, they were dropped and therefore these probabilities do not add to one.

Evaluation of Predictors

We said in Chapter V that the value of information (experiment) is the difference between the expected monetary value of the data problem and the no-data problem. That is, it is the difference between the weighted average monetary return of the Bayes strategy and the maximum expected monetary return, using the prior probability distribution.

For the rainfall predictor, the weighted average return of the Bayes strategy is:

$$\bar{u}^* = \sum_{k=1}^{6} q_k u_k^*, \text{ where } u_k^* \text{ is the expected profit, using the rainfall}$$

predictor, and q_k is the $P(Z)$ distribution, that is, the probability of the predictor forecasting the specific predictions. Now:

$$u_k^* = \int_a^b \pi_k p_k^1(G)dG + \int_b^c \pi_k p_k^2(G)dG \qquad \text{and}$$

$$\pi_k = R_y y_k^* - r_N N_k^*, \qquad\qquad\qquad \text{where}$$

N_k^* is the optimal nitrogen level corresponding to the kth prediction, (Bayes strategy in Table 11.3) and y_k^* is the yield response associated with N_k^*.

The maximum expected monetary return, using the prior probability distribution, is:

$$u_o^* = \int \pi_o p_o(G)dG \qquad \text{and}$$

$$\pi_o = R_y y_o^* - r_N N_o^* \qquad \text{where}$$

N_o^* is the optimal nitrogen level (see Table 11.3, no-data actions) using the prior probability distribution, and y_o^* is the yield associated with N_o^*. The optimal nitrogen level, N_o^*, is found by solving the following equation for N:

$$E\left(\frac{\partial y}{\partial N}\right) = \int_a^b \left(\frac{\partial y}{\partial N}\right) p_o^1(G)dG + \int_b^c \left(\frac{\partial y}{\partial N}\right) p_o^2(G)dG$$

where $p_o^1(G)$ and $p_o^2(G)$ are the probability density functions corresponding to the two segments of the prior cumulative distribution in Figure 11.B.

Therefore, the value of the rainfall predictor is given by

$$V_B = \bar{u}^* - u_o^*.$$

The value in cents per acre for the rainfall predictor (assuming it forecasts growing season rainfall) and the value of a perfect predictor of growing season rainfall is given in Table 11.4. The value of the perfect predictor is given by:

TABLE 11.4

**VALUE OF RAINFALL PREDICTORS FOR VARIOUS
LEVELS OF SOIL MOISTURE AND SOIL NITRATE**

Soil Texture Coefficient	Soil Nitrate	Predictor	
		Predictor Growing Season Rainfall	Perfect Predictor Growing Season Rainfall
Percent	ppm.	Cents per Acre	
3	1	7.9	36.0
3	2	6.9	30.0
3	3	5.8	25.0
3	5	3.5	15.0
3	7	1.1	5.0
6	1	7.9	34.0
6	2	6.7	28.0
6	3	5.6	22.0
6	5	2.4	10.0
6	7	0.1	1.0
9	1	7.6	31.0
9	2	6.3	24.0
9	3	4.5	17.0
9	5	0.5	5.0
9	7	0.0	0.0
12	1	6.4	25.0
12	2	4.0	17.0
12	3	1.6	9.0
12	5	0.1	1.0
12	7	0.0	0.0

$$V_P = \bar{\bar{u}}^* - u_o^*, \qquad \text{where}$$

$$\bar{\bar{u}}^* = \int_a^b \pi^* p_o(G)dG + \int_b^c \pi^* p_o(G)dG \quad \text{and}$$

$$\pi^* = f(G).\text{[9]}$$

[9] With perfect information the growing season rainfall is known to be G, and the optimal level of nitrogen application N^* can be determined solving

$$\frac{\partial y}{\partial N} = \frac{r_N}{R_y}.$$

Now the Bayes strategy for the perfect predictor of growing season rainfall is continuous and can be written as:

$$N^* = f(G), \text{ provided}$$
$$N^* \geq 0.$$

If G_c is the level of rainfall at which $N^* = 0$, then π^*, the profit from applying N^* given that rainfall is G, can be expressed as:

$$\pi^* = f(G) \text{ if } G \geq G_c$$
$$\pi^* = 0 \quad \text{ if } G < G_c.$$

The value of the predictor (growing season rainfall) in determining strategies for nitrogen application to wheat is low, with a maximum value of 7.9 cents per acre. The maximum value of the perfect predictor, 36 cents per acre, provides a useful guide to the potential improvement of growing season rainfall predictors as far as wheat production is concerned. Of course, these values may differ widely for other types of crops.

SUMMARY

We hope that this chapter provides an introductory idea of the potential value of decision theory to problems involving climatology, as well as pointing out some of the empirical and conceptual challenges that arise in its application. The fact that weather forecasts are increasingly being formulated in terms of probabilities (there's a 60% chance of rain today) suggests that decision theory may see greater application in the future in those fields where weather affects optimal decisions. Agriculture is one such obvious field. But increasing public concern with environment suggests many other applications. For example, controls on industrial burning of waste products are being implemented in some areas to reduce air pollution. Often the form of control simply involves restricting of burning to those periods when weather conditions are forecast to be "favorable for burning." Similar controls might be imposed on agricultural pesticide use by restricting spraying to periods when forecasted wind and moisture conditions are expected to minimize the probability of offsite damages.

Hopefully, the applications of decision theory in this and earlier chapters will alert the reader to the possibilities for empirical application in still other fields. Clearly, the applications here presented barely scratch the surface of possible problem areas to which decision theory tools are relevant.

CHAPTER XII

Guidelines for Application of Decision-Making Framework

The central role played by Bayes' formula in the decision-making framework presented in this book should now be clear. The framework presumes that there are a number of possible states of nature, one of which will occur when a particular action is taken. The problem is to obtain some information about the probable states of nature in a particular situation and then to incorporate this information into the decision framework. Bayes' formula provides a means for carrying out these stages. From Chapter II, Bayes' formula is:

$$P(A_i|E) = \frac{P(A_i)P(E|A_i)}{P(A_1)P(E|A_1) + \cdots + P(A_n)P(E|A_n)}.$$

The $P(A_i|E)$ is the posterior probability distribution, which is a weighting of the prior probabilities $P(A_i)$ by the conditional probabilities $P(E|A_i)$, that is, the likelihoods of acquiring the specific information E given the possible values of the random variable A_i.

The prior probabilities need not be treated as being objective or empirical, but rather, as we have seen, often involve subjective judgment. When a prior probability is chosen which is not identical to a historical frequency, the differences indicate the extent to which elements of subjective or personal evaluation may be involved. We have tried to emphasize throughout the empirical applications presented in previous chapters that truly objective or empirical probabilities are rarely obtainable. We believe that the usefulness of the Bayesian decision-making framework rests on the possibility of incorporating these personal, subjective beliefs directly into the analysis. The distinguishing feature of this approach to decision-making lies more in the philosophical issues underlying the techniques than in the techniques themselves.

Bayes' Formula and the Philosophy of Science

We believe that some of the philosophical issues raised by a decision theory approach have broad implications for social science research methodology. To point out some of these implications, we might view the process of research methodology as pictured in Figure 12.A. In the social sciences, as in the physical sciences, there are two routes leading to scientific conclusions. One of these is by the logical route (right-hand side of diagram) from abstraction to the mathematical model, and then by the rules of logic and physical interpretation to conclusions that take the form of hypotheses or, more specifically, the probability of hypotheses, $P(H)$. The other route is by the statistical route from observation to the statistical model to conclusions that take the form of likelihood statements $P(E_A|H)$, where E_A stands for the evidence which the analyst obtains from observations, and H stands for the hypotheses to be tested. The hypotheses are the same ones that are generated by the mathematical model on the right-hand side of the diagram. From these two routes emerge scientific conclusions in the form of information $P(H_i|E_A)$. We recognize that the new form in which the information appears is obtained from Bayes' formula where we have substituted H_i, the possible hypotheses, for A_i. Thus, the posterior probability $P(H_i|E_A)$ comes from the weighting of the $P(H_i)$ by $P(E_A|H_i)$ in the formula:

$$P(H_i|E_A) = \frac{P(H_i)P(E_A|H_i)}{P(H_1)P(E_A|H_1) + \cdots + P(H_n)P(E_A|H_n)}$$

It should be noted that the prior probability of H_i is often quite subjective as it may be based on sparse evidence; in many cases, it may be little more than a hunch on the part of the scientist. Furthermore, the likelihood function $P(E_A|H_i)$ may also be subjective with little empirical foundation and considerable speculation by the scientist (statistician). The only objective part of the procedure, so far, is the use of Bayes' formula, that is, objective in the sense of employing the mathematical rules of logic to derive posterior probabilities from given prior and conditional possibilities.

Generally the scientific process is given further objectivity by subjecting the hypotheses to empirical testing as shown in Figure 12.A. In the physical sciences this usually means conducting experiments in which further evidence is obtained to see if one can materially alter the odds on a hypothesis in its favor or against it. In the social sciences, however, large-scale experimentation under the control of the scientist is quite limited, and he must depend on other individuals and groups to run his experiments for him. These experiments really take the form of the everyday actions taken by decision makers using, in part, the information $P(H|E_A)$ supplied by the body of scientific conclusions available at that point in time. To be consistent with our earlier terminology we can think of scientific conclusions as being the information provided by the analyst.

FIGURE 12.A

THE PLACE OF BAYES FORMULA IN SCIENTIFIC PROCESSES[a]

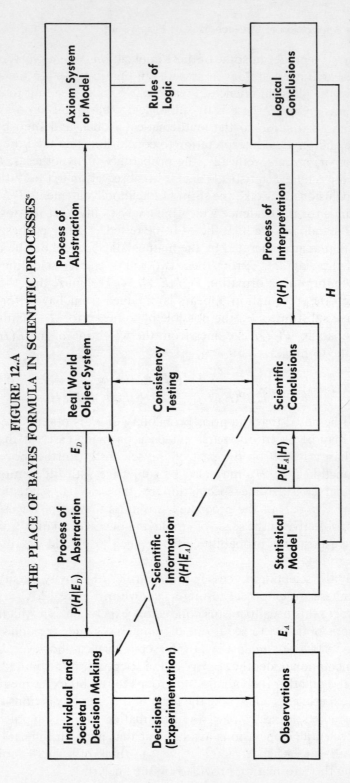

[a] This figure is an adaptation of a diagram by George G. Judge, "The Search for Quantitative Economic Knowledge," *American Journal of Agricultural Economics*, Vol. 50, No. 5 (December 1968), and based upon another by C. H. Coombs, H. Raiffa, and R. M. Thrall in R. M. Thrall, C. H. Coombs, and R. L. Davis, eds., *Decision Processes* (New York: John Wiley & Sons, Inc., 1954).

At the same time the decision maker has been carrying on his own observation and abstraction of the real world, and has formulated his own information $P(H_i|E_D)$, where E_D stands for the decision maker's evidence. He may be supposed to arrive at this form of probability statement via Bayes' formula, however rough and unconscious his use of the formula might be. To arrive at a decision, the decision maker has to put together the two pieces of information $P(H_i|E_D)$ and $P(H_i|E_A)$, which he will do theoretically by multiplying the two distributions and normalizing. However, the legitimacy of this multiplication depends on whether the two distributions are independent of each other. It is quite unlikely that the two distributions are completely independent in a world of modern communication, which leaves the problem of how to combine the two distributions. We have no suggestions on this problem for the moment, and leave it as one of the unsolved philosophical issues of the social sciences.

The fact that individuals and groups are in charge of the social scientist's experiments leads to two other more practical difficulties. One is that the scientist does not know whether society's experiments are well designed to test his hypotheses, that is, unlike physical scientists, he does not know if the experiments are designed to refute his hypotheses or are so designed that they contribute only to confirming evidence. This problem means the social scientist must be a more careful observer than his counterpart in the physical sciences, and that he must be more critical of his data. It does not mean that hypotheses cannot be tested in the social sciences; it just means the analyst must try harder to refute his hypotheses.

The other difficulty arises in trying to find solutions to social problems. Social scientists who try to persuade individuals and groups to make the decisions that are consistent with the scientist's probability distributions must remember that a distribution with one large peak is the most persuasive. However, for scientists to agree among themselves on prior distributions and likelihood functions so that a single peaked distribution will emanate from Bayes' formula is something unheard of in the social sciences. It is difficult to state which disagreements among social scientists contribute most to the lack of solution of social problems; however, it is the opinion of the authors that it is the lack of agreement on prior distributions that contributes most. This is, no doubt, partially due to the multi-valued theory prevalent in social sciences, that is, that a large number of hypotheses are consistent with the same body of theory. While we make no pretenses at having solved these difficulties, we do believe that looking at the problem through "Bayesian glasses" helps to clarify the issues.

Decision-Making Research[1]

We have discussed a number of research results, especially in the appendix to Chapter III, which illustrated that utility is measurable in a practical decision-making context. On the one hand one could conclude that, since utility is measurable, decision makers implicitly base decisions on maximizing utility, and therefore that our decision-making framework is descriptive of what decision makers actually do. On the other hand, one could also conclude that, since utility can be measured, the framework can be used to say how decision makers should make decisions. In other words, is the decision-making framework that we have discussed in this book descriptive of actual decision-making, or is it prescriptive for decision making?

There have been a number of attempts to ascertain whether decision makers use the decision criteria we discussed in Chapter IV. However, we do not know of any research that has attempted to verify all components of the decision framework, as we have presented it, in actual decision-making situations. We should not fault these researchers for not considering the Bayesian approach in their research, for it is only recently that this framework has been fully recognized. As we look back upon their efforts, however, we recognize that, in one way or another, they hit upon certain aspects of the total framework. Two studies that we will discuss here were made by J. L. Dillon and E. O. Heady in Iowa in 1957, and by F. D. Sobering in North Dakota in 1960.[2]

The Dillon-Heady study was intended as an empirical assessment of the descriptive role of the decision-making model as a "game against nature" and an empirical evaluation of the possible role of the Laplace, Savage regret, and the maximin criteria for solving games against nature. The decision setting was the choice of a 1957 feed-lot program by cattle feeders under price and weather conditions that would prevail under four states of nature. The decision makers were 77 Marshall County, Iowa, owner-operator cattle feeders between the ages of 30 and 50. These cattle feeders were interviewed four times at six-week intervals to check for patterned responses and reliability of responses.

One phase of the study involved noting the extent of agreement be-

---

[1] Psychologists have contributed both to the theoretical and empirical aspects of decision theory. For a review of this work, see R. Duncan Luce and Patrick Suppes, "Preference, Utility, and Subjective Probability," *Handbook of Mathematical Psychology*, ed. by Luce, Bush, and Galanter, (New York: John Wiley and Sons, Inc., 1965). This paper also contains an excellent list of references for anyone wanting to pursue this literature.

[2] John L. Dillon and Earl O. Heady, "Free Competition, Uncertainty, and Farmer Decisions," *Journal of Farm Economics*, Vol. 43, No. 3 (August 1961); Frederic David Sobering, *Farm Management Decisions within the Framework of Game and Decision Theory Models* (unpublished M.S. thesis, North Dakota State University, March, 1963).

tween the general game theoretic model and the respondents' stated decision-making processes. Farmers were found to simplify their range of alternatives as postulated by the model. In fact, only three farmers considered more than five alternative programs. The farmers' choice of program placed major emphasis on the uncertain characteristic of several key factors, for example, the uncertainty of weather and cattle prices. Twenty-four of the 77 interviewed said they considered alternative feed-lot programs in terms of payoffs, varying according to the states of nature that might prevail. Only 12 of the 77 farmers, however, could be said to be consistent with the model in the sense of thinking about a fairly complete payoff table in making their decisions.

Another objective of the Dillon-Heady study was to assess the possibility that the Laplace, Savage regret and maximin criteria could improve profit possibilities in actual feed-lot decision problems facing the 77 farmers. Each farmer's alternative feeder programs were taken as a set of actions. Each farmer was then asked his most probable buying and selling price for cattle under four possible states of nature. Given the farmer's most likely price, he was asked which alternative he would select, and the number of cattle to be fed. Payoff matrices were calculated from the price data supplied by the farmers and the three criteria applied to obtain a solution that could be compared with that given by the farmer. In every problem setting, the respondents would have been able to increase their net return by at least 19 percent, on the average, by using one of the criteria. The researchers concluded that the model and the criteria tested do not have a descriptive role in explaining actual decision making. Unfortunately, the study did not explicitly test the Bayesian decision model.

In the North Dakota study conducted by Sobering, 90 farmers were asked, among other things, to choose among four actions, each of which represented an equal annual investment, and having the payoffs as shown in Table 12.1. The payoff table was constructed such that a person using a maximin criterion would choose Action B, while the maximax criterion chooses Action C, the minimax regret chooses Action D, the Hurwicz pessimism-optimism criterion chooses B or C, depending upon the value of the α index, and the Laplace criterion chooses Action A. The frequency of farmers' responses, given certain conditions that were explained in asking the question, is given in Table 12.2. The conditions referred to the short run versus the long run, and whether the farmer had an outside source of income to supplement his income from the particular decision being made.

From Table 12.2 one can observe that a definite difference was found in the choice patterns. The minimax solution was chosen most frequently

TABLE 12.1
PAYOFF TABLE OF FOUR CHOICES OF ENTER-PRISE AND FOUR STATES OF NATURE USED IN NORTH DAKOTA STUDY

State of Nature	Action			
	A	B	C	D
θ_1	$2500	$1700	$ 0	$ 0
θ_2	0	800	0	0
θ_3	5500	3000	10,000	8000
θ_4	3500	2500	0	2000

when no supplemental income was available, while when supplemental income was available, the Laplace criterion solution was chosen most frequently.

While the researcher concluded from his study that farmers use different decision criterion, as interpreters of these data we would conclude that different farmers have different utility functions and attached different subjective probability distributions to the four states of nature. The results could just as well be explained on this basis as by saying that different criteria were used to solve the problem.

Based on these studies, we would be unwilling to say that the decision-making framework of this book is not descriptive of real world decision making. Without further testing, however, we would not conclude either that it is totally descriptive of all decisions. What we would hypothesize

TABLE 12.2
FREQUENCY OF FARMERS' CHOICES AMONG THE ACTIONS OF TABLE 12.1[a]

Action Selected	Decision Criterion	Problem Setting			
		No Supp. Income		Supp. Income	
		Short Run	Long Run	Short Run	Long Run
A	Laplace	21	35	42	55
B	Minimax, Hurwicz[b]	60	52	21	23
C	Maximax, Hurwicz[c]	6	0	20	8
D	Minimax Regret	3	3	7	4
Total		90	90	90	90

[a] Sobering, *op. cit.* p. 55.
[b] With α index larger than 35/39.
[c] With α index smaller than 35/39.

at this point in time is that the entire framework is descriptive and could be tested in simple enough decision situations. We would not expect it to be descriptive in very complex decision situations like those examined in Chapters VII and XI. In the latter cases we would expect that decision makers would want to make a conscious application of the decision framework to insure them of consistency with their procedures which they employ in simple decision situations. Hence, we would conclude that the decision framework is descriptive of decisions in simple settings and should be tested in that kind of situations; and that the decision framework is prescriptive when it comes to complex decisions, that is, decision makers would find themselves making more consistent decisions by following the framework than by not following it, or doing what they are now doing.

In reviewing the studies discussed briefly above, as well as other studies of management in business and agriculture, it seems clear that there has been a lack of a consistent framework around which to build theory and conduct empirical research.[3] By conceptualizing the problems of uncertainty and information seeking in the decision-making framework of this book we believe that future research on managerial processes and related aspects of motivation, communication, and organization can proceed more meaningfully.

USE OF DECISION THEORY BY RESEARCH WORKERS

This book has concentrated primarily on the use of decision theory principles in improving various kinds of decisions made by businessmen. However, these principles can also be of considerable value in solving various decision problems facing research workers. We illustrate with two typical examples, one dealing with physical experiments and the other in the area of econometrics.

Investment in Production Response Research

A common problem facing research workers is whether additional experimentation is in some sense worthwhile. To take a problem well known to agriculturalists, will additional experimentation in refining estimates of a production function response surface improve decision making sufficiently to justify the cost of the experiment? Anderson and Dillon[4] have

---

[3] See, for example, G. L. Johnson *et al.*, *A Study of Managerial Processes of Midwestern Farmers* (Ames: Iowa State University Press, 1961).

[4] J. R. Anderson and John L. Dillon, "Economic Considerations in Response Research," *American Journal of Agricultural Economics*, Vol. 50, No. 1 (February, 1968).

provided significant insights into this problem by casting it in a Bayesian decision framework. The gist of their argument is summarized in this section.

To avoid the problems of calculating public benefits and costs from research, Anderson and Dillon simplify the problem by considering it from the viewpoint of a private farmer (or group of farmers with homogeneous resource situations and utility functions) who finances his (their) own response research (for example, on fertilizer) and fully exploits the knowledge gained. The additional experimentation is judged to be worthwhile if it increases the expected utility of this individual farmer (or group of farmers).

Suppose that results are available from a local experiment conducted in the past. This constitutes the *prior* information. Now suppose another experiment is conducted and the two experiments combined using Bayesian principles.[5] The combined results can be considered the *posterior* information. An *ex post* evaluation of the additional experiment can now be made, that is, was it worthwhile? In making this evaluation we should use the best information available, namely, the posterior information. Thus, using the posterior production function, we first calculate the expectation (E'') and variance (V'') of profit, using the fertilizer rates that are optimal for the posterior function. (The expenses of conducting the experiment are included as a cost in calculating E''.) Next, again using the posterior production function, we calculate the expectation (E') and variance (V') of profit, using the fertilizer rates that were optimal for the prior function. Assuming a utility function that depends only on the expectation and variance of outcomes, the expected utility U'' using E'' and V'' is compared with the expected utility U' using E' and V'. If $U'' > U'$, the additional experimentation was justified, and vice versa.

The above analysis could provide a valuable *ex post* assessment of experimental work. As Anderson and Dillon point out, "If the last experiment conducted in a series has not proved economical, it is unlikely that further similar work will do so." However, the more interesting general question is whether a future experiment will be economical, and if so, how much experimentation is optimal? To answer this question, Anderson and Dillon use "preposterior" analysis.

The preposterior analysis begins by simulating experiments of different sizes by Monte Carlo techniques. Experimental outcomes are generated, based on random variables of regression coefficients and error terms whose expectations and variances are the prior equivalents. In general, a larger

    [5] H. Raiffa and R. Schlaifer, *Applied Statistical Decision Theory* (Cambridge: Harvard Business School, 1961), p. 343.

experiment reduces the variance of profit, but also eventually reduces the expected profit because of the higher cost of the larger experiment. Again, the optimal size of experiment, if it is profitable at all, is that size which maximizes expected utility. The results can also be conveniently summarized in a E-V framework.

The above sketch is intended to illustrate a first approach to decisions involving the allocation of research funds. As Anderson and Dillon recognize, a number of difficulties remain, particularly in extending the analysis to the public domain. One might also question the general advisability of using only data from the prior experiment(s) in simulating experimental outcomes in the preposterior analysis. Bayesian principles would allow the experimenter to inject his own prior subjective information into the analysis at this point. To take an extreme case, if only one previous experiment existed, and it had been conducted in a year of abnormal weather or disease conditions, the experimenter would be justified in revising this information subjectively as a basis for Monte Carlo preposterior analysis.

Applications in Econometrics

In econometrics the purpose of estimation is generally (1) predicting of future values of dependent variables with given independent variables, or (2) making decisions on certain controlled independent variables that will accomplish some objective.[6] While the distinction in purpose is clear, it has become conventional to use the same statistical procedures for estimating unknown parameters in both prediction and decision models. Using conventional least squares estimation procedures for a decision maker ignores his utility function. If one were to take a decision theory approach to estimation, one must use not only prior information about the unknown parameters but also the decision maker's utility function. Estimation procedures in the decision-making spirit are suggested by Walter Fisher for the linear decision model. Further work of this type is needed to make full use of the decision-making framework in econometric research.

A philosophical problem (which is often confronted by econometricians) is the discrepancy between what the econometrician claims to be his hypothesis and the procedures followed in testing the hypothesis.[7] The analyst says his hypothesis is based on economic theory; for example, he hypothesizes that the quantity of output of product X is linearly related in

[6] Walter D. Fisher, "Estimation in the Linear Decision Model," *International Economic Review*, Vol. 3, No. 1 (January 1962), pp. 1–29.

[7] H. Theil and A. S. Goldberger, "On Pure and Mixed Statistical Estimation in Economics." *International Economic Review*, Vol. 2, No. 1 (January, 1961), pp. 65–78.

logarithms to some set of input variables A with positive coefficients. He then carries out a least squares analysis of some seemingly appropriate type to provide estimates of parameters in the linear relation. He finds that one of the coefficients on an input is negative. He does not accept this negative estimate, but rather reshuffles his data and may delete or add variables. It is well known, and frequently ignored, that exact probability statements can no longer be made if the original hypothesis was rejected, but now the same data are to be used to test another hypothesis. This approach of claiming a hypothesis is derived from economic theory, and yet not using the hypothesis at some point in the analysis, is an inconsistency that is made blatantly clear by the spirit of Bayes' formula. Bayes' formula makes use of the prior information or the probability of the prior hypothesis. Thus the difficulty with the conventional approach is that the analyst has ignored his prior knowledge which, in this case, is his theory. His prior knowledge tells him that the coefficients should be positive, and it is exactly this information which should be used in his estimation. It would be more consistent to incorporate such knowledge into the prior hypothesis right from the start than to exclude it from the hypothesis, and then reject it afterwards when the results contradict the omitted knowledge.

In practice the conventional tools of regression analysis cannot be used to incorporate prior knowledge. In recent years, however, statisticians and econometricians have been developing tools to handle prior knowledge in estimation problems. A review of these procedures is provided by Judge and Yancey in a University of Illinois paper that also contains an extensive list of references on the subject.[8]

GUIDES FOR DECISION-MAKING

There have been a sufficient number of empirical studies to show that decision makers adopt different management practices because they have different attitudes toward risk (utility functions), and that these attitudes can be measured and compared. These conclusions imply that extension personnel, business and farmer consultants and advisors should allow for their clients' attitudes toward risk in their recommendations. At a minimum, information should be provided to the decision maker in a format that makes the risk elements apparent. Widespread availability of high speed computers is making it increasingly practical to generate probability

---

[8] George G. Judge and Thomas A. Yancey, "The Use of Prior Information in Estimating the Parameters of Economic Relationships," Quantitative Economics Workshop Paper No. 6801 (Urbana-Champaign: University of Illinois, Dept. of Economics, May, 1968).

distributions, even for highly complex decision alternatives.[9] In presenting such results, we would recommend the framework of this book in which the alternative actions, possible states of nature, and the monetary pay-offs from state-action combinations are made explicit. This format would allow the decision maker to attach his own subjective probabilities to the states of nature and evaluate the monetary payoffs intuitively in terms of utility.

Many consultants and advisors believe, however, that a single valued recommendation must be made. Particularly in this case should the risk preferences of the clients be allowed for in the advice. For an individual decision maker, this will require that his utility function be derived.

In the case of a group recommendation, we believe that the consultant should use a group utility function as an aid in arriving at his recommendations. When utility functions are used to allow for risk in making a group recommendation, the consultant makes explicit the interpersonal comparisons of utility that otherwise are implicit in making a group recommendation.

In a study reported by Officer, Halter, and Dillon, two different methods of deriving group utility functions were used, and an assessment of the errors between the group recommendation based on the group function and the decision maker's actual decision was made.[10]

An obvious method of deriving a group utility function is to take the average of the individual's utility functions, that is, average the coefficients of the individual functions. Another method is to take the median of the individual utility function as the group function. When these two methods were applied to the five farmer's utility functions that were given in Table 3.7 of the appendix to Chapter III, the comparative errors against the farmer's actual decisions were as shown in Table 12.3.[11] The comparative errors from using the farmers' individual utility function and the criterion of minimizing expected monetary cost are also shown.

The average error is .64, which compares favorably with the average error of .86 for the average group utility function and .71 for the group decision to minimize expected cost. Still, it compares most unfavorably with

---

[9] A. N. Halter and G. W. Dean, *Simulation of a California Range-Feedlot Operation*, California Agricultural Experiment Station, Giannini Foundation Research Report No. 282 (May, 1965).

[10] R. R. Officer, A. N. Halter, and John L. Dillon, "Risk, Utility, and the Palatability of Extension Advice to Farmer Groups," *Aust. Jour. of Ag. Econ.*, Vol. 11, No. 2 (December 1967).

[11] The group's average utility function, found by averaging the coefficients of the utility functions in Table 3.7 of the appendix to Chapter III, after standardizing the coefficients for unit of scale, was:

$$Du = .86462926x + .00124773x^2.$$

The median function was that derived for individual 1, Model 3, of Table 3.7 of the appendix to Chapter III.

TABLE 12.3

COMPARATIVE ERRORS OF THE GROUP DECISION METHODS,
INDIVIDUAL UTILITY FUNCTIONS, AND MINIMIZING
EXPECTED MONETARY VALUES[a]

Subject	Average Utility Function	Median Utility Function	Individual Utility Function	Cost Minimization
1	9	2	2	4
2	10	5	4	3.5
3	4	7	3	10
4	15	8	1	4
5	5	10	3	14
Total Error	45	32	13	35.5
Average Error[b]	.86	.64	.26	.71

[a] An error is defined as occurring when the criterion predicted a different decision to that made by the farmer. The degree of error was measured by the total amount, in months, by which the decision made under the criterion differed from the farmer's decision over the 10 fodder reserve choice situations presented.

[b] Average error is the error per subject per decision.

the average error of .26 for making decisions using the individual utility functions. In terms of this particular study, it would seem that a risk-oriented group utility function approach can provide better recommendations than a more traditional approach such as expected cost minimization, which makes no allowance for risk.

The use of a utility function for making group decisions does not overcome problems of interpersonal comparisons of utility. The shortcomings in using group utility functions must be balanced against the economic benefits of making a group recommendation. Although this approach is open to misinterpretations, it is concluded that this essentially behavioral approach is generally superior to alternative approaches of maximizing expected monetary outcomes or simply consulting a conjurer. Obviously, further research is required before a definite statement can be made on the use of group utility functions.

We have few reservations in stating that the framework of this book has many practical uses in the process of decision making in agriculture, natural resources, business, and government. One of the authors has co-authored a practical decision guide for Australian farmers that is finding a wide audience among consultants and advisors.[12] We believe that further such efforts should be pursued in business, natural resources management, and government.

[12] J. P. Makeham, A. N. Halter, and John L. Dillon, *Best-Bet Farm Decisions*, Professional Farm Management Guidebook No. 6 (Armidale, N.S.W., Australia: University of New England, 1968). Available for $A1.50.

A FINAL WARNING

If the decision makers use the decision framework of this book, all of their decisions will be "good" in the sense of maximizing expected utility. Unfortunately, we are still dealing with uncertainty, and a carefully reasoned decision might still have a bad outcome in any particular instance. We do not guarantee good outcomes — just good decisions!

APPENDIX A
PROBABILITY THAT t LIES BETWEEN $-t$ AND $+t$
Degrees of Freedom

t	1	2	3	4	5	6	7	8	9
0.0	.0000	.0000	.0000	.0000	.0000	.0000	.0000	.0000	.0000
0.1	.0634	.0706	.0734	.0748	.0758	.0764	.0768	.0772	.0774
0.2	.1256	.1400	.1458	.1488	.1506	.1520	.1528	.1536	.1540
0.3	.1856	.2076	.2162	.2208	.2238	.2258	.2272	.2282	.2290
0.4	.2422	.2722	.2840	.2904	.2944	.2970	.2990	.3004	.3016
0.5	.2952	.3334	.3486	.3566	.3618	.3652	.3676	.3694	.3710
0.6	.3440	.3906	.4092	.4192	.4254	.4296	.4326	.4348	.4366
0.7	.3888	.4436	.4656	.4774	.4848	.4898	.4934	.4962	.4984
0.8	.4295	.4924	.5178	.5314	.5400	.5458	.5500	.5532	.5556
0.9	.4666	.5368	.5656	.5810	.5906	.5972	.6020	.6056	.6084
1.0	.5000	.5774	.6090	.6260	.6368	.6440	.6494	.6534	.6566
1.1	.5302	.6140	.6484	.6670	.6786	.6866	.6922	.6966	.7002
1.2	.5578	.6470	.6838	.7036	.7162	.7246	.7308	.7356	.7392
1.3	.5826	.6768	.7156	.7366	.7496	.7586	.7652	.7702	.7740
1.4	.6052	.7036	.7440	.7658	.7796	.7890	.7958	.8010	.8050
1.5	.6256	.7276	.7694	.7920	.8060	.8158	.8228	.8280	.8322
1.6	.6444	.7492	.7920	.8152	.8296	.8392	.8464	.8518	.8560
1.7	.6614	.7688	.8124	.8356	.8502	.8600	.8670	.8724	.8766
1.8	.6772	.7864	.8304	.8538	.8682	.8780	.8852	.8904	.8946
1.9	.6916	.8022	.8464	.8698	.8842	.8938	.9008	.9060	.9102
2.0	.7048	.8164	.8605	.8838	.8980	.9076	.9144	.9194	.9234
2.1	.7170	.8294	.8734	.8964	.9102	.9196	.9262	.9310	.9348
2.2	.7284	.8412	.8848	.9074	.9210	.9298	.9362	.9410	.9446
2.3	.7390	.8518	.8950	.9170	.9302	.9388	.9450	.9496	.9530
2.4	.7486	.8616	.9042	.9256	.9384	.9468	.9526	.9568	.9602
2.5	.7578	.8704	.9122	.9332	.9456	.9534	.9590	.9630	.9662
2.6	.7662	.8784	.9196	.9400	.9518	.9594	.9646	.9684	.9712
2.7	.7742	.8858	.9262	.9460	.9572	.9644	.9694	.9730	.9756
2.8	.7816	.8926	.9322	.9512	.9620	.9688	.9734	.9768	.9792
2.9	.7886	.8988	.9374	.9558	.9662	.9726	.9770	.9802	.9824
3.0	.7952	.9046	.9424	.9600	.9700	.9760	.9800	.9830	.9850
3.1	.8014	.9098	.9468	.9638	.9732	.9788	.9826	.9854	.9872
3.2	.8072	.9146	.9506	.9670	.9760	.9814	.9850	.9874	.9892
3.3	.8126	.9192	.9542	.9700	.9785	.9836	.9868	.9892	.9908
3.4	.8178	.9234	.9576	.9728	.9808	.9856	.9885	.9906	.9922
3.5	.8228	.9272	.9506	.9752	.9828	.9872	.9900	.9920	.9932

Degrees of Freedom

t	1	2	3	4	5	6	7	8	9
3.6	.8276	.9308	.9632	.9772	.9844	.9886	.9912	.9930	.9942
3.7	.8320	.9340	.9658	.9792	.9860	.9900	.9924	.9940	.9950
3.8	.8362	.9372	.9680	.9808	.9874	.9910	.9932	.9948	.9958
3.9	.8402	.9402	.9700	.9824	.9886	.9920	.9942	.9954	.9964
4.0	.8440	.9428	.9720	.9838	.9896	.9928	.9948	.9960	.9968
4.1	.8478	.9454	.9738	.9852	.9906	.9936	.9954	.9966	.9974
4.2	.8512	.9478	.9754	.9864	.9916	.9944	.9960	.9970	.9976
4.3	.8546	.9500	.9768	.9874	.9922	.9950	.9964	.9974	.9980
4.4	.8578	.9520	.9782	.9884	.9930	.9954	.9968	.9978	.9982
4.5	.8608	.9540	.9796	.9892	.9938	.9958	.9972	.9980	.9985
4.6	.8638	.9558	.9806	.9900	.9942	.9964	.9976	.9982	.9988
4.7	.8666	.9576	.9818	.9906	.9946	.9966	.9978	.9984	.9988
4.8	.8692	.9592	.9828	.9914	.9952	.9970	.9980	.9985	.9990
4.9	.8718	.9608	.9838	.9920	.9956	.9972	.9982	.9988	.9992
5.0	.8744	.9622	.9846	.9926	.9958	.9976	.9984	.9990	.9992
5.1	.8768	.9635	.9854	.9930	.9962	.9978	.9986	.9990	.9994
5.2	.8790	.9650	.9862	.9934	.9966	.9980	.9988	.9992	.9994
5.3	.8812	.9662	.9868	.9940	.9968	.9982	.9988	.9992	.9996
5.4	.8834	.9674	.9876	.9944	.9970	.9984	.9990	.9994	.9996
5.5	.8856	.9684	.9882	.9946	.9972	.9984	.9990	.9994	.9996
5.6	.8876	.9696	.9888	.9950	.9974	.9986	.9992	.9994	.9996
5.7	.8894	.9706	.9892	.9954	.9976	.9988	.9992	.9996	.9998
5.8	.8914	.9716	.9898	.9956	.9978	.9988	.9994	.9996	.9998
5.9	.8932	.9724	.9902	.9958	.9980	.9990	.9994	.9996	.9998
6.0	.8948	.9734	.9908	.9962	.9982	.9990	.9994	.9996	.9998

Partly from "Student," "New tables for testing the significance of observations," Metron 5: 18–32, 1925; and partly from new computations.

Degrees of Freedom

t	10	11	12	13	14	15	16	17	18
0.0	.0000	.0000	.0000	.0000	.0000	.0000	.0000	.0000	.0000
0.1	.0776	.0778	.0780	.0782	.0782	.0784	.0784	.0784	.0786
0.2	.1546	.1548	.1552	.1554	.1556	.1558	.1560	.1562	.1562
0.3	.2296	.2302	.2306	.2310	.2314	.2318	.2320	.2322	.2324
0.4	.3024	.3032	.3038	.3044	.3048	.3052	.3056	.3058	.3062
0.5	.3722	.3730	.3738	.3746	.3752	.3756	.3762	.2766	.3768
0.6	.4382	.4394	.4404	.4412	.4420	.4425	.4430	.4436	.4440
0.7	.5002	.5016	.5028	.5038	.5046	.5054	.5060	.5066	.5072
0.8	.5576	.5594	.5608	.5620	.5630	.5638	.5646	.5652	.5658
0.9	.6108	.6126	.6142	.6156	.6166	.6176	.6186	.6194	.6200
1.0	.6592	.6612	.6630	.6644	.6658	.6668	.6678	.6686	.6694
1.1	.7028	.7052	.7070	.7088	.7102	.7114	.7124	.7134	.7142
1.2	.7422	.7446	.7468	.7484	.7500	.7512	.7524	.7534	.7544
1.3	.7772	.7798	.7820	.7838	.7854	.7868	.7880	.7890	.7900
1.4	.8082	.8110	.8132	.8150	.8168	.8182	.8194	.8206	.8214
1.5	.8364	.8382	.8405	.8424	.8442	.8456	.8470	.8480	.8490
1.6	.8594	.8620	.8644	.8664	.8680	.8696	.8708	.8720	.8730
1.7	.8800	.8828	.8852	.8870	.8888	.8902	.8916	.8926	.8936
1.8	.8980	.9006	.9030	.9050	.9066	.9080	.9092	.9104	.9114
1.9	.9134	.9160	.9182	.9202	.9218	.9232	.9244	.9254	.9264
2.0	.9266	.9292	.9314	.9332	.9348	.9360	.9372	.9382	.9392
2.1	.9380	.9404	.9424	.9442	.9456	.9470	.9480	.9490	.9500
2.2	.9476	.9500	.9518	.9536	.9548	.9562	.9672	.9580	.9588
2.3	.9558	.9580	.9598	.9614	.9626	.9638	.9648	.9656	.9664
2.4	.9626	.9648	.9664	.9680	.9692	.9702	.9710	.9718	.9726
2.5	.9686	.9704	.9720	.9734	.9746	.9754	.9764	.9770	.9776
2.6	.9736	.9754	.9768	.9780	.9790	.9800	.9806	.9814	.9834
2.7	.9776	.9794	.9806	.9818	.9828	.9836	.9842	.9848	.9854
2.8	.9812	.9828	.9840	.9850	.9858	.9866	.9872	.9876	.9882
2.9	.9842	.9856	.9866	.9876	.9884	.9890	.9890	.9900	.9904
3.0	.9866	.9880	.9890	.9898	.9904	.9910	.9916	.9920	.9924
3.1	.9888	.9898	.9908	.9916	.9922	.9925	.9932	.9936	.9938
3.2	.9906	.9915	.9924	.9930	.9935	.9940	.9944	.9948	.9950
3.3	.9920	.9930	.9936	.9942	.9948	.9952	.9954	.9958	.9960
3.4	.9932	.9940	.9948	.9952	.9956	.9960	.9964	.9966	.9968
3.5	.9942	.9950	.9956	.9960	.9964	.9968	.9970	.9972	.9974
3.6	.9952	.9958	.9964	.9968	.9972	.9974	.9976	.9978	.9980
3.7	.9958	.9964	.9970	.9974	.9976	.9978	.9980	.9982	.9984
3.8	.9966	.9970	.9974	.9978	.9980	.9982	.9984	.9986	.9986
3.9	.9970	.9976	.9978	.9982	.9984	.9986	.9988	.9988	.9990
4.0	.9974	.9980	.9982	.9984	.9986	.9988	.9990	.9990	.9992
4.1	.9978	.9982	.9986	.9988	.9990	.9990	.9992	.9992	.9994
4.2	.9982	.9986	.9988	.9990	.9992	.9992	.9994	.9994	.9994
4.3	.9984	.9988	.9990	.9992	.9992	.9994	.9994	.9996	.9996
4.4	.9986	.9990	.9992	.9992	.9994	.9994	.9996	.9996	.9996
4.5	.9988	.9990	.9992	.9994	.9996	.9996	.9996	.9996	.9998

Degrees of Freedom

t	10	11	12	13	14	15	16	17	18
4.6	.9990	.9992	.9994	.9996	.9996	.9998	.9998	.9998	.9998
4.7	.9992	.9994	.9994	.9996	.9996	.9998	.9998	.9998	.9998
4.8	.9992	.9994	.9996	.9996	.9998	.9998	.9998	.9998	.9998
4.9	.9994	.9996	.9996	.9998	.9998	.9998	.9998	.9998	.9998
5.0	.9994	.9996	.9996	.9998	.9998	.9998	.9998	.9998	1.0000
5.1	.9996	.9996	.9998	.9998	.9998	.9998	.9998	1.0000	
5.2	.9996	.9998	.9998	.9998	.9998	.9998	1.0000		
5.3	.9996	.9998	.9998	.9998	.9998	1.0000			
5.4	.9996	.9998	.9998	.9998	1.0000				
5.5	.9998	.9998	.9998	.9998					
5.6	.9998	.9998	.9998	1.0000					
5.7	.9998	.9998	1.0000						
5.8	.9998	.9998							
5.9	.9998	.9998							
6.0	.9998	1.0000							

Degrees of Freedom

t	19	20	25	50	100	200	∞
0.0	.0000	.0000	.0000	.0000	.0000	.0000	.0000000
0.1	.0786	.0786	.07884	.07926	.07946	.07956	.0796556
0.2	.1564	.1564	.15676	.15770	.15812	.15832	.1585194
0.3	.2326	.2328	.23334	.23458	.23520	.23552	.2358228
0.4	.3064	.3066	.30744	.30914	.31000	.31042	.3108434
0.5	.3772	.3774	.37856	.38072	.38182	.38238	.3829250
0.6	.4444	.4448	.44610	.44878	.45014	.45082	.4514938
0.7	.5076	.5080	.50960	.51282	.51444	.51426	.5160725
0.8	.5664	.5668	.56876	.57250	.57440	.57534	.5762892
0.9	.6206	.6212	.62330	.62756	.62972	.63080	.6318798
1.0	.6702	.6708	.67310	.67788	.68028	.68148	.6826894
1.1	.7150	.7156	.71818	.72340	.72602	.72734	.7286678
1.2	.7552	.7558	.75860	.76420	.76702	.76844	.7698605
1.3	.7908	.7916	.79454	.80044	.80340	.80490	.8063990
1.4	.8224	.8232	.82620	.83232	.83538	.83694	.8384866
1.5	.8500	.8508	.85386	.86010	.86324	.86480	.8663856
1.6	.8740	.8748	.87784	.88410	.88724	.88882	.8904014
1.7	.8946	.8954	.89844	.90466	.90776	.90932	.9108690
1.8	.9122	.9130	.91606	.92192	.92512	.92664	.9281394
1.9	.9272	.9280	.93098	.93678	.93968	.94112	.9425668
2.0	.9400	.9408	.94352	.94916	.95180	.95314	.9544998
2.1	.9506	.9514	.95402	.95920	.96176	.96302	.9642712
2.2	.9596	.9602	.96274	.96754	.96990	.97106	.9721932
2.3	.9670	.9676	.96992	.97434	.97648	.97752	.9785518
2.4	.9732	.9738	.97584	.97954	.98176	.98270	.9836050
2.5	.9782	.9788	.98066	.98424	.98596	.98678	.9875806
2.6	.9824	.9828	.98458	.98778	.98926	.98998	.9906776
2.7	.9858	.9862	.98774	.99056	.99186	.99248	.9930660
2.8	.9886	.9890	.99028	.99276	.99386	.99440	.9948898
2.9	.9908	.9912	.99232	.99446	.99542	.99586	.9962684
3.0	.9926	.9930	.99396	.99580	.99660	.99696	.9973002
3.1	.9942	.9944	.99524	.99682	.99248	.99778	.9980648
3.2	.9952	.9956	.99628	.99762	.99816	.99840	.9986258
3.3	.9962	.9964	.99708	.99822	.99866	.99886	.9990332
3.4	.9970	.9972	.99772	.99868	.99904	.99918	.9993262
3.5	.9976	.9978	.99822	.99902	.99930	.99942	.9995348
3.6	.9980	.9982	.99862	.99928	.99950	.99960	.9996818
3.7	.9984	.9986	.99892	.99948	.99964	.99972	.9997844
3.8	.9988	.9988	.99916	.99962	.99976	.99982	.9998554
3.9	.9992	.9992	.99936	.99972	.99982	.99988	.9999038
4.0	.9992	.9992	.99950	.99980	.99988	.99992	.9999366
4.1	.9994	.9994	.99962	.99986	.99992	.99994	.9999586
4.2	.9996	.9996	.99970	.99990	.99994	.99996	.9999734
4.3	.9996	.9996	.99978	.99992	.99996	.99998	.9999830
4.4	.9998	.9998	.99988	.99996	.99998	.99998	.9999892
4.5	.9998	.9998	.99988	.99996	.99998	.99998	.9999932

Degrees of Freedom

t	19	20	25	50	100	200	
4.6	.9998	.9998	.99990	.99998	.99998	1.00000	.9999958
4.7	.9998	.9998	.99992	.99998	1.00000		.9999974
4.8	.9998	.9998	.99994	.99998			.9999984
4.9	1.0000	1.0000	.99995	.99998			.9999990
5.0			.99996	1.00000			.9999994
5.1			.99997				.9999996
5.2			.99998				.9999998
5.3			.99998				.9999998
5.4			.99999				1.0000000
5.5			.99999				
5.6			.99999				
5.7			1.00000				
5.8							
5.9							
6.0							

Answers to Chapter Questions

CHAPTER I
Answers

1. You are on your own.
2. Follow the steps of Chapter I for what you consider reasonable strategies, or enumerate all of them.

CHAPTER II
Answers

1. (a) .367   (b) .835   (c) .867 assuming 1200 voters.
2. $.2^{10}$; independence of predictions; well would you?
3. .35 by conditional probability formula.
4. .306 by conditional probability formula. (Remember to normalize distribution of cut.)
5. .169
6. (a)

P(Urn)		P(Ball|Urn) R	G	Posterior Probabilities P(Urn|R)	P(Urn|G)
½	Urn A	⅓	⅔	.455	.526
½	Urn B	⅖	⅗	.545	.474

Value of information: $(.545)(.367) + (.526)(.633) = .533$.

(b) With replacement:

P(Urn|R on 1st draw)		P(Ball|Urn) R	G	Posterior Probabilities P(Urn|R)	P(Urn|G)
.455	Urn A	⅓	⅔	.411	.480
.545	Urn B	⅖	⅗	.589	.520

P(Urn|G on 1st draw)					
.526	Urn A	⅓	⅔	.479	.553
.474	Urn B	⅖	⅗	.521	.447

Value of information: $[(.589)(.370) + (.520)(.630)] (.367)$
$$+ [(.521)(.365) + (.553)(.635)] (.633) = .543.$$
(c) Without replacement:

		P(Ball|Urn)		Posterior Probabilities	
P(Urn|R on 1st draw)		R	G	P(Urn|R)	P(Urn|G)
.455	Urn A	0	1	0	.527
.545	Urn B	.25	.75	1	.473

P(Urn|G on 1st draw)					
.526	Urn A	½	½	.526	.526
.474	Urn B	½	½	.474	.474

Value of information: $[(.527)(.864) + (1.0)(.136)] (.367)$
$$+ [(.526)(.5) + (.526)(.5)] (.633) = .550.$$

7. $P\{A_1 \text{ or } A_2 \text{ or } A_3\} \leq P\{A_1\} + P\{A_2\} + P\{A_3\}$

8. In obtaining action probabilities.   Because the z_i are independent of one another.

9. $P(I) = \frac{1}{2}$ $P(II) = \frac{1}{2}$
   $P(R|I) = 3/10$ $P(R|II) = 6/10$
   (a) $P(\text{Red Chip}) = P(I)P(R|I) + P(II)P(R|II)$

$$= \frac{1}{2}\left(\frac{3}{10}\right) + \frac{1}{2}\left(\frac{6}{10}\right) = \frac{9}{20}$$

   (b) $P(II|R) = \dfrac{P(II \cap R)}{P(R)} = \dfrac{P(II)P(R|II)}{P(R)} = \dfrac{1/2 \cdot 6/10}{9/20}$

$$= \frac{6/20}{9/20} = \frac{6}{9} = \frac{2}{3}$$

10. $P(A_1) = f(1,1) + f(1,2) + f(1,3) + f(1,4) + f(1,5) + f(1,6)$

$$= \frac{6}{36} = \frac{1}{6}$$

$$P(A_2) = \sum_{x=1}^{6} f(x,6) = \frac{6}{36} = \frac{1}{6}$$

$$P(A_1 \cap A_2) = f(1,6) = \frac{1}{36}$$

$$P(A_1 \cup A_2) = P(A_1) + P(A_2) - P(A_1 \cap A_2) = \frac{11}{36}$$

11. We would interpret this to mean that the probability is 8/20 to you.

12. Answer: 4

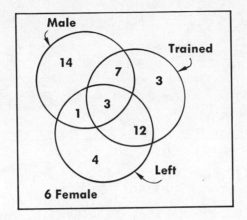

Ans.: 4

13. Since A_1, A_2 is a partition of the sample space for this experiment, Bayes' formula can be applied.

$P(A_1)$ $= 0.8$ priors
$P(A_2)$ $= 0.2$
$P(E|A_1) = 0.7$ conditional probabilities
$P(E|A_2) = 0.3$

Letting E be the event "fair weather when predicted"

$$P(A_1|E) = \frac{(0.7)(0.8)}{(0.7)(0.8) + (0.3)(0.2)} = \frac{0.56}{0.62} = \frac{28}{31}$$

or approximately 90%.

Calculation of conditional probabilities:

$$P(\theta_1|z_1) = \frac{(0.7)(0.5)}{(0.5)(0.7) + (0.3)(0.5) + (0.2)(0.1)} = \frac{35}{52}$$

$$P(\theta_1|z_2) = \frac{(0.2)(0.5)}{(0.5)(0.2) + (0.3)(0.3) + (0.2)(0.5)} = \frac{10}{29}$$

$$P(\theta_1|z_3) = \frac{(0.1)(0.5)}{(0.5)(0.1) + (0.3)(0.2) + (0.2)(0.4)} = \frac{5}{19}$$

$$P(\theta_2|z_1) = \frac{15}{52}; \; P(\theta_2|z_2) = \frac{9}{29}; \; P(\theta_2|z_3) = \frac{6}{19}$$

$$P(\theta_3|z_1) = \frac{2}{52}; \; P(\theta_3|z_2) = \frac{10}{29}; \; P(\theta_3|z_3) = \frac{8}{19}$$

15. $P(A_1 \cup A_2 \cup A_3) = P(A) = 1$

$$P(A_1) = \frac{1}{12} + \frac{1}{4} + \frac{1}{4} = \frac{7}{12}$$

$$P(A_2) = \frac{1}{4} + \frac{1}{4} + \frac{1}{3} = \frac{10}{12}$$

$$P(A_3) = \frac{1}{4} + \frac{1}{3} + \frac{1}{12} = \frac{8}{12}$$

Hence,

$$1 = P(A_1 \cup A_2 \cup A_3) \le P(A_1) + P(A_2) + P(A_3)$$

$$= \frac{7}{12} + \frac{10}{12} + \frac{8}{12} = \frac{25}{12}$$

16. (a) $P(A) = .25, P(\tilde{A}) = 1 - P(A) = .75$
    (b) $P(A \cup B) = P(A) + P(B) - P(A \cap B)$
    $$= .25 + .30 - .05 = .50.$$

    (c) $P(A|B) = \dfrac{P(A \cap B)}{P(B)} = \dfrac{.05}{.30} = \dfrac{5}{30} = \dfrac{1}{6}$

17. $A_1 \cup A_2 = A_1 \cup (\tilde{A}_1 \cap A_2)$ from Problem 16.
    But A_1 and $\tilde{A}_1 \cap A_2$ are disjoint, so we apply Property #3 and get
    $$P(A_1 \cup A_2) = P[A_1 \cup (\tilde{A}_1 \cap A_2)] = P(A_1) + P(\tilde{A}_1 \cap A_2)$$
    Now $A_2 = (A_1 \cap A_2) \cup (\tilde{A}_1 \cap A_2)$ and the two sets $A_1 \cap A_2$ and
    $\tilde{A}_1 \cap A_2$ are disjoint. Applying Property #3 again gives
    $$P(A_2) = P[A_1 \cap A_2) \cup (\tilde{A}_1 \cap A_2)] = P(A_1 \cap A_2) + P(\tilde{A}_1 \cap A_2)$$
    or $P(\tilde{A}_1 \cap A_2) = P(A_2) - P(A_1 \cap A_2)$
    Substituting $P(\tilde{A}_1 \cap A_2)$ into the above equation yields
    $$P(A_1 \cup A_2) = P(A_1) + P(A_2) - P(A_1 \cap A_2).$$

18.

	Ph.D.	M.S.	
Male	5	11	16
Female	1	3	4
	6	14	20

Let M = subset of male students
                    F = subset of female students
                    P = subset of Ph.D. students
                    S = subset of master students

$$P(P|M) = \frac{P(P \cap M)}{P(M)} = \frac{5/20}{16/20} = \frac{5}{16}$$

$$P(S|F) = \frac{P(S \cap F)}{P(F)} = \frac{3/20}{4/20} = \frac{3}{4}$$

19. Probability of win with various strategies and different number of balls in urn.

Number of Balls in Urn (X)	Probability of Win with Strategy		
	1	2	3
0	0	1	0
1	0.1	0.9	0.18
2	0.2	0.8	0.32
3	0.3	0.7	0.42
4	0.4	0.6	0.48
5	0.5	0.5	0.50
6	0.6	0.4	0.48
7	0.7	0.3	0.42
8	0.8	0.2	0.32
9	0.9	0.1	0.18
10	1	0	0

CHAPTER III
Answers

1. a. Transitivity.

   b. Consider the following choice situations:[1]

SITUATION 1:

	Option 1		Option 2	
	Prob. of State	Gain	Prob. of State	Gain
θ_1	1	$500,000	.1	$2,500,000
θ_2	0	0	.89	$ 500,000
θ_3	0	0	.01	0

Which do you prefer, Option 1 or Option 2?

SITUATION 2:

	Option 3		Option 4	
	Prob. of State	Gain	Prob. of State	Gain
θ_1	.11	$500,000	.1	$2,500,000
θ_2	.89	0	.9	0

Which do you prefer, Option 3 or Option 4?

Many people will prefer Option 1 to Option 2, and Option 4 to Option 3; but this is inconsistent, as can be shown with almost any hypothetical utility function that will satisfy the preferences from Situation 1.   The preferences imply:

SITUATION 1: $U(\$2,500,000) > .1\ U(\$2,500,000) + .89\ U(\$500,000) + .1\ U(\$0)$

---

[1] This example comes from Leonard J. Savage, *The Foundations of Statistics*, (New York: John Wiley & Sons, Inc., 1954), pp. 101-104.

SITUATION 2: .1 $U(\$2,500,000) + .9$ $U(\$0) > .11$ $U(\$500,000) + .89$
$U(\$0)$, but these are inconsistent with utility function of figure below,
since:

SITUATION 1: 3.8 > .1 (4.0) + .89 (3.8) + .1 (0) = 3.78

SITUATION 2: .1 (4.0) + .9 (0) = .4 which is not greater than
.11 (3.8) + .89 (0) = 4.18, hence preferences in Situation 2
must be Option 3 > Option 4.

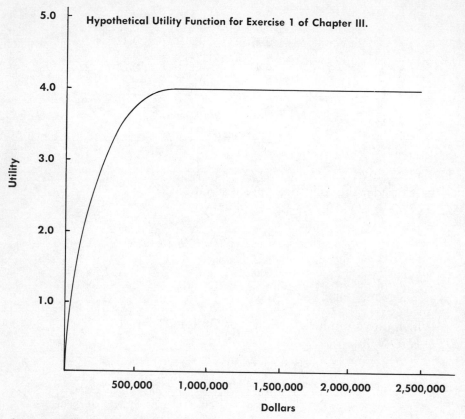

Hypothetical Utility Function for Exercise 1 of Chapter III.

2. a. $u(M_2) = p\, u(M_1) + (1 - p)\, u(M_3)$.
   b. M_1 = happy life.
      M_2 = miserable life.
      M_3 = possibility of hell.
   c. If the probability of M_3 is small enough, a choice could be made.
3. a. Independence of irrelevant alternatives.
   b. Bounded.
4. a. True. Expected utility of any fair bet is greater than utility of cer-
      tainty.
   b. Yes. Expected utility of this unfair bet is greater than utility of $20.

c. False. $\dfrac{11}{20}$ ($10) + $\dfrac{9}{20}$ (−$15) < 0.

d. False. Preference is prior to utility.

e. True. u' is a linear transformation of u.

f. False. Option 1 provides the highest expected utility.

g. False. His utility function must be bounded somewhere.

h. True.

i. False. Consider $0 < m < 1$.

j. False. Only for values greater than 2.7 (approximately).

k. False. Not for values greater than 2.7 (approximately).

5. You're on your own.

CHAPTER IV
Answers

1. (a) $P(\theta_1) = .304$, $P(\theta_2) = .696$.

   (b) a_2

2. Plot $\sigma^2 = \dfrac{u(a) + .02[E(X)]^3 - .18[E(X)]^2 - E(X)}{.5[-.12E(X) + .36]}$

3. You are on your own.

4. 6

5. Yes

6. Cannot tell.

7. a_4 is optimal and $> a_2$.

8. It is also optimal.

9. You are on your own.

10. $(\tfrac{2}{3}, \tfrac{2}{3}, \tfrac{3}{8})$.

11.

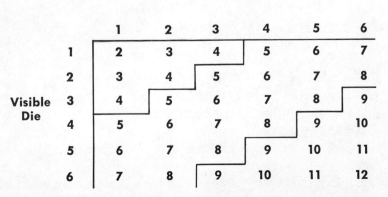

Hidden Die

Visible Die	1	2	3	4	5	6
1	2	3	4	5	6	7
2	3	4	5	6	7	8
3	4	5	6	7	8	9
4	5	6	7	8	9	10
5	6	7	8	9	10	11
6	7	8	9	10	11	12

Conditional Probabilities

		$P(\theta_i)$	1 or 2	3 or 4	5 or 6	$P(\theta_i)\,P(z_3\mid\theta)$
			z_1	z_2	z_3	
≤ 4	θ_1	6/30	5/6	1/6	0	0
5 and ≤ 8	θ_2	20/36	7/20	8/20	5/20	5/36
≥ 9	θ_3	0	.3/10	7/10	7/10	7/36
						12/36

$$P(\theta_2 \mid z_3) = \frac{5/36}{12/36} = \frac{5}{12}$$

CHAPTER V
Answers

1. Graph No. 1

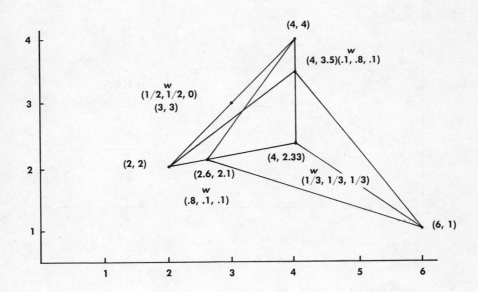

2. Graph No. 2

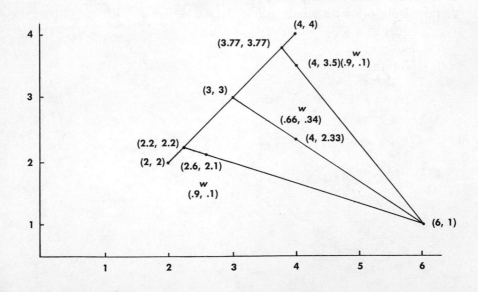

3. Graph No. 3

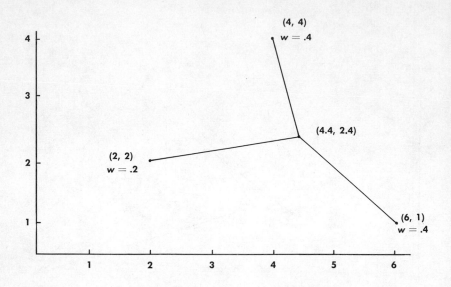

4. Yes. No.
5. (a) Not convex.
   (b) Convex.
   (c) Convex.
   (d) Convex.
6. Depends upon which prior you choose.
7. (a) Using prior distribution (.3, .3, .4), action a_1 with expected gain equal to 5.333.
   (b) Nothing.
   (c) Nothing.

8. (a), (b), (c) Graph 8(a), (b), (c).

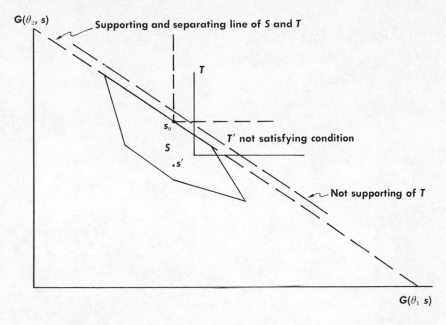

(d) a and b have same sign, $a + b \neq 0$.

(e) Sum to one, w and $1 - w \geq 0$.

(f) At $\bar{u}$: $(1 - w) G_1 + w G_2 = c'$. For all points of S, $(1 - w) G_1 + w G_2 \leq c'$.

(g) Hence, admissible strategy S_0 represented by $\bar{U}$ maximizes G_1 and G_2, and is therefore a Bayes strategy for the weights $1 - w$ and w.

9. (a) Graph 9(a).

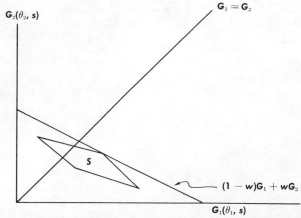

(b) Maximin strategy is always less than or equal to Bayes' solution.

10. Tested, 2 out of 2 with desired characteristic.
11. (a) .25
    (b) $600.
12. Depends upon your assignments of losses, prior probabilities, and conditional probability densities.

1955